THE VETERANS' YEARS

BARRY BROADFOOT

THE VETERANS' YEARS

COMING HOME FROM THE WAR

Douglas & McIntyre
Vancouver/Toronto

85 86 87 88 89   5 4 3 2 1

Douglas & McIntyre Ltd., 1615 Venables Street,
Vancouver, British Columbia V5L 2H1

Canadian Cataloguing in Publication Data

Broadfoot, Barry, 1926-
    Veterans' years

   ISBN 0-88894-473-X

   1. Veterans - Canada - Biography.
2.Canada - Social conditions - 1945-1971.
I. Title.
UB359.C2B76 1985   362.8'6'0971   C85-091360-8

Design by Barbara Hodgson
Typeset by Pièce de Résistance
Printed and bound in Canada by Imprimerie Gagné Ltée.

Photo Credits
Endpapers: The Vancouver *Sun*
Frontispiece: Department of National Defence Photo
Chapter openings: City of Toronto Archives, Globe and Mail
    Collection: p. 5, 99131; p. 57, 98619; p. 83, 98047; p. 117,
    98474; p. 147, 98052; p. 181, 99173; p. 215, 98478

To LORI,
the right girl

Contents

THE VETERANS' YEARS

Preface

How many of us remember that glorious summer and autumn of 1945 when the cruel war against Germany and Japan ended?

How many of us remember those sunlit days when we returned to civilian life with high hopes, great dreams, smiles on our faces—and precious little money in the pockets of our uniforms?

The German armies had been pounded into submission along the Rhine and beyond. The war against Japan ended with the blinding flash of the world's first atomic bomb exploding over the industrial city of Hiroshima. Winston Churchill—whose people saw him as a magnificent leader of the free world during wartime but not as a man to lead Britain in peace— rose in the House of Commons to explain the enormity of the bomb, and failed. But he did say that the world as we had known it would never be the same. Once again, the old man was right.

Certainly Canada would never be the same; it was not even the same country that had entered the war in September of 1939. Just as we had emerged from a colonial to a semi-autonomous state after World War One, so we emerged from World War Two as a genuine nation with world stature.

Canada's contribution had been massive, heroic, and freely given. In a nation of barely more than 12 million people, more than a million men and women had worn the King's uniform and over 40,000 had died in the service. More than 1,100,000 civilians had worked in war pro-

duction. The rest, old and young and many who were still children, had
kept the country going by doing the necessary chores, duties, and jobs.

The Army in 1939 consisted of 10,200 men, and at victory it was
700,000 strong. The fledgling Air Force's 4,000 men had soared to 250,000
men and women; forty-eight squadrons flew in the defense of Britain
and thousands of other air crew served in the RAF. More than 19,000
died, a colossal percentage. The Royal Canadian Navy, with its six
destroyers, grew to 100,000 men and women and 480 ships. Its corvettes,
frigates, and destroyers convoyed 180 million tons of food and vital supplies on the deadly North Atlantic convoy routes to keep Britain in the
war.

Then it was over and the men and boys began coming home. Each
in his own way asked himself: "Home to what?" A new Canada, certainly, with new ideas, morals, perceptions formed while they were away,
a different way of life into which they had had no input. These million
in uniform, whether serving in war zones or in Canada, had existed apart
from the nation. Now it was their turn to make their voices heard.

Canada was not much more populous—only one million more people—
but it was undeniably bigger, stronger, more willing to take chances. Much
had to be done and the veterans had the muscles to do it. New lands
and resources had to be explored, towns built, cities made larger. New
roads, bridges, dams were needed. Industries established during the war
had to be refitted for peacetime, and the flood of nonspendable wartime
dollars demanded more and better goods, from shirts to stoves. Farms
had to be modernized and new ones broken to the plow with tractors,
not horses. Universities and colleges geared up to handle the huge in-
flux of veterans. Small businesses had to be revitalized, and competition
sharpened as the returning servicemen started up the ones they had been
planning amid the drudgery and dangers of war.

The veterans, though they did not quite realize it then, were entering
a huge vacuum, one created by the cautious growth of the 1920s, the
no-growth of the Great Depression, and the six years of war when every
sinew, every idea, and every dollar were channeled by government decree
into this nation's astonishing war effort. Canada, in effect, had marked
time for almost three decades. In 1945 the road to the future lay open
and our lives were what we wished to make of them.

That is what this book is about. It is an exuberant book. It is a book
about successes, for they far outnumbered the failures. It is not about
the Army sergeant who rose to the presidency of a university, or the
Navy able seaman who built a run-down family repair shop into a rival

of General Electric. It is about the short term, those first and so important few years when the veterans' compasses swung, then shivered on
a bearing, then steadied at true north, and their course of the future was
fixed.

So who remembers? It was long ago and the average veteran's age is
now sixty-six—but they remember it well. The train ride home, the
welcome by happy citizens, the first days of walking down familiar streets
or beside ripening fields of wheat. Learning how to be a civilian again,
to live again with a wife, and often children, greeting old friends and
hearing, "Well, John, what are you going to do now that all the excitement is over?" and often fumbling for an answer.

But there was no fumbling when I interviewed them. Through letters-
to-the-editor in daily and weekly newspapers and veterans' and senior
citizen journals, I asked them, and they responded with long letters—
more than 500 of them—asking for interviews, and a few even sending
tape cassettes.

As I had for my five other books of oral history—"living memories,"
I think, is a better phrase—I toured much of Canada with my tape recorder
interviewing them. I ate more carrot cake and drank more coffee and
tea than I care to think about. Generally, I found most veterans quite
affluent. The years and Canada had been good to them. Their war service had been invaluable, they all admitted, making them so much more
determined, more experienced, more clued-in.

Many talked to me about the value of education, especially of a university degree or trade school and the on-the-job training that the government provided, making this country the world's leader in veterans'
rehabilitation. Others told about eagerly signing up for loans and grants
to buy farms or start their own businesses. Still others had said to hell
with all these frills and had gone back to their former employers, often
at the same dull job, or back to Dad's farm. As for the tens of thousands
who had never had a job, who had enlisted from the ranks of the
unemployed of the Depression, or who had jumped from high school
into uniform, they talked about their search for the right job, and often
it was just not there. Most of the 45,000 women in the services married
within a few years and so did the men; there was also a sharp increase
in divorces, many because of wartime marriages so hastily solemnized.

The great majority, as I found them, felt that it had been a good war,
the great experience of their lives. But I also encountered frustrations
from those long-ago days, hidden until now. Deep anger resurfaced in
some vets over injustices real or imagined. Hatred of some opportunistic

employers still remained. Rebuffs by civilians still rankled as memories flooded up, and many declared that the folks at home had not seemed to know that a war had been raging elsewhere. I met some vets who are still contemptuous of young men their age who sought refuge in university and war production—"those miserable draft dodgers." But ironically there did not seem to be the same contempt for Canada's Zombies, the men who were called up but refused to sign to serve overseas. They felt, perhaps, that being in uniform still robbed these men of the delights of civilian life.

The country had to keep moving ahead and the veterans were the ones who were going to take over the controls, eventually. They molded and shaped Canada and made it strong, and we should never forget it. How many took over the controls consciously? Probably very few. Self-interest predominated, naturally. Their goal in 1945 was to get ahead. They wanted careers, jobs, homes, families. They wanted success, security; they wanted to live in peace and, hopefully, in prosperity.

They still remember that summer of great expectations. I can stop any man on the street who was a veteran and ask him about those days and he'll snap out an answer, about time and place, facts and figures, and he'll elaborate—word, sentence, chapter, and verse—on the high hopes and great dreams, on the smiles on their faces and the precious little money in their pockets. They wear their memories of coming home, as they do their war experiences, as a badge of honor.

And that is why this book was joyous to research and write.

Barry Broadfoot
April 16, 1985
Nanaimo, B.C.

1 BACK ON
CIVVIE STREET

1 BACK ON CIVVIE STREET

It was over!All Canadians had waited weeks for that flash: "Victory in Europe!" Wild and happy celebrations erupted in cities and towns on both sides of the Atlantic.

Then came the massive job of bringing the hundreds of thousands of men and women in service back into civilian life, with the least possible disruption to them and to the nation. And fast! The servicemen demanded it. Overseas assembly points were jammed. Troopships, lights ablaze now, streamed home. Trains rolled across the country and discharge depots were clogged. By July 1945 the trickle back to Civvie Street had become a flood.

Those first hours and days and weeks are still vivid to the veterans, even forty years later. They came home to find no one waiting for them at the station—or a houseful of family and friends ready to welcome the hero. They were greeted by wives and sweethearts they barely remembered—and children who didn't remember them. Family farms beckoned, old jobs were waiting, university was a challenge—or the future seemed a blank. Some memories are joyous, some poignant, some bitter, and some sad, but all had one thing in common: the urge to put the war behind and get on with the business of living normally again. It had been a long time. It had been too long!

"WE MADE CANADA"

A good question. What did happen to all of us? I can say this:
All of us, male and female, whatever we did, we all came out of a tremendous experience and I don't think any generation which came after us
experienced the same experience. And they never will. Today, it will
be bang! Then it is all over.

I don't think many of us thought of our service as a great sacrifice.
I didn't. I thought of it as a job—somebody handed us a job and we did it.

I think most of us didn't come back looking for a free lunch. I just
do not think that is the Canadian way of thinking. We had been matur-
ing when our country was at war, and in the Canadian way, if our country was at war we enlisted and fought for our country and that was all
there was to say about it.

There were the opportunities for everyone, such as the chance to go
to any university or college in Canada. You didn't have to be the son
of a banker to go to university. You could be the son of a farmer in New
Brunswick, which I was. You could go to a trades school and learn welding
or masonry or carpentering or typing and shorthand. There were men,
and I know of a couple, who went West with that gleam in their eye
because the Department of Veterans' Affairs would also let you get a farm.

In every case it was up to the individual. Nobody pushed him, nobody
pushed her. There was the opportunity to better yourself and it was all
there between the covers of that little gray booklet they gave us and
in it, it said, if you were a veteran these are the opportunities. All you
had to do was ask.

I went to the University of New Brunswick. My father had gone there
and that is where I went. I just picked up the thread of my life, no big
deal, you might say. I gave Canada, the people of Canada, four years
of my life and they said, fine, now we're giving you the chance. I'd earned
it, but I didn't have to take it.

I will say this. Every town, city, province, and this dominion of ours,
they all were made into better places by the influence of the veterans.
You might say, if you wish to accept my point, that we made Canada.
The Canada that we live in today, yes, and with all its faults, we made it.

We became the lawyers, the entrepreneurs, the doctors, the architects,
and the businessmen and the workers, yes, the guy with the pick and
the shovel and the Stanley plane and the Caterpillar tractor, and we
all pitched in. Our wives did, too. There was this huge new mass of

people all working like the very devil to make something of themselves. Just as people always will.

The war was a very bad thing, a terrible thing. But there will always be some form of human conflict and I'd say, from limited experience you could say, that Canadians who served Canada came out and were better for it, their families were better for it, and their country was better for it.

We lost our inferiority complex during the war when everybody pitched in and showed each other what Canadians could do. Hey, look! We've done this and this and that. Aren't we something, eh? That's the way it went.

I'm not sure many people today look on it this way, but that's the way it was. The country you know today, despite its faults, and face it, they really aren't *that* many, but the country we know today, the veterans put together. There is no other way of looking at it. We were the generation blessed with opportunity and we took it! Yes. We took it.

"THEY DIDN'T WANT TO KNOW"

An officer told me the only way I would get home in a hurry was to volunteer for the Pacific and I did, so that got me home quickly. A ship, from Liverpool. God, when I think of it. Maybe 10,000 or 15,000 men and when she had been a passenger liner before the war she might have carried a thousand passengers.

Our draft was small and they hooked about eight coaches on to a regular train and we were fed like in barracks. Food was brought in in big cans, kettles, huge bowls, you know, and you just dug in, and we were fed only twice a day—and it was at seven in the morning and six at night— and there was nothing to do. A few guys had cards or dice. Naturally dice, because there were some guys who had become gamblers overseas and if they didn't play crooked they played straggly, and I never went into those games.

But what really made me mad, made me wonder if coming home would be all that it was cracked up to be, was there were four MPs on our section. Two at a time would walk through the section, and this was day and night, looking at us as though we were crooks. I often wondered if those types became regular policemen for cities or the Mounties when they got out. They didn't do much. They just looked mean.

Another thing. Naturally we had officers with us. The sergeants and corporals ran the show, like they always did, but we had officers in charge. Four of them, I think. They didn't bunk in with us in those old, creaking cars. They were up in the passenger section, berths, good food naturally, a fine time, and I guess they did a lot of chatting with the civilians about what a great bunch of heroes they were in the war.

I should put in here that I was a sergeant, too. There were other sergeants and corporals, too, but we were just passengers. It was Army sergeants who were in charge, just as it was Army MPs who were the tough guys.

It burned me up. A sergeant air gunner with twenty-seven missions is just one step away from a pilot officer or flying officer with twenty-seven missions, but why should we get the dirty end of the stick? I'll tell you. That was the way it was, and that's the way it will always be.

I think it was five days from Halifax to Winnipeg. It was about Whitemouth when I started to get excited because we were nearly home and we were into settled country, and that old steam whistle was blowing for every crossing and it started to rain and I've enough of a Manitoba grandfather's farming blood in my veins that I remember thinking, it would be great for the crops. It was July 17. It fell heavily the rest of the way, real heavy, and Winnipeg when you come in from the eastern side isn't the prettiest way to approach your home town, lots of grubby little houses, but it sure looked terrific to me. I saw a milkman's horse and wagon going down a street and I thought, God, I'll be having fresh milk and cream soon.

My mom was there and so was my dad. He'd knocked off the day at the CNR roundhouse. The big welcome, you bet. Laughing, everybody hugging, kissing. There was no band or anything like that. I think that stuff came later when the regiments came home as regiments. Then a band and the mayor and stuff. We were just a bunch of airmen and the war wasn't over by then.

We got a taxi home. That surprised me. I don't know why but I thought it would be like England. Wartime restrictions, shortages, rations, no private cars. You know what it was like.

Okay, it wasn't. This was Canada and there wasn't, or I mean there hadn't been, a war for 8,000 miles either way. Everything looked the same. The streets were clean and there were cars and the boulevards were mowed, and I kept wondering, and I said to my father, "Dad, how did you make out in the war? Was it tough?"

The old man laughed and said, "Eddie, my boy, the Cartwrights survived. Your mother didn't get her booze," and he patted her knee and said, "Did you, Mother?" and because she never touched a drink in her life I knew who had been getting it.

There was a big dinner. Nothing had changed. We all sat down and had one hell of a big dinner and we talked and talked and we drank beer and whiskey and got a little loud and I'm sitting there and this is when I began to wonder. First the taxi, then the dinner, then the talking and boozing and horseplaying around and I thought, nobody has asked me what it was like over there. Flying, freezing, on the watch all the time, London, rations, only girls were whores if you wanted them and could afford them, and waiting around outside Liverpool for a while and the ship ride and the train ride and not one of these people had yet asked me, "Hey Eddie, what was it like over there?"

I felt like standing up, half-drunk that I suppose I was, and saying, "Hey, I'm twenty and I've been in a war for two years and all you're doing is talking about who's had a baby or who's done this or that," and then I thought, "Oh, to hell with it. They don't really want to know." It was not until later, after I had got things squared away, after I'd talked with some of my buddies who were back, I guess it was only then I came to the truth that they didn't really want to know what happened, and didn't care.

THE LAWYER AND THE PARTY

Coming home. Well, there's one thing I can tell you about which you won't, I bet, have anybody else telling you about this business of coming home.

The Carters, that's us, lived on a farm. Dad and Mom had three quarters, and he rented a quarter off an old lady who lived next to the northeast quarter, and we had another quarter a mile away, mostly bush and marsh hay and some pasture, so that's where the stock was kept. That part of Manitoba was good country. South of Russell there.

So here's what happened about coming home. Mom and Dad had six kids. Robert, Bobbie, he was the oldest, and then came Garnet and then Millie and then Eva and later there was Jean, and I was sort of the tail-end pup, I came along at the end. Bobbie joined first. Goddamn it, he was raring to go and he went down to Brandon and joined up in the Army because the Navy and the Air Force weren't ready to take fellows yet, but he didn't care. He was going to have some fun. About two years later Garnet doesn't tell anybody anything, but he just gets on a bus one day and goes into Winnipeg or Saskatoon, can't remember which, and he comes back four days later and he's in the Air Force and he's got about ten days before he has to go back.

Then Millie marries a guy from down Hamiota way and she's off with him, living on his old man's farm and things are getting a little tight. Then I get my call. Dad says he's going to fight it. He says he knows he can get an exemption for me, but I says to him, you try and exempt me and I'll go to Toronto and enlist, and he said he would, so I went to Winnipeg and I joined the Army. The Air Force weren't taking guys then.

To show you how dumb I was, only eighteen, I had to go to a drugstore and give the druggist some money and ask him to phone the police in Russell to tell them to tell my dad I was in the Army and I would be home in four days for a week and I'd help with the crop and then I'd be gone. That's how dumb I was. I didn't know how to use a long-distance phone.

Our dear mother died before I joined and Dad died in January of the last year of the war, so by the time we were set to come home we'd dried all our tears, and Bobbie and Gee and me had kept in touch and we arranged we'd meet in London at the services club, the Canada Club, at a certain time after the war, and by golly we made it. A real booze-up, I'll tell you that for sure.

Now, here's the crazy part. By some crazy luck we're all on the same ship together. Fifteen thousand or so troops, Army, Navy, Air Force, nurses, officers, everything, and there we are, and the second day Bobbie and I run into each other. About two days later, damned if we don't run into Gee. There's no booze-up this time but we put together a plan. We'd get our discharge leave and then we'd meet in Brandon and be big stuff and hire a taxi and all arrive home together. So when we reached Halifax Bobbie phoned the elevator operator in Russell and he drove out and told the girls who were still on the farm and by golly, we hit her right on the head, and the day we said we'd be coming home we did, all three of us, in that taxi with our gear and presents and all.

The place looked the same. Eva and Jean weren't married and they rushed out with their boyfriends and we danced a jig and stomped and ripped and roared and had a great old time. I remember Millie, she'd come up from Hamiota with her husband and kid, she took a camera and the three of us lined up and that's the only picture there is of the three of us together in uniform. Bobbie, Gee and me. Still got it. In that album over there.

We talk a bit about Mum and Dad a bit and we all walk around the yard a bit and things look fine. Then Millie says we should go to the house for some wine and cookies. Well, sir, when we get there, in the parlor there's a fussy little guy sitting there and we're told he's a Mr. Garber, Gervin, Gardner, something.

He says he's a lawyer and he goes into a lot of mumbo-jumbo about Mum and Dad and how he's dead and we know that and property rights and titles and estates and wills and the worst lot of baloney you ever heard of. Then he says it is now time to read the will because he's delayed it, being the family lawyer, which I didn't know about. So Bobbie tells him to get on with it. I suspect something's coming. I know Bobbie does.

Okay, mister, he starts to read and I'm getting it right away. Dad has made a new will, and the three of us are going to get a dollar each or something like that and the girls are going to get it all. Lock, stock, and barrel, including the six horses I'd owned when I left. We had been had, as you might say, and when it sunk in, Bobbie stood up and he pointed at this lawyer. He was trembling. He, well, his face was white, and he said quietly, "If this is true, you shyster, you ain't leaving this goddamned room alive," although he didn't use the word "goddamned."

Millie popped up, my favorite sister Millie, and she said, "It's only fair. When the girls were working their fingers to the bone and me coming up from our farm to help, you three guys were over in England and France having a swell time. It's only right we get this place and everything that's on it and all the money in the bank that we made off it. You guys had your fun and now we're going to have ours. Aren't we, girls?"

Well, sir, I thought that was going to be the end of the Carter bunch. Murder. Men, women, and children.

Then the girls and the lawyer started to laugh and somebody yelled and the door to the living room opened—we were in the kitchen—and a whole bunch of people, cousins, friends, kids, old ladies, came streaming in and laughing and shouting, "Welcome home!" and guys were carrying bottles of beer and cases of beer and the ladies turkeys and pies and they stood in a big circle around the three of us and they started singing, like to "Jingle Bells":

> It's a joke, it's a joke,
> A big joke all the way,
> Glad you're back, glad you're back,
> Pockets full of pay.

And it was a joke. The lawyer was a fake. A lawyer, naturally, but one who'd moved into town while we were away. All the mumbo-jumbo and talk of Dad's will was a joke. The girls had cooked it all up. Soon Bobbie and Gee and me were laughing and dancing as much as any of them, and that started off the party. It lasted until early morning and I've never been as drunk again as I was that night and never eaten so much food and never danced so much and never kissed so many pretty local girls, and it was just one hell of a party.

So, in a few days this lawyer gets us all together again and the will gets done with and the whole business is split six ways, three boys and three girls, and we decide to sell it because you can't split a farm with stock and buildings and machinery six ways, and that is what we do.

I went farming on my own with my share and what I've got from the government, and I farmed for thirty-two years.

That's the best I can do for you. You'll have to write about that lawyer and that party. That was something else again.

"THAT WAS COMING HOME"

I was wounded in Holland. Who wasn't? They sent me by air ambulance to a hospital at Aldershot for a patch-up, and when they had sewed me up a bunch of us were sent home.

I hadn't written or telegraphed I was coming. I was quite sure they didn't even know where the hell I was because I wasn't a good letter writer at all, and they were even worse. I mean, my mother wasn't. The old man could barely sign his name. I was just going to walk into the yard and up to the door and they'd know I was there because the dogs would be barking. They wouldn't know me. Hell, I'd been away four years.

I didn't get far when a truck comes up behind me and stops and it's a neighbor, and I hop in and sure, he recognizes me, but there's some kind of people you could have gone to the moon and walked on it and they'd seen it on the television and they wouldn't say more than "Ho, youse back. Ha'nt heard of you for a long time. Coulda thought youse mighta been dead." Real ignorant people around there way back from the highway. This guy was one of them. A dumb English, but smart enough to keep out of the Army.

I said if I had been dead he would have heard about it. It would have been in the Olds paper or *The Bulletin.* You know what he said? That he didn't read the papers, that it was full of lies. I know the kind of lie he was talking about, when the Olds papers said he was fined for running a still. That was a lie to him. It was a good thing he left the district when he did, the next year.

He stopped at the lane and I hiked up to the house and right away I could see nobody was home. Seeding was over and summer fallowing done and I could see good rains were bringing the crop along just right, and when I got to the yard there was chickens scratching and the dogs barking and a bunch of cattle over by the windmill making a fuss. I climbed through the fence and went over to the trough and it was down to the last two inches, so I figured they had gone to Sylvan Lake for the day, a picnic. They'd have left after breakfast and someone had forgotten to pull the bar to get the windmill spinning, and when I did that I went back to the house. Nobody inside.

I walked around the big kitchen. Boy, but did I ever know that kitchen and had I ever thought about it. The woodshed by the door, next to the wash-up stand. I touched the old stove, it was a Majestic, with my hand and it was still warm and it was noon then, so I figured they must have left about ten and hell, what was I going to do?

When you're on a farm and you don't know what to do when nobody is around, then there is no place I know where there is so much of nothing to do. I spent some time going around the house. There was a new radio. In the hall, where the stairs go up, by Jesus, there was a phone. So I could have phoned them from Edmonton. Who would have thought the old boy would have sprung for a phone? I hadn't noticed the poles coming in so they must have strung them from the next road allowance, and that would have cost the old boy a penny or two.

So here I was in the farmhouse where I was born, right in one of those three bedrooms upstairs, and it is early July and I'm out of the goddamned Army and I'm right back home in sunny Alberta and my uniform is all I've got because I check out my old bedroom I shared with my kid brother and there's not a snitch or snatch of my clothing. I think of putting on a pair of overalls that are hanging in the kitchen and I say to hell with it, I didn't come back to be a stupid farm boy. I been in London and Amsterdam and Montreal and Winnipeg and, I thought, I'd better strike out Winnipeg. It's no better than that dump Edmonton. That's what I was thinking, Barry. I'm standing in the kitchen, and I've got three hooks and a few medals coming to me and a bunch of money, about $770, so the officer in Edmonton told me, and the money I'd sent to Mom to put in the bank, so I've got more money than the old boy ever made in any year.

A lot had changed around the house. A phone and a new radio. Big

deal, I guess I thought. So I went around the farm kind of seeing it for
the first time and it looked kind of run-down. I guess you wouldn't know,
but my eye could see it. A fence needed mending. The barn door was
hanging a bit wonky on the rail, not true. The pig yard looked the same,
at least one foot deep in pigshit and mud, not counting what was on
the pigs. But all in all, it was not too bad. The machinery looked okay.
Nothing new, naturally. I knew that. Let the government spend millions
on damn-fool war and waste it like you would never believe—and believe
you me, I could tell you some of the things I saw over there that would
chill you—but don't give the farmer any decent equipment so he can
grow more wheat and beef. I am not the only one who thinks that the
farmer was just as much a part of the war effort as the guy firing a gun
in a big Sherman. No sir, I can get quite upset about that, the stuff about
he went and *he* didn't go, so the one who didn't go and stayed back on
the farm, he was a traitor or a Zombie or something. That, my friend,
is bullshit. I can get awfully vexed when I hear somebody after all those
years say that So-and-So who is now a big shot up in Red Deer got there
because he stayed home and did well, while the guy who is talking was
at the war. That guy, probably, was home on the farm and working his
guts out, and he was like my folks and they got maybe a day of a picnic,
a deer hunt in the fall, maybe going to a bonspiel come spring and the
ball tournament Dominion Day in Olds or somewhere.

Hell, I'm off and running. Whoa!

I remember, by the time I done the big circuit and found everything
fairly jake, I went over and shut off the windmill and went into the house
and scrounged around to eat and there's not much. I could see when they
got back it was going to be a cold supper. I went out to the ice house,
beside the well, in a concrete shed, a low affair, where we kept the cream
cans, and there's part of a pork roast and some cold potatoes and I goes
back to the house and gets a plate and a big knife and off comes a big
slice of pork and some potatoes and then I see these strings. Well, I guess
I said to myself, I'll be goddamned and then triple-damned. Did I ever
know them! At the end of every string was a bottle of Mom's home-made
wine. Dandelion, usually. Chokecherry. Plum. No, carrot and rhubarb wine
came later. So I hauls up one string and there's a bottle, and on a little
bit of paper glued on it, it says "Dandelion." The next said, oh, I forget.
Anyway, I heads myself out of there and over onto the lawn and there
I am sitting under a little clump. Poplars. They never grow high in that
part of the country. You'll never see a sky-high one. God said they would
be prairie shrimps and they were. I yanked the cork out of the dandelion

wine and took a slug and brrrrr, cold, I remember it today. I'm lying under trees and the sun is shining down and the clouds are going past and I'm munching cold pork from one of our hogs and eating cold potatoes like they was French fries and taking another slug, and I take off my tunic and throw it away, away, away goes the Army, the whole goddamned lousy lot of it, away, away, away, and I'm having fun.

Of course I remember all this. Every old soldier has something to say about that one time. This is mine.

I'm lying there drinking, from one bottle, then the other, and I go to the ice house and get two more and I drank that whole afternoon away, on a big slice of cold pork roast and two cold potatoes, and I was getting drunk, although I didn't mean to. I guess anybody who starts drinking at noon doesn't really mean to get tight, does he? But that popskull! My mother could have made a fortune selling it. She sure could make dandelion wine.

I guess it was about five when I heard the car coming down the lane and I get up and sure as hell, there were those four dead soldiers and I knew it was no sense in getting up because I was better off on the ground so I just sat down again and when they came through the gate to the house I yelled something like "Hullo, there" and they stared and then they came running over.

They could count and they could see I was somewhat pissed, but that didn't matter, and as I've heard it told, there was great rejoicing.

Well, I guess, you could say that was about it.

Next morning I waked up and I hear the separator going in the kitchen, that steady hum-hum-hum, and so I know Kenny and my sisters have finished with the milking and time to be eating and I go downstairs and it was like it always was. There's greasy eggs and thick bacon hacked off a slab and there's coffee and we sit down and eat and Dad says he wants to have a family talk. Okay, I don't know what a family talk is, since we never had one before, but I'm willing.

I thought maybe they might want to hear about me in the war but nobody asks and I think, maybe I told them all last night but I don't remember, so I says, okay, let's have a family talk. Mom and the girls are doing the dishes and Dad and Kenny and me go into the parlor. That's what a family talk is going to be about in this household. No women folk. Okay.

Dad said he'd figured it all out. If I stayed I'd get one-third of the profits. Kenny would get one-third, and he'd get one-third—but he'd get all the money from the sale of beef. That's how he'd figured it. Our thirds were for grain and I could see he was being cagey. I asked, what if there's no crop, we're hailed out, dried out. Rust. Sawflies. Hoppers. You know, the works? He sort of spread his hands out on the table palms up as if to say, that's the way she's going to be.

I wasn't exactly hotheaded, but I said if that was the way he had it figured, I'd just take off to town for the day and look around and see some of the gang. He said okay, and I pumped her full of purple gas from the drum in the shed and I hightailed off and I came back late that afternoon. I'd been in the beer parlor all afternoon where I thought maybe somebody would want to hear about those English and Dutch girls and so on, maybe see my scars, but nobody did. It was the same old thing. Crops. The Grain Exchange. Trucks. The weather. Whose daughter had gone to Edmonton to visit for five months with her aunt, and wondering which guy had stuck it into her and why the hell didn't he marry her like in the good old days.

That was coming home. Getting screwed at home and getting ignored in town.

"WHAT WAS IT ALL FOR?"

I remember lying in a debarkation hut near the Devil's Punch Bowl at Hindhead, not wanting to go back to Canada because it represented the unknown. I kept asking myself what the hell was I going to do after being out of Civvie Street for five and a half years and who was I going to be able to talk to?

Overseas, fear wasn't in it, except, as an after-shock, because everybody thought the other guy would get killed. But now I was scared. Better the devil you know than the devil you don't. It's true what they say. War is a game invented by old men for young men to play.

I was still glooming about all this when I climbed up the gangplank on the *Ile de France* with 25,000 other bods, and the sight of Halifax Harbor a week later didn't improve matters any.

In fact I don't even remember getting to Regina, but there I was standing with the flock in a reception shed, listening to the sundry well-meaning bigwigs making speeches of welcome. I lasted halfway through the first one before I stepped over the rope and tried to hide my thoughts behind Eric Wells who had come to meet me.

I had the usual ribbons and sergeant's stripes up, none of which I'd earned compared to some of the boyos I'd known and loved. The ribbons were standard stuff, the kind you get for being on time at pay parades. So two weeks later when I was demobbed I dropped my uniform in a garbage can and struggled to get adjusted to another life.

I spent a long time wondering what it was all for, anyway? Still do, in a way. Many of the kids today look at servicemen as gun-happy anachronisms who sit around Legion halls swilling beer and fighting the war *ad nauseam*. The post-war generation doesn't, of course, know what it is talking about, but what else are they to think when they look around and find that yesterday's enemies are today's friends?

What they don't know is that veterans have long since decided that hate is self-defeating and it is better to forgive and forget. I'm still working on it. That's why you'll find more pacifists in the Legion halls than you will on the street. Having said that, I still get goddamned mad when I see the Legionnaires scorned by banner-waving pacifists who've never heard a gun go off. So let them keep away from the Legion halls and the cenotaphs. Let those who were killed and those who were wounded— and most of them were kids—let them rest in peace.

We don't need history lessons from amateurs.

What we would like is a pacifist who has the grace to shut up and listen to the ghosts at the eleventh hour of the eleventh day of the eleventh month. That's the time when the dwindling few get tears in the eyes for the ones who didn't make it home.

Forgive me for getting sidetracked. We were talking about what it was like to come home. Bloody lonely, that's what it was like. Getting a job was easy, though. I worked a night desk in a Regina newspaper, seven to three in the morning, but my clock somehow was always wonky and I'd sleep until four in the afternoon.

All I could afford was a room at the YMCA and I shared a room with a guy, but I'd hang around downtown after work until he left for work so I never saw him. Then I got up and was gone by the time he came in from work. All I know about him was from his clothes, and he wore outrageous ties. He made model airplanes and he ate apples. I figured I wouldn't like him.

I had bucketed around for thousands of miles in 1945, only to come to a dead halt in a room with a singing radiator in a city I didn't know. The one friend I had lived in Moose Jaw forty miles away and I spent every weekend with him until my wife came back from England.

He was the only guy I knew who spoke a language I understood.

It took me four years to get over all that. Maybe more.

During that time I resented the Zombies and the stay-at-homes. But finally I came to terms with the realization that service and survival were merely the luck of the game and each man goes where his will and his conscience leads him.

Having said that, I get to thinking once in a while that all wars are stupid. What helps, though, is the conviction that some wars are less stupid than others.

"OUR SON DIDN'T COME BACK"

About November the town and the Legion in Swift Current gave us a party, figuring everybody who was coming home would be home, and it was a good bash, speeches and entertainment and dancing and food and quite a few of us had crocks out in the trucks and cars, so not all that much had changed from before the war.

A lot of guys who joined up weren't there, naturally. The troops had taken an awful kicking during all the heavy fighting, and I suppose more than half of the guys in bomber crews hadn't made it back, and there were the ones who thought this kind of a welcome-home party was a lot of baloney. But anyway, the hall was packed and we were on our best behavior. None of this "Please pass the effing butter" kind of thing. A good party.

I was meeting a lot of guys I hadn't seen for a long time and it was hi, let's get together, how about the beer parlor Saturday afternoon, and give me a ring soon, you know, and then I saw this couple sitting by themselves in the corner.

It was the Johnstons, mother and father, and I'd played with Johnny all my life until they'd moved to Regina about the time the war broke out, so I knew them well. I hiked over there lickety-split and after saying hello, hello, I said I was glad to see them back in town and where was Johnny these days?

As soon as it came out of my mouth I knew, and Mr. Johnston said, "Kenny, our son didn't come back. His plane was shot down over Germany."

Well, what do you say? You didn't know. They knew you didn't know. But it went through me like a shock. It just did. I stood there mumbling, saying I was sorry, and then I felt myself give a big sob and there they were. Tears. Just a gush of them and it was all over.

Mrs. Johnston stood up and she said, "Kenny, I know, I know. When you're in Regina come and visit us. We're in the phone book. Thank you for asking about John, and we love you," and I guess I nodded and I headed for the outside. I wasn't crying by then, but I just wanted to get out of all that sound and laughter and music and feel some fresh air on my face.

Here, you've been away for three years and things were pretty rough a lot of the time, I'll say that, and you come back and run into a couple who are just visiting town and come to a party like that and suddenly, damn it all, you realize there was a war and you've been in it and your chums have died and you wonder, what in hell was it all about?

"THE SERVICES MADE US"

Let's talk turkey. Let's talk facts. Let's talk reality. The services made us. I was Army. It applies to Joe Air Force and Jim Navy. Everybody.

We were all amateurs and by that I mean that when we enlisted or were called up we were amateurs in life. Kids. That's what we were. A great majority of us. Out of high school and one or three meaningless jobs because that's what life was then. The Depression, my friend, didn't exactly end when Hitler invaded Poland. In Western Canada, B.C., everywhere, there was still that old Depression lingering around. You ask the guys who joined up in 1939 and a lot of them will tell you they joined up for excitement. Adventure. Baloney. They joined up because they had no jobs and the Air Force, the Army, the Navy offered them clothing, three square meals a day, medical treatment, travel, and in a hell of a lot of cases more money than they'd seen in a long time. Another thing. The money that had to be sent back home to the wife by guys who joined up kept a lot of those families going.

I'm saying we were amateurs in the game of life, because we couldn't participate in the game and that was making money, getting married, establishing a home, taking out a mortgage, having kids.

When we got out you could hardly call us kids. Not in my case. Now, I joined the infantry in November of '42, a year out of high school. I knew nothing. By some fluke, somebody who pushed the buttons and cranked the levers said that Bob Robinson, myself, a kid from Regina, me, he wasn't the right sort for infantry, so after my advanced training at Shilo I was put into the RCE, the engineers. That reduced my chances of going overseas because engineers were needed in Canada, too. I learned carpentry, and it wasn't rough carpentry either. Finishing work. Who do you think put in the officers' mess at Vimy Barracks and at Shilo? Us. Me. I learned carpentry and welding and plumbing and other trades, too, and I got a trades education. It was a form of college. I was learning something which would help me on Civvie Street and I'm damn glad for it.

A lot, many many, probably most of the fellows who went overseas and came back in one piece, sure, they didn't have trades. Throwing artillery shells at a German town you can't even see, or cleaning out a village in Italy, is an experience you'll never forget—but after ten years, when everything has long been forgotten, all you've got to show for it is two or three overseas stars and you don't even know where you've put them. What I'm saying is, I was lucky. The Army gave me a bunch of trades I could work at.

If my kids had ever asked me what I did in the war, I would have said, "Sonny, I built H-huts for soldiers to sleep in and I repaired plumbing in the showers so they could keep clean," and if the little bugger had said, "But Daddy, that's not really fighting," I would have whopped him. Everybody did his share. If you were shipped overseas, then it was your kind of luck. I can look anybody in the eye. I joined up to fight the Germans. I just didn't, that's all.

But I did have the jump on a lot of guys. A flying officer comes back and because he's learned some manners in the officers' mess and has a DFC, which they handed out like Grapenuts for breakfast, he thought he was too high and mighty to go out on a construction site and pick up a hammer and start pounding, and pound for eight hours a day. That's my brother-in-law I'm talking about. So he sat around Regina for six months after discharge and finally took a job selling life insurance. The only guys he knew that he could sell to were other guys like himself. From the Air Force. He found they were selling insurance, too. No, I'm not kidding. That's what happened to Ben. Then he got smart and went to university and he's way better off than me now, but that's another story.

I got out and within forty-eight hours I was working for an outfit which was tearing down a commonwealth training station. The war was over. I was tearing down, not building, but it was work and I was getting a fair wage. I think it was seventy-five cents an hour. That was good then. A lot of fellows were getting less.

It was good quality. I'll say this, the Canadian government didn't scrimp when they built wartime bases and camps. No sirree. The best. It worked this way. A station would be decided to be obsolete. The bid was put out. The high bid was usually a company that had a reputation in

Saskatchewan or Alberta. What I'm saying is that some of the companies which built these bases also got the bid to tear them down, and they made a fortune. You know, selling the lumber and plumbing, light bulbs even. There were still shortages for a lot of stuff.

My father had a '38 Chev pickup, which I drove to work, and I'd hang around after work and every night I'd pop a few good two-by-twelves into the back or maybe a small keg of nails somebody had found in one of the shops. I'd pop these in and take them home. I got the old henhouse of my mother's, and I filled up that old henhouse and when Helen and me got married the next spring I had most of what I needed for a house. I mean this was *good* lumber. B.C. Number One Grade. Not a knot in a carload. You don't get that stuff now.

I quit that job to get married and then we went on a holiday, a honeymoon to my aunt's summer home on Lake Winnipeg, and when I came back and found how much I had taken, I was sure surprised. I didn't think it was stealing. It just seemed like it was everybody's stuff and there was so much of it. One guy took plumbing stuff from this company's warehouse and nobody noticed anything was missing. No inventory. I guess it was, if it was not nailed down it was for the taking.

Anyway, I built a house and every time I go back home I drive around and look at it and it is one fine house. Every nail in it I drove myself.

That house got me my second start, but I got my real start in the Army, and that's what I've been trying to say.

We went in as amateurs and I came out as not an amateur and for that, the war was a good thing for me because it taught me how to operate, to function in the world outside—and I'm going to tell you something. The world outside, and that's Canada, it operated all during the war as if there was no war going on. Sure, there was a war but the civilians felt it was for their benefit. It was, too, you know, I can't think of a single civilian in the city or on the farm who didn't do good out of the war. I found that out early. Just talk to people. The war was just good times to them. That's why I stole that lumber and that other stuff. I had to catch up. I thought I had a pretty good right to catch up. I did. I did. But good.

Was I bitter? Hell's bells, no. Maybe if I'd been over there getting shot at, yes, maybe I'd be bitter. No, stepping out of those Army wool pants for the last time was a great day for me. I came out into Civvie Street a hell of a lot smarter than when I went in. It almost put me on the same level of smartness as most civilians. You bet.

"SORRY, CHIEF"

I've got no grudge. If you've been an Indian as long as I have, you learn that grudging don't do you one damn bit of good. No sir, not one damn bit, but when I joined the Army in Regina in September of '40, the guys in Fort Qu'Appelle, they said the Army don't take Indians. But I can tell you this, they sure did.

You still didn't have a chance even when you were in uniform in Canada, and when we were going overseas in '41 the train would stop at these towns and the ladies, the Red Cross or something, they'd be handing out sandwiches and candy bars and smokes. You really had to put your hand out right in front of them if you was an Indian before they'd give you anything. I remember that.

I liked England. The girls and the people, they liked us. You'd go to a little inn, a pub, you know, near the base and they'd buy you beer and slap you on the shoulder and none of this English stand-offishness, you know, but like they were glad to see you. They thought Indians were like the guys who killed General Custer and it was fun, we'd ham it up, the other Indian fellows like me, you know. We'd go, well, once one night four of us, we painted up our faces and took off our tunics and underwear and we went up to this pub and pushed in the door and we jumped in, screaming and jumping around in our war paint. That was fun, you know. I remember that.

Then me and the boys went to Sicily and there was just the Italians there at first and they were nothing. But then we found what war was going to be like when we met the Germans. I got my first wound there, and I got two more the same night in the Liri Valley, an awful place to be if you were a soldier, and then further up, I was sent back in with some replacements and I was sent up to the front with these guys. Like the lieutenant, he probably said, we'll put these guys up front there because they don't know nothing from nothing and if they get killed then it will be no loss to us. That was the kind of things some officers did.

Then I got wounded again in the stomach and they sent me to Malta to hospital and then I came back to Canada, and I was a corporal with four wound stripes and nobody at Camp Shilo had those, I'll bet.

I got out in December of 1944, a week before Christmas. They didn't want a guy like me around, you know. Go show your four wound stripes to the guys on the reserve, they said. No they didn't. I made that up. But that's what they meant, you know.

There were a few Indians around Regina then and I knew where to find them and we got pretty drunk for a week and I wound up in jail for being drunk, and the uniform and my being in Italy didn't mean a thing. That judge, he just said fifteen days, and this was three days before Christmas. But there was a Salvation Army man in the court and he asked to speak to the judge and after he talked to him the judge said, "Suspended."

I had been in jail two days by that time, so I was sober and there was no good place I could have lunch that would take me. You think I am fooling you? Wouldn't serve an Indian hero? I can show you five guys who can tell you the same as me. You'd sit down and the waitress would come over and say, "Sorry, chief." You didn't blame her. You blamed the Greek or the Chink who was watching her from the cash register. You'd pass him and you'd like to say, "Fuck you, you Chink!" but you didn't. What was the use? I guess you'd think, he's got to think of his wife and kids. If his customers see an Indian eating next to them they won't come back. I'll tell you this, they wouldn't get away with it now around here. Not with some of the young fellows we got on the reserve now. We don't want to push these things, but by God, this was our land. You guys took it away from us with a whole shitpile of bad promises.

I ate in the bus station where they had to serve Indians.

I went home and it was the day before Christmas, and everybody says, "Hi, Louis" and "Good to see you, Louis," and I feel good. Except I had no presents, but my family and relatives and friends, they didn't care because I was home and I was alive, you know. We think of those things. Not what presents somebody can give to us for Christmas but that we went away to the war and got all shot up and now we're home and everybody has got big smiles on their faces and they're just glad to see me home for Christmas. And I'm glad to be home.

"WE WERE ALL BITTER"

When I got home to London I didn't know what I wanted to do. I guess you could say I was nervous, jumpy, fidgety. Irritable, I guess. At least I remember my mother saying that's what I was. I could have told her that if she'd been in a German prisoner-of-war camp for fourteen months, then she'd be irritable, too. So I looked around. I wasn't going to make up my mind yet.

I got a job driving taxi. It was easy work and I'd always been nuts about cars anyway. Some of my business was hauling around people like me, veterans who just couldn't sit in their parents' parlor after dinner and listen to the radio, and I guess they'd suddenly jump up and call for a taxi and that was me. They'd want to do something. Anything. There were a few bootleggers in town but outside the city limits and that was the territory of the OPP, so they were pretty safe. I made good money. Sometimes I'd come back at midnight and go into one of these blind pigs and the guys would say, stick around. They weren't ready to go yet and I'd tell them I would have to put the meter on because the boss was taking a long look at my fares out to the blind pigs, but he did like the money.

So if they wanted to keep the meter running, fine, and I'd sit in the bootlegger's place. It was always the living room with the shades down. There would be maybe a dozen people there. I'd have a beer on the house, maybe two, and listen to the guys talk. Mostly veterans. I don't remember much talk about the war. Most of them seemed pretty restless. Like me. This is all memory, but over those months and a lot of different guys, I'd say most of the talk was about getting jobs. That seemed to be number one. They wanted a girl to get married to. They wanted a job to support her. To have kids. Nobody as I remember would have said they wanted a wife just to screw her. No, they wanted to start families and get a house or buy a small business, start one, get into something where they could make money.

If one guy said he was browned off about the guys, maybe school chums, who didn't go into the services, then you got quite a bit of flack flying around. Sure, you're right. I was bitter about that, too. Damned bitter at times. We all were.

Especially me. Why shouldn't I be? I was the one who got captured when our kite went down and I was the one on that last march, in February, when they made us take off our boots and they gave them to the German Army and we had to march hell and gone over half of Germany, about a thousand of us. Prisoners. Our feet wrapped in rags, canvas, you name it.

But it was all talk. Rye talking. Beer talking. They'd forget about it next morning. Until the next time. Or the next time they saw one of their school chums of four years ago looking like a million bucks with the pretty wife and a kid beside him, and he's still in his uniform because he can't get into his civvie clothes or can't buy any because he hasn't got the money. Or something.

Anyway, I heard a lot of that kind of talk. Not angry talk. Not shouting, you know. Just talk about the unfair way the exemption board did this or that, but this would be farm guys who had got exemptions to help the old man run the farm. Or a business, and the son had to stay home to keep it going because it was essential to the war effort. Those words. "Essential to the war effort." How many times did I hear that?

And you know what? You get seven or eight guys talking this way and it is late at night and they're a few sheets to the wind and someone says, like, "Okay, he was smarter than us. He stayed out." And you know what? They'd agree. Yeah, old So-and-So was smarter.

So there was some bitterness but only when somebody got them going on the subject. Usually the one person who had a real bitch about it. But they knew nothing could be done. There would always be these guys with wealthy fathers, influential fathers, or uncles who would get them off the hook. I guess it happens in every war you want to name.

"LIVE AND LET LIVE"

Let's put it this way. I chose to enlist and I did because I wanted to. They chose to stay out and if they had to look at themselves in the mirror every morning and ask themselves, "Why am I not serving Canada?" I would say that is something they had to deal with. It was their problem, I guess.

Back to your first question. Sure, I could have been bitter and mean and resentful and make a lot of dirty remarks if I wanted to. It all depended on the guy. I just chose to do it my way. Leave well enough alone.

I honestly don't think it was much of a problem for anyone. If it was a problem, then maybe it said a little about him, too. I've always been an easy kind of person about somebody else's weaknesses. Live and let live.

"I STILL FEEL THE SAME WAY"

To this day I can't meet a man my age without somehow trying to find out if he was in the war, and if I find out he was, then fine, but if he wasn't, I feel contempt for him.

My wife says, why should you worry? She says you did your part and you came back and you've made a good life for all of us and we're retired and everything is fine. She's right, you know. The war was a long time ago. I have to agree with her, but I still feel that way.

I get thinking, and I think about losing my right leg and how when I came back there was a lot of things I couldn't do. I couldn't play baseball, which I loved. You need speed and agility for that. With a wooden leg?

What I'm talking about is coming back in February of '46 and going to church with my folks that first Sunday and there were a lot of the fellows I'd been to school with. A couple were even important at that age. Twenty-two, if you'll believe it! And I knew they'd all snuck out of service, wangled their way out. They were as healthy as I was.

That day I couldn't talk to those fellows. I'd known them all my life and they came up to me and were happy I was back and I was thinking, how can you even look me in the face if you're the least bit honest? I could not figure out what made them tick. I mean, did they look in their shaving mirror every morning and say, "No, I am not a coward"?

The way I look at it, it is as simple as that. Just that!

Sure, I've had to work with people like that. All my life, in fact. No doubt. But I couldn't call them friends, real ones, and I know that's harmed me because Red Deer is a small city and was a lot smaller then. I can't help it. I can't see them as honest and decent people. Even now.

"HE DIDN'T HIRE ARMY GUYS"

You know, the first job I ever went for, it was like this. The guy in the government employment office read me off a list of jobs they had and after he finished I asked him what the best-paying one was and he said carpentering, but what the hell was I to know about that?

He read off truck driver and I said, how much is that, and I think it was eighty-five cents an hour and I thought that was pretty good, so he gave me the form after I'd filled it out and down I went to this coal and wood company on Cambie Street.

The girl took me in where the manager was and he looked at my form and looked at me. I said, did he have a job, and he said yes, but he said it was coal and wood driving and the driver had to load and unload the stuff at homes and he had a policy of not hiring guys who had been in the Army. Now did you ever hear of anything so fucking stupid? Just after a war, and he wants men and there's hundreds of Army guys around.

I asked why and he said something like this. He didn't hire Army guys because we were lazy, we'd spent three years of the war sitting around doing nothing in England and going up to Scotland to screw the girls, and then we went to France and killed a few Germans and screwed a lot more girls and come home, and didn't we think we were a bunch of heroes?

That did it. I'd taken a fair amount of shit since I'd got home but nothing like what this fat Bohunk was throwing at me, and I walked around his desk and he half got up and I knocked that garlic-eating slob down and then I got my tail out of there.

There must have been a cop car half a mile away because they picked me up at the bus stop just across the street and down to Cordova Street, and the old cop who was in charge of the car said we'd better go and see the sergeant first. The cop said this was Sergeant McGregor or Mc-Something, and he told him what I'd done and the sergeant asked me my side of the story. I told him, straight. I was an Army vet, and I was sent there for a job and what the big Bohunk said to me and that I'd plowed him into the middle of next week.

I even put in the part about screwing the Scotch girls. That did it. He said that if the guy wanted to lay charges, then they would have to haul me in, but if he didn't, I was free to go and good luck.

Then he said, "Good man. I didn't like what he said about the girls in Scotland."

Now, imagine that. And the next thing he said was, and get this, will you, and forty years later it still makes me give a laugh or so, he asks me if I wanted to join the force. I mean, he said would I consider join-ing the force. He thought a man with a name like mine, McRae, would be a good man. I said yes and he took down my name and address and when the time came for getting recruits I looked the registration form they sent me over and I thought, no, five years in the Army is enough. The police force, too much like the service, I figured.

I got a job in a supply house, easy work, got promoted, married the boss's wife's cousin and in a few years they moved me to Calgary to open a store and, well, I guess that's all I have to say, I guess. Short and sweet. I still remember that slob of a Bohunk. Splat! I sure smoked that one at him.

TWO WRENS AND A MODEL-A

I enjoyed the whole thing. It was the Navy and it was just a darned good thing to feel you were wanted and doing a part in winning the war. I think the most disappointing thing for all of us was that so few of us got overseas. I'd have killed just to have gotten over to Newfiejohn, let alone 'Derry in Northern Ireland, where all the excitement was. Imagine just pining away to be posted to St. John's in Newfoundland? But I was stuck in Ottawa as switchboard operator at headquarters. Oh, so dull. Three years of it, but I was wearing the WREN uniform and that was something, and then there was the social aspect of it, too. I'm joking. It was almost nil. There were so many girls in Ottawa and so few men who we thought were eligible. We didn't actually look too kindly on the ranks. They were just like us—Joe boys. But it was all okay. An experience.

Then we got out. I was discharged on June 28, I believe, and that harvest I worked on my dad's farm. He had a new Massey Harris, self-propelled. It cost him more than $3,000, so you could see he had done quite well out of the price of wheat during the war. He let me run it, his pride and joy. That horrified my mother, but it was so simple. Like one of these lawnmowers you see on the golf course. You just sit and steer. Dad paid me a man's wage and so I had about, August, September, oh, about three hundred dollars coming to me and I said I'd take his Model-A as my wages. That suited him just fine. He figured he'd got two months' work out of me for nothing as he wasn't using the Model-A.

There was a girl I knew in Brandon named Alice Dunne. We decided we'd go to Vancouver in the car, and her brother was a mechanic and he gave the old Ford—black, you remember—he fine-tuned it and the tires were good. The tenth of October away we went. We wore our uniforms. Navy for me. Army for her. The best thing we ever did. The smartest move. We were going to go down through the States. You could go to Vancouver by road through Canada but it was not very good. Besides, we wanted to see the States, and we did.

From the time we rolled over the border and into North Dakota we had nothing but fun. Most of them had never seen a woman in a Canadian uniform and we couldn't buy a meal. You'll not believe this, but we often wouldn't be allowed to pay for our hotel or cabin. They didn't have motels then. "No, you are our guests." That sort of thing. If we had a flat, and we had a few, the first car or truck would stop and out would hop some old geezer or truck driver and bingo, the tire would be changed. And when we got to the next town the tire would be patched and sometimes we just couldn't pay for it. "No, we don't want your money," they'd say. I'll tell you, servicewomen in Ottawa certainly weren't treated that way. Sometimes we felt like we were dirt. It just shows how differently they thought of the people who served their country.

Well, as you can imagine, it took us a long time to get to Vancouver. I'm surprised we ever got there! We were having so much fun and spending so little money that we decided to see California. Might as well.

Everything's on the house. A real party. I could have written a book about it. Those wonderful Americans. You'd go into a café and have a big meal and when you went to pay, the waitress would say, "That gentleman over there has taken care of it," or "The boss says it's on the house." All the time. All the way to California and all the way back up through Oregon along the coast. Through Washington and then, well, you can imagine. Once we crossed into Canada we were just a couple of women, a WREN and an Army CWAC, just two women driving an old Model-A. The party was over. Back to work. Hello Canada, you don't like us anymore.

Vancouver was beautiful. We drove in during a fog at night and you couldn't see twenty feet in front of you, and I remember we stayed at the Dufferin Hotel. Next morning I looked out and the sun was shining and it was about ten in the morning and there was a kind of farmers' market going on down below on a vacant lot. And then I looked up and there were the mountains. My God! I shrieked to Alice something like, "Look! Real honest-to-God mountains!" It was a Saturday and I'll never forget that day. We'd heard of Stanley Park. Who hadn't? And we chugged around it, chug-chug, and it was unbelievable. That day, wow! I still get excited thinking. It was so free, so easy. Even the people seemed different. People out walking and people playing tennis and it was the end of October.

We got talking to a couple at Siwash Rock where we stopped and they gave us the name of a place in Chinatown. I remember it: the Sai Woo Restaurant. We went there. I didn't know Chinese food from Romanian food, but there were two policemen eating in the booth across from us and they said they'd order for us, and they did—about five dishes. Shrimp, crab, beef, greens, fried rice, probably. Anyway, it was a feast, and we asked these cops where there was some excitement in town and they suggested the Georgia Hotel. That's where we went.

The beer parlor was like I thought an English pub would be, and we went in. We were wearing civilian clothes now, two women sitting alone. The next table had four women and two men. They were college students and in almost a jiffy we were all sitting together. When the lights blinked, meaning closing time, gentlemen, we were all great friends and nothing would do but that we go on a party.

You couldn't party forever but you could party a lot, so we both got jobs. That wasn't too difficult. I clerked in a stationery store on West Pender where they also sold books and magazines, and that way I got to meet lots of people. Everybody was a regular customer and they all worked in the area and you saw them in the coffee shop and shopping. Alice and I got a small apartment in an old house on Broughton Street and we had a great time. The Georgia Pub was still our social center and Chinatown was where we ate. To this day I've never grown tired of Chinese food.

In about a month I sold the Model-A for $400 to four of the college students who were always in the pub. They plastered it green and red, Christmas colors. You'd see it buzzing around town for three or four years and then I guess it quit on them.

All this time there were things I wanted to do. Open a dress shop was one of them. Work my way to Hong Kong on a freighter. Hide myself away in a little cabin up Hollyburn Mountain for six months and write a novel. Lots of things, but I never did them. Instead, I got married to a vet, an Army sergeant.

One day about 1955 I was having coffee, looking out the window, and I thought, I haven't seen Alice for a long, long time. I phoned and there was great peals of joy at either end of the line, and then I asked her what she was doing and she said, "Married, two kids, stuck in a rut, and sitting here drinking coffee," and I said, "Same here."

A few days later we met for a couple of beers in the Georgia Pub before lunch and walked down to Chinatown and gabbled away like we used to, but it wasn't the same as when we were young and happy and in Vancouver after the war. We were just a couple of old hausfraus. Sad, isn't it?

SOLD FOR BACK TAXES

I'm not saying that every soldier got treated rotten when he got home. Maybe only one in ten did, or maybe one in fifty, but it happened to me and that's all I can go by.

For two years before I joined up, and that was in '41, I worked all winter in the bush cutting pulp. The pay wasn't good but it was getting better—the war, you see, and guys leaving to join up—and because I wasn't spending a cent for about five months I saved a lot. And I worked for a summer camp, American tourists, guiding, and I had quite a bit of money in my bank account.

I, well, my parents were poor and they didn't speak English and they kind of kept to themselves, and before I went overseas I bought this little house. Eight acres and a little house and my dad could earn enough peddling eggs and vegetables around the town and doing work for neighbors, so he could keep the place together. And there was the twenty bucks I sent home for four years and so I thought everything was going okay at home.

Then I get home. There was no welcome in that town. Oh, the Legion got a bunch of us together a few months after most of us got home and gave us a bunfeed, and the reason they done this, they wanted us to join the Legion. That's the only reason those World War One old guys gave us a little party, costing maybe fifteen bucks. They wanted us to join, but they'd still be running everything and, believe me, it took something to get those old fogies out of the top jobs in that Legion. It was their private club, yeah, and we could drop in and have a game of darts and a beer, but anything to do to make that Legion a better place, then you could just forget it. They seemed to think their war was the only one ever fought and if they had stopped and heard about our war, it might have stiffened the hair that grew out of their ears. A couple, when they had us for their bunfeed, even wore their World War One medals for show. Like, see I got this one for being in England and this one for looking after a bunch of horses in Belgium. You know, that kind of thing. Why, I haven't even sent away for my medals. Yeah, you have to write away for them. Now it's forty years past and I don't want them now and I didn't want them then.

Anyway, anyway, no more about the Legion. What I'm talking about is the town, and I won't give you the name. But when I get home and there's nobody to meet us, about a dozen, nobody but the station agent and his dog, I walk home with my duffel and there's the folks and we're gabbing away in Ukrainian and having a fine old time. Mom is zipping around the kitchen making a feast and Dad and I are sipping that rotgut he made. Just throw some potatoes and even the peelings and other stuff into a pot and let her stew up and put it through a ten-buck still and you've got yourself a couple of quarts of powerful stuff.

He's talking Old Country, as you could guess, and I'm pretty rusty in it. I hadn't talked it for maybe four years, but I got part of it and it's to the point that somehow it's mixed up with taxes and the town hall and some bastard. I get it out of him that there are letters involved. You know, something from the town hall, the town clerk.

Oh, he has them and he brings them out and I go over them and it's pretty plain to me. The old man hadn't paid the taxes for three years. The notices are there. Hell, the whole shooting match comes to something less than eighty bucks and then there's the poll-tax things. Now, you're asking about how all this comes about? It's simple. The old man doesn't write English and he doesn't speak it, and if he'd been smart he'd of sent those letters off to me and I'd of looked after them, but he didn't. My mom and dad are Old Country and if you don't know what that is, then you can guess.

There's another letter and it says that the property is going to be sold at auction, for taxes. That letter, I look at the date and that is June first, the day of the tax sale. Now here's a nice mess, a really nice mess. We're into January and that's, let's see, that's eight months past and that sale has to have happened.

Next afternoon I go hotfooting down to the lawyer and he sees the letters. You know, that son of a bitch didn't even welcome me home. You'll find out why in a moment. He read the letters and he said that the tax sale was over and the house had been sold. No, nothing could be done about it. A legal auction, right there in the law books said unpaid taxes, they sell the house to pay the unpaid taxes, and that is it. The town gets their money that way. Get it? But here I was in England and across the Channel part of the time, the old man can't figure out what the letters say, so these letters addressed to me on Craig Street, the house, they don't get to me. That's why I don't have me a house to come home to to get a head start on learning how not to be a veteran anymore. Not a soldier, I mean.

I thank him and he smiles at me. Nice guy, eh? I go out and I'm walking down the street and I figure I'm going to the beer parlor and throw back maybe thirty or forty beers when suddenly it hits me. How come, how come if the sale was held seven, eight months ago and my house is sold, how come my mom and dad are still living it it? Yeah, I think, how come?

I'm right outside the Commercial Block on the main drag just then and there's a law firm in there, a couple of old guys who must of been there in 1905 when the town was started, and I go up the stairs and in the office and I see one of them, Mr. Crawford. Mr Crawford, I says, and I explain everything I've told you and show him the letters and everything, and he puts the letters down and he cleans his pipe and he fills it with Wood and Water—ha, ha, I mean Field and Stream, that nice-smelling stuff—and I can see him now.

Then he looks at me and he says, "Mr. Gregorchuk, have you got roughly one hundred dollars?" I say yes, I have, and that I've got even more. And I say that once I finish my thirty days of leave and get my discharge I'll have a lot more from my grants. Maybe seven hundred more.

I also say I'll have a job by then and I'll have more. I thought I'd lay it on thick.

Now, I'll tell you what this old Mr. Crawford said, and it was this. He said I was to wait until May 31, wait until two o'clock in the afternoon on May 31, and then I was to go to the town hall and I was to ask for the tax file on my property, and when the clerk brought it I was to ask him how much was owing on it and I was to pay him, the clerk, get a receipt, and ask if there was anything else against the property. Then he called in his secretary and he dictated all this and he told her to type it up and give it to me right away and then he said, "Well, we'll just let that bastard stew in his own juice."

I asked him what he meant and he said he'd tell me later, and just go and enjoy myself and get out of the Army and be sure to be at the town hall at that time on that date. I remember he said, "Don't let wild animals keep you away and bring at least a hundred bucks."

Then it comes to May 31, and I put on my suit and a white shirt and a tie, and I go to the town hall, and at two P.M. I walk up to the counter and I ask for the file on my property. The clerk kind of goes huuuhhhh? I say it again and I give the legal description and he says, well, maybe he can't find it, these things are filed away. And there's this voice behind me and it booms out, "You get that file, sonny. You get it here right away." Nobody was going to talk back to that voice and there's the clerk, scooting away to get it.

In a few minutes he's back and the voice, Mr. Crawford, of course, tells him to tot up what's owing, the works, everything, delinquency payments, everything, and the clerk does. The guy's shaking and he's older than me. One of these guys that didn't think it was important enough to put on a soldier's suit and go to war. Nicer to stay home and marry the prettiest girl in town. You know.

It came to $99.14, and that included the five-buck poll-tax I hadn't paid on the property, too, and the clerk stamped things and gave me a receipt and that was it.

One other thing. I remember it to this day. When it was done, this old lawyer pointed a finger at this town clerk, just pointed his finger, and he said "Beware."

Mr. Crawford invited me back to his office and he pulled a forty out of a filing case and we had a drink, and then he said he was going to tell me something. He said the taxes on that property came to about seventy-five dollars and it had sold for ninety-five and that the owner, the buyer, was a company with a name I can't remember, and he said

the main shareholder was my lawyer; the other was his wife. The guy
who had run the sale through before I joined the Army and the guy who
a few months before had told me it was sold and nothing could of been
done. He didn't, you see, say I had one full year to pay the back taxes.
His buying my place would have been no good then. He'd be out on
his ass.

This lawyer—no name because he's still breathing good clean air, back
in the home town—he stood to make a lot of money once he got his
hands on the place. Mr. Crawford said the government had plans for
the place, building an equipment yard, a place for storage and trucks,
an asphalt pile, sand, a mixer, and the like. The war was over and spring
was here, and there was going to be a lot of roadwork for two or three
years, and you know governments; they get their eye on a piece of land
and no matter if there is something just as good or better half a mile
away, no, they want that land and they was going to get it. Mr. Crawford
said the lawyer stood to make several thousand dollars on that land. I
don't know how, but he said several thousand dollars.

So who made the several thousand? Three guesses and the first two
don't count. I did. Mr. Crawford run the deal through with me and the
government. Just sign here, sign there, Mr. Gregorchuk, and I moved
my house and garage—it wasn't but two days work—to a piece of six acres
I bought for three hundred dollars not far away and I guess you could
say that was that.

But going back, we had about six good drinks and I figured it was time
to leave Mr. Crawford. She's about five o'clock and this secretary of his
is making tut-tut noises at us, and I say thanks and he said he was glad
to help, very glad, and I walk down the street and here's this lawyer
coming to me. He's red in the face and when he gets to me he says,
kind of mean and low, "You fucking potato head, Gregorchuk."

Well, I knew what was up. He phoned that clerk or the clerk phoned
him and told him the jig was up. He'd been euchred by this Bohunk, me.

I says to him, a lot of whiskey talking in me, I says that if I ever meet
him on the sidewalk of that town I'm going to take my knife and cut
off a good big length of buggy rein at the nearest hitching post and I
was going to tie him to that post so tight he couldn't move and then
I was going to look behind that mare or that team, and if there was any
horseshit, I was going to smear it all over his face and his fancy shirt.
I said it and I'm telling you, there were a couple of people heard me say it.

In the six years we lived in that town, not once did I meet that bastard
on the street. Not once. Every time he'd see me coming he'd duck into

a store or cross the street. I used to laugh. The whole town knew about it, too, because after the war things had been so good during the war for the farmers that nobody came to town anymore with a horse and buggy. No one. Cars and trucks, that's what they drove, and I've never seen one of them that drops a pile of shit.

"I WAS NO LONGER A WREN"

Oh, I can remember. I was so lonely. So lonely I could die. I was out of the Navy and I was home in my mother's nice warm home and there were all the girlfriends I still had in town, and there I was bawling my head off.

What it was all about, you know, was that I missed my pals, the other girls, the ones I had been with at Stadacona for two years. They were closer to me than my mother and sisters back there in Ottawa. They were my buddies, and there I was, missing them terribly and my mother coming to look in my door every three minutes and not knowing what to do.

This was the second day after I got all the papers signed and was discharged, and when I stepped out on the street I realized I was no longer a WREN. I was so proud to be a WREN and serving my country and, you know, backing up my brother Lennie in the Army and my cousins right across Canada who had joined up.

I remember. They had planned a big party for the day, the time I walked into the house free and clear of the Navy. Little Jean coming home. All happy and ready to be something. Somebody. Something. Well, I had been something as a WREN and like all the girls I had worn that uniform oh so proudly. The big party. I walked in the door and there were about two dozen people. Gosh, you would have thought I had won the war instead of just being a typist in Halifax headquarters, but I went along with them—but you know what? It was more like their party than one for me. I was just the excuse to have a party.

Next morning I guess everybody had a hangover but me because I didn't drink and it hit me: I wouldn't see Nora and Aggie and Janet and Frances again, although it didn't work out that way. Janet has died but the rest of us get together when we can. But next morning there was this terrible feeling of let-down, that I was alone, and because I'd been told what to do and when to do it and how to do it every day for the past two and a half years, I just felt lost. That's when all the crying started.

It is all like yesterday. At noon my mother brought me up two eggs boiled and some toast and honey and a pot of tea, and I certainly tucked into it. No breakfast, you see. The crying jag had just hit me when I realized I was so alone.

But when you're twenty-one you bounce back. Oh, how I can laugh at myself now. Little Jean, the family cry baby. My mother sat down and had a talk with me and got it out of me, and she told me I'd have to buck up. We'd go down to Sparks Street and start buying me some nice clothes that the Civil Service girls were wearing now and that set me off again. Bawling. But the storm clouds cleared and I dried my eyes and fixed my face, and when I came downstairs my mother asked me where I'd got that lovely perfume. I said I'd bought it in the women's canteen at Stadacona. "Oh," she said, "we civilians can't buy that kind of perfume. It just isn't available." I thought like saying, well, you didn't serve your country, that's why! But I didn't.

So, we went shopping that afternoon and you know, we'd thought there were no nice things, dresses and things, because of the war effort. I know it was so in Halifax. But there were nice things and buying these things perked me up no end.

It was a nice and clear sunny Ottawa day. I can remember it now. My mother had arranged we would meet friends of hers for tea at the Chateau Laurier, and when we got to their table the man stood up while we were seated by the waiter. I thought, oh my, isn't this grand! Far better than the mess hall. Far better than those crowded and awful and noisy restaurants in Halifax. There was small sandwiches and butter tarts and tea with lemon and I remember thinking, maybe, after all, I'm going to enjoy being a civilian. In the taxi home I remember clutching my bags and packages and thinking, what will it feel like having lovely underwear on and this lovely dress and these stockings and these pumps? Girl talk. Girl thoughts.

You know what I am trying to say? I had my good bawl and then it was back into real life again. After all, service life could never be called real. It is the most unreal life for a person I can think of. So just a dash of shopping and a dash of male chivalry and a dash of civilized teatime and there I was, almost removed from it all and I was still wearing my uniform.

What I'm saying is, coming home was easy. I had been away. It had been a wonderful time. The excitement. The good feel of the marching on parade. The girls. My wonderful friends. But suddenly it was all over. Done and gone forever. We all had lives to begin living and there was no time to think of that wonderful adventure. *Now* was the time we had to think of. The real adventure was ahead, and I knew I would miss terribly my friends for a while because they were the only ones I had. But again, the old Presbyterian common sense of mine. Things change. Make the best of it.

And I guess I did, like so many.

"I NEVER FORGOT HER"

I got off the boat in Montreal. Whitey Dawson and I caught a cab and headed for downtown Montreal. We said we wanted a good Canadian meal and the driver said his brother owned a restaurant on St. Catherine, so we said okay, take us there.

I guess I was expecting a dump, but it was a really fine place and we sat down at a nice table and I remember it because there was flowers on it. We ordered double scotch and water to start things off. I'd been dreaming of this. You'll never know what it was like in London. The rationing, I mean. I look at the menu and it says pork chops. "Chops" means more than one, so I ordered six.

The waiter didn't bat an eye. The guy asked if we'd like a bottle of wine and Whitey said sure. We were loaded. There was a lot of gambling going on in that ship and I had a roll of bills that would choke Seabiscuit, and Whitey hadn't done too bad either. The waiter went through all that foofaraw with the cork and the tasting, a sip of the wine, and I didn't know what to say, so I just said it was good. Then our meal came and by God, there were my three chops on the plate and a little side plate with the three others and Whitey's steak was big. There we were, eating meat and potatoes and drinking wine, and Whitey says something like this, "In June of '42 the ration for one Englishman for one whole week was two of those chops you got there, *if* you could get them. Now you're eating one Englishman's rations for three weeks, and you don't even think about it," and I guess we both laughed. I guess that's when we realized we were back home again.

Six of us were traveling in a small draft so we were going on a passenger train, I guess I called it a civilian train. I sat at the window and watched every mile of the country going by and wondering, what will I do? I was twenty-one years old and I'd been away from home since I joined up in '42. I didn't know what to do. I really felt lonely. I didn't know anybody. Not even the guys on the train. Whitey was only a guy who was in the same camp with me for two weeks waiting for a ship to go home and we'd hit it off pretty well, but he was getting off in Calgary and I'd be alone and, frankly, it scared the hell out of me.

I didn't have a girl. None of the girls I knew at school had written me, although there was a teacher in the Chilliwack High School who had girls draw names out of a hat, to be pen pals, you see. Whatever happened to pen pals? You never hear of them now. Anyway, this girl wrote me about a dozen letters when I was in England and then in France and Holland, but they were little-girl letters, but I sure appreciated the socks she'd knit. Woolen ones. They weren't any better than Army issue, but you felt you had a bit more class wearing them. That was the only letter writer I had except my brother, who wrote twice, both times at Christmas, and said the farm was going okay, and so on and so on but nothing, really.

Don't think I'm going to say I went back to Chilliwack and married the girl who wrote me and sent the socks. No, it didn't happen. I could have looked her up, I guess. Anyway, I didn't.

When I said good-by to Whitey, getting a couple of words and a shake before his family hit him like a bunch of football tacklers, I felt alone and wandered around the station a bit and then I got back on the train and there was a girl sitting in the vacant seat, Whitey's, next to me. She was twenty and her husband had been killed in a plane crash in Germany just before the war shut down and now that she had some widow's money, I guess you'd call it, she was going to take a long trip and try and forget her sorrow. You can guess that we were both in the same boat, not knowing what to do with our lives, and yet, when I look back we were so young. She was a very young twenty and hadn't really known much of her husband. I was twenty-one and hadn't known much about girls and, I guess, life in general. I was just a farm kid from the Fraser Valley.

I remember one funny thing, right at the start. She said her mother was English and you know how some of those English women are. She'd named her Rowinda. I thought it was a name she'd made up but no, it was a name. She had a sister Melinda, which wasn't bad, and the other sister was called Belinda, which was a name I recognized. So when she realized how stupid a name like Rowinda was, she became Betty, which was the nickname for Elizabeth. I told her my mother had named me Debrett, which was stupid, too, so I'd enlisted under the name of Brett, which was what I'd been called in school. That sort of thing kind of made us good friends right off.

We talked all the way to Vancouver—no sleep—talked sitting in our seats and in the dining car, and when we got to Vancouver we put her bags and mine in the baggage room. It was about eleven in the morning, and I hired a taxi and we had the driver just drive us for about two hours. I was seeing civilization again and she was seeing Vancouver. Then we got out at Chinatown and she hadn't eaten Chinese food before, so we had a big meal. I could tell you even today just what we had. We were still talking a mile a minute and I guess that taxi driver wondered what the hell we were doing because we weren't looking much at Stanley Park.

We were just two people together and we hadn't even held hands on the train or anything. I mean I just felt good about her and I didn't want her to leave, but it was time to say good-by and I can remember, to this day, walking back to the station with her and getting out her two bags. They were green. I said I would phone for a taxi and when it was coming we stood on the curb in the sunshine and she heard the whistle of a freighter and she asked what it was. I said it was a deep sea ship. She said she hadn't seen one and I said I'd take her across the harbor on the North Van ferry and she said yes, she'd like that, but just then the taxi came racing up and we knew that it was not the right time. Not the right place. Not anything. It was too early, I guess, and too late.

She said she'd write me and I said I'd write her and the taxi driver put her bags in the trunk. She leaned over and gave me a kiss and said, "Good-by, Brett, good-by, and thank you," and I gave her a little hug and then I kissed her on the mouth and she kissed me back. She got into the cab and I waved good-by.

I never forgot her. I wanted to write. I know she would have written back. But you know, and this is crazy, in all those hours of talking and not sleeping I hadn't told her my address, and she hadn't given me her address. So how many Betty Calders were there in Calgary forty years ago?

I didn't try and write her and I went back to the farm and picked up where I'd left off, but I'll always remember her, for all the things we talked about and how she sort of reintroduced me back to Canada again and that wonderful meal in Chinatown and me kissing her, and that was the first time I had ever kissed a girl.

"THEY CALL ME FB"

There certainly was an adjustment. No doubt of that. You were back in the arms of your loving family although they looked at you in a strange way, although they didn't know they were doing it.

When I got back it was just before Christmas, so there was the usual family dinner at my grandmother Parsons's house, the main farm. Like the family farm. It was tradition that we eat at Grannie's.

You know, somebody asks you, "Where were you when President Kennedy was shot?" Everybody knows. The point is, do you remember your first Christmas dinner back home? I do. Before dinner there's about twenty or more of us sitting in the living room and I think I'll tell them about the Christmas before. Italy, '44. I get halfway through it and then figured, hell, Maury, this isn't the right kind of story to tell. It's a good story but pretty damned gory and gruesome. The Germans had broken a truce on us, you see, and mortars started to land around us and, by gosh, we sure as hell found ourselves back in the war pretty quick. So I snapped her off right there and everybody had that kind of funny look on their face as if to say, my gosh, we've got to humor this guy. He's been in a bad war. Actually I didn't have too bad a war. In fact I enjoyed it.

So there we are, about twenty of us and then Grannie Parsons calls us all into the kitchen. Now that was a whopper of a kitchen. They don't build them like that anymore. The cream separator was there. The table would pull out and seat a threshing crew and there was a big stove over there and a small one where you're sitting. Two turkeys, not one. Everything. Then the meal starts after grace said by my grandfather and then grace said by my sister's smallest kid, little James, who is about four then. Cute as a button. He zips through it and in we pitch. I know people are watching me, so I'm careful to use a knife and fork and thank somebody when they pass the cranberry sauce. And then there's one of those pauses, nobody's saying a single word, and I say, "Please pass the fucking butter."

It came as natural as breathing. "Please pass the fucking butter." I'd said it a hundred times in the past, without the please, naturally, because I was being polite. It was about two seconds before I realized what I'd done.

Nobody said a thing until my grannie, good old Grannie, she said to my sister, "Lil, Maury asked for the butter."

Well, that tore it and everybody starts in eating and chattering and laughing and breaking crackers and we had a great and grand old time, a real Parsons Christmas. We had the opening of the gifts around the tree after dinner which was Christmas Day, not Christmas Eve, and there were dozens for me. I was the guy who'd been away four years, you know. They just piled up around my feet. It was one hell of a Christmas.

Nobody, none of my brothers or uncles, none of them mentioned what I said. Hell, it was just the natural thing to say. That word was used as a noun, adjective, verb, adverb, by everyone. It was just a word. 'Cept you didn't say it in front of your grannie.

Next week I'm in town and I go to the pool hall to shoot a couple of games and to see what guys are back, and I walk in the door and I hear a voice say, "Hey, FB, stay right there and I'll go and get some soap to wash out your mouth." I didn't get it but then I did. FB, fucking butter, and I guess my brother, one of them, had talked it up around town and now they were calling me FB. Oh, I didn't mind. One nickname is as good as another and, besides, I never did like Maury as a nickname. Always thought it was too sissy, like a painter would have.

I stayed around for another year and that's all anybody called me, including my grannie, and how she knew I'll never know, but when folks from way back look me up they say, "Hey, FB, it's me, Johnny Jones, and how about we get together for a little drink or two?" Meaning at my house, of course. I don't mind. It's always good to see people from the old town. Old towns are good to come from. Not to stay in.

"IT ALL STRAIGHTENED OUT"

A lot of Army guys came back in rough shape. In Europe, like the last days of the war in Germany, there was a lot of booze lying around. So, there was a lot of drinking and some guys I know came back and they were real boozers. Sitting in the beer parlor. Waiting when the door opened. That sort of thing. Not many of these types had any plan for their lives and I figured, Christ, man, you've been through a war and got out with a full skin because you were lucky and God or whoever does it has handed you your life back. You're just sitting on your butt handing out your back pay to some guy and then going into the can and pissing it up against the wall. That didn't make sense.

Everybody had to adjust. We'd been away too long and everything had passed by. The parade had gone on down the street. You couldn't hear the music of the brass band anymore. The crowds had all gone home. That left you sitting with a glass in your hand in a tavern wishing you had someone to talk to about what it had been like.

Well, like we all did, these guys with the glass glued to their hand, they had to smarten up, too.

They did. Oh, yes, they did. I think old Mackenzie King and his gang thought they were going to get a bunch of killers home on the troop trains. You know, it never happened. You know, when killing just was a part of your life and you'd knock out a German tank and roll on by and it's on fire and you'd think, "God, there's five guys in there being turned into fish and chips." It was him against you, and you were still alive. That kind of thing produced quite a few boozers.

But I think that it all straightened out, and soon. Guys just decided the civilians at home didn't give a shit about what they had done, so they had better start being civilians again and catch up. That's why so many guys went back to university. To college. Got a better education. You didn't talk about it then. You just knew you'd better start being better than the next guy because the better guy got the better job, and that was it. By God, that was it, and that's the way it worked out. Right down the line.

But back to the boozers. Sure, there were a lot. There had to be. That was one hell of a jolt for a lot of us, coming back home, and I think the attitude of the civilians was tough, too. You know: "Okay, you've been lazing around in the Army for four years, so let's see if you know how to work."

Maybe the fellows you'd see waiting for the tavern to open in those first few months were guys who were just pissed off with civilians as they found them and sat in the taverns because it was a way to get away from the civilians. Could be.

There sure were a crappy lot of them, you know. The civilians, I mean.

"THE MOST WONDERFUL MOMENT OF MY LIFE"

This is about how I came to Canada. I was an English girl living with my parents in Surrey, south of London. I joined the Air Force as many, many English girls did—the Army, the Navy, and the Air Force—and I wonder if they could have carried on the war without us. For four years I was in the tower at Bigan Hill—that's where a Canadian squadron was based—and one night at a dance at the grange hall in our village I saw this Canadian officer, and I said to myself, I'm going to marry that man. Oh, he was handsome.

And like any girl worth her salt can do, I got him to dance with me and that's where it began. He was the only man I was ever serious about and things just went along and we got married.

Things were starting to get hot in the East and they needed experienced pilots, so he went to India and then Ceylon, and then the war was over. I had a chance, one of these things where they said, you've got three days to decide, and it was if I wanted to catch a ship to Canada. A war bride ship, although there were others on it. I made some awful fast arrangements and I was to go out to Canada and when he got back from the East he was to follow me.

Now what happened was this. I didn't know it but some of the fellows could volunteer to fight the Japanese in the Pacific, and for some reason he did. I didn't know this and when, the very day my ship sailed, he arrived back in England, he phoned my folks and they said I had already gone to Canada. That very day. They had just got home from seeing me off.

Oh, I guess you can figure out the rest. Fred roared back to his base and talked with the chap, probably the adjutant, and things were pushed hard and there he was, flying in a plane across the water back to Canada while my ship was probably only halfway across the Atlantic.

About ten days later the train carrying the war brides pulled into the Regina station and his parents were there to meet me. All smiles. All hugs. I loved them on sight. The Jamiesons were fun people, as they say, and once they had got my baggage and it was checked in the baggage room and all these things, they said, "Now, Ellen, we'll take you to the restaurant in the hotel and you can have lunch and then we'll pick you up in an hour because both of us have got to see a lawyer and that will take time." So they took me to the Hotel Saskatchewan and to the door of this big restaurant and Mr. Jamieson pointed and he said, "You go to that table over in that corner, the one by the window, and wait for us there."

I looked and there was a man sitting there. His back to me. I said it was already taken and they said, "Don't worry. He's a friend of ours and he'll keep you company while we're gone."

Oh, I was a proper English girl then and I walked slowly toward the table and suddenly I had a funny feeling and I started to run and he got up and yes, it was my Freddie. Something about the shape of his head I recognized, after eighteen months away. I couldn't believe it, I just couldn't. I started to cry and he was laughing and then I was laughing and then that poor dumb sap started to cry and people were looking at us, I know, and I guess they were smiling. I know they were smiling when I sat down and my eyes cleared. It was the most wonderful moment in my life.

Then Freddie said, "Listen, El, do you know I haven't kissed you yet?" and we both got up and kissed long, a long time, and I know that people in that restaurant didn't know what was going on, but they started to clap.

We talked for about ten hours straight and his folks didn't come back and next morning Freddie told me we'd have to be outside the hotel door at nine o'clock—and here comes this car up Broad Street and his father is driving and he had bought a bottle of champagne. About 150 miles up the road we stopped by a schoolhouse and went into the yard and had a picnic.

Mr. Jamieson asked me if I knew Freddie when I saw him at the table, and I said if I had met him on the street here, because you see I thought he was still in Ceylon or somewhere, and if I'd met him on the street, in a nice suit and a hat, I would have just passed him by. Why? Well, I'll tell you. If you are not expecting to see someone, and also it is thousands of miles away from where you would expect to see him, then you would not recognize him. Remember, too, I had only seen him in his officer's uniform.

But then I said there was just something. Maybe I did recognize the shape of his head or the way his shoulders were. Or maybe—well, something just told me to run.

I loved the way the Jamiesons did things. They loved a joke. I think that may have been why I fell in love with Freddie—his sense of humor— although when I first saw him at the grange I knew that was it. In those days a girl should not have put such high hopes in marrying a pilot in Bomber Command. So many girls did and were widows a week, a month later.

When I read your letter to the editor in the Toronto *Star* I didn't think I had anything to contribute, and also, I was not a Canadian veteran. Then, I thought, he might like that story about the meeting in the restaurant that morning in Regina. That, really, must have been the most important moment in my life. A new husband and a new life in a new land. It didn't quite work out that way. The Air Force still had him. I thought it out once. When you're a kid off the farm and you get your pilot's wings and a commission and see strange and exotic lands, I guess it gets into your blood and there is nothing you can do about it. Like the call of the sea, you might say.

"THE SERVICE WAS GOOD ENOUGH FOR ME"

Naturally I can't say how it was with the Army and Navy but I know this, we didn't sit around the hangars and in the huts talking about our future when we got out. I don't know. It just didn't seem to be the type of conversation you talked about.

Oh sure, we talked about getting home, all the time, but one fellow wouldn't suddenly say, "Hey! I've just decided I'm going to become a doctor," and another would say, "I'm going to be the greatest engineer in Canada." Most of us had been hanging around England for maybe three years and we were so far from the Canadian scene that, well, Canada was just one hell of a long way away. It was another country that we didn't know much about anymore.

I got back in February of '46. It was cold when I got back to Montreal. Don't kid yourself, Montreal is not a nice city in the winter and I found out there were no jobs. All the jobs were taken by those guys who were sent home in July and August of '45 and believe me, there were no jobs. I tried for three straight weeks and the only job I was offered was dishwashing. I asked the owner if that meant I might get a chance to become a waiter and he said no, his customers liked French waitresses and he said, besides I didn't look like a waiter. What the hell is a waiter supposed to look like?

After three weeks I quit and I had my money coming in from the government and I was staying with my parents. Suddenly it struck me, "Hey, this isn't the way I had hoped it would be." I knew I missed my buddies and the whole part of being a team and the fun of it. Yeah, I know. There wasn't all that much fun in England, but I was living kind of a useless life. I thought it was me. I thought maybe I was the misfit. That could be it, I thought. Maybe I wasn't used to civilian life. After all, I never had been a civilian. High school, one year at McGill just fooling around, into the Air Force. I didn't know what it was to work, go in at nine and come out at six and catch a streetcar home. Have a house and a wife.

I thought about it, and that summer I took a trip out to the West Coast and I picked up odd jobs. That fall I hitchhiked home and got home in late September and I'd made up my mind. I didn't tell anybody. I just went down to the recruiting office and they said sure, we need aircraft mechanics for all these new planes we're going to buy. That was when the Russian bear started to snarl and roar in earnest. Sure, Corporal, c'mon back in. We'll even give you your stripes back. I thought, no more worry, no more thinking about jobs, no more nothing. In three weeks they sent me a letter and I reported, had my medical. Can you see lightning and hear thunder? You know. I was in.

Let me tell you, it felt good.

To make a long story short, I stayed in until '67. Centennial year. I was nothing more than a sergeant, but in the Air Force that was a cozy rank. Very secure. It got me a twenty-six-year pension.

No, some just were not prepared to make it on Civvie Street. I guess somewhere in the back of this old bean there was always the thought that the service was good enough for me, so why knock yourself out with a bunch of civilians? Besides, even though I didn't have anything against them, I mistrusted civilians from the day I got out the first time. Their life just didn't seem real to me somehow.

"A SHINY NEW PRIVATE AGAIN"

There comes a time when you just say fuck it.

I don't know how many times I would come back to that little room I rented from the Italian woman and look at that pistol I'd brought back from Germany and I'd be thinking, I can make a good living with this thing.

Oh, don't get me wrong. I didn't. What I'm saying is, I was pretty discouraged. I can remember the day. Like the day President Kennedy was shot. What were you doing? Everybody seems to remember. Well, I can tell you this, the day I wasn't shot was on December 21 and I had come back from working in the coal bins, lousy work for worse-than-lousy pay, and it was my wash night. My night in the tub was Thursday and I found the old Italian lady had a flock of their cousins and nieces and uncles and the whole damned crew there, and she said I couldn't use the tub that night. Remember, the twentieth was just before Christmas and so I packed up my clothes and a few books and my gun and other things and I walked out. I didn't even tell her she had lost a roomer.

Dirty as I was, I got a cab and I went to a hotel where they didn't mind a guy looking like a chimney sweep and I spent an hour scrubbing myself down to the bone. I was red and shiny and then I went downstairs and proceeded to drink as much beer as I could until 10 P.M., and then I got a cab and he took me to a boot. I knew the people. He was a war vet, and a mortar had banged him up. I've always liked blind pigs. The people who go to them may be rough, but they're honest.

Next day all shined up I went down to the recruiting office and the sergeant did look me over kindly, I would say. A lot of questions and then he said that they weren't doing any business that day as it was the day before Christmas, so I was to come back the day after Boxing Day. I went to the coalyard and got my pay and fooled around town. I couldn't go home for Christmas and I didn't know anybody well enough to ask myself for Christmas dinner.

It was lonely, sure, but what could I do? My folks farmed outside of Oxbow, Saskatchewan, and that's all the folks I had.

I was betting they'd take me back into the Army again and I felt good, so when the day came, I was there with my papers and everything I had and sure, two days later, there I was, not a sergeant like I'd been, but a shiny new private again and that suited me fine. I knew I'd get a stripe or stripes soon.

Yes, you can ask that question. No, I didn't consider myself a failure in Civvie Street. Remember, I did what one hell of a lot of guys did in the two or three years after the war. It wasn't that I couldn't have made it out on Civvie Street. I had been a sergeant—that counted for a hell of a lot. No, I just didn't care about it, otherwise I wouldn't have been working my butt off humping ice on the truck in summer and working like a slave in the coalyard in winter. I didn't care.

It was only when I joined up again that I cared. I knew I was doing something worthwhile and what was good for me and that's a good combination.

About the gun? Well, I did nothing. It was a souvenir. A German officer's pistol. A Luger. It was worth something. I mean, I remember how I got it and that was something but no, I sold it. For fifty dollars. Too cheap, but I didn't want it. It was a dangerous thing to have in the Army.

"THE WAY I SEE IT"

There was myself, all Bristol fashion in my naval lieutenant's uniform, a hero if you want to believe stories in the newspapers, but all I really did was zip around some hot spots of the English Channel in my sub-chaser looking for subs or anything that looked like enemy that we could sink, capture, or take pot shots at. It was a good war and we had white sheets on our beds most every night and now I was going home and I didn't know what the hell to do. I did have the connections, you know, but I wasn't quite sure how my skill at navigation and handling a crew of four and bearing down on a French fishing boat which might have held a German cannon was going to work in the Vancouver business world.

It didn't, of course. Everybody was glad to see me and nobody wanted to hear one single word of my experiences and besides, I wasn't about to tell them. I drifted along for a few weeks, going down to the yacht club and chatting around with the old gang, just being pleasant, saying I was looking around if anyone asked me what I was going to do, crewing for some of the yachts in the Outer Harbor races and just being, well, I suppose being like a character in a Scott Fitzgerald novel, without the heavy drinking and the world-worn and weary attitude.

About September, when things started to turn around after the summer and our crowd decided it was time to go to work again, I still had nothing and I thought, you'll have to take a more positive attitude. Oh, I did. I did. In about three weeks I exhausted most of the contacts I had made and there were a lot of smiles and a few vague promises and invitations to house parties and such, but nothing I could stick in a letter and put a stamp on.

I said I was uptight, didn't I? Yes, a modern word but it applied. Here I was, twenty-six, and nobody to look after me when I was sick, nobody to give me a filling, nobody to give my rig a pressing, and no one to feed me and billet me. What I'm saying is, Vancouver was a damn nice place to be if you were in the Navy, the Royal Canadian Navy as a lieutenant, and when everyone was giving their all for King and Country to get *out* of the blooming outfit, I was coming around to the point of view that it would be very nice to be back *in.*

Hell, I didn't want to sell insurance, for Christ's sake!

You had to sit down with yourself on a quiet morning without a thing on your mind and think about the advantages and disadvantages of signing up again, and I can tell you this: the disadvantages took up very little space on the red ink side of the ledger and the advantages just stretched away out of sight on the black ink side. You know, I was still undecided and as I was in the club at the time and it was just 11:30, and when the steward came around with my first drink of the day I told him, "Here's a quarter." Then I told him to flip it on the table and as it spun I said, "Heads I go, tails I don't." And it came up heads.

So I joined the Navy again. My old friend for four years. My castle, my kitchen, my chef, my servants, my ship, my buddies, and all the rest that goes with it, including many perks which they don't have today.

So that's it. It wasn't that I couldn't hack civilian life again. It was that I just couldn't seem to get the feeling that it was the right life for me, and as I said, I certainly put out a lot of bait and nobody bit and as I also said, I was goddamned if I would sell insurance. You know that look a man gets when a friend in the insurance business leans a little toward him at the bar in the club and says something like, "Barry, perhaps we could have a little talk soon about your future"? Well, that was never going to happen to me, whether it was insurance of any other kind of job.

I came out with one great pension for twenty-five years of service and I was just under fifty and plenty of job offers because the Navy is still the superior service, as you know, old infantry-man, hah! No offense. I looked around for a position of some sort that did not have that infernal everlasting and blasted government interference and I found chartering would be just my cup of champagne. A good boat, beamy, with a clipper bow and a full stand-up cabin, main stateroom, small cabin, galley, Australian iron wood, Philippine mahogany, Burma teak, solid as a rock, a half a fortune in furnishings, and with my contacts in the Bay area, the San Diego Yacht Club, here, on the prairies, I can charter her any time and at rates I don't believe: minimum, one week, and max, two weeks, and that's long enough for the nastiness to surface in most people aboard a small vessel. I've had the same cook for ten years and he doubles as engineer and deckie and sail-hoister.

She's my life. I sleep aboard, live aboard, and in a few years when I get fed up with spoiled honeymooners who have a daddy rich enough to pay my rates and plain mean and cantankerous middle-aged women and their husbands who just want to drink and fish, I'll just pull her up to some government wharf in a nice village, town, and that's where I'm going to swallow the hook.

The wharfinger will come along some morning and find no activity aboard and he'll open her up and there I'll be, dead in my cabin and with a lovely smile on my face. At least that's the way I see it.

"I NEVER ADAPTED TO CIVILIAN LIFE"

I'd come over from Saskatchewan to Edmonton to join up and when the sergeant asked me my age I said eighteen and he said I was too young to join up, come back when I had another birthday. So I went to the end of the line again and when he asked me how old I was I said nineteen and he said, "And don't you ever forget it either."

There were times at first when I thought I'd write home and say, "Mom, I'm too young," but I didn't and I wound up in England and in '42 I was a sergeant. An officer who didn't like me, he put me in charge of a detail to bring back mines from this area which had been cleared. We were standing beside the truck when it was loaded and it just blew. Four were killed and the other fellow was critically hurt and I was blind in one eye for a while, deaf, and in hospital I had my face grafted back on and, well, I spent a long time in hospital before I was shipped back to Canada.

But going back. When our regiment had finished training in Canada we were given one of the most noble efforts of the war to perform. Guarding the Welland Canal. Three regiments on guard on that thing. There was nothing to do in Niagara Falls, so one night a buddy and me, we go to this YMCA dance and it is a tame affair. No booze, of course, and we're just about ready to walk out and have a beer when I spotted this girl and I said, "I'm going to marry that girl." My buddy said I was mad, but I went back and asked her to dance and we danced well and a hostess couldn't date any of the troops, so she met me and my buddy after, around the corner. We went together for a month before I was shipped to Halifax and then overseas. She wrote every day and then the accident happened.

Eventually I got back to Canada and we got married in one week's time.

My wife still says it was touch-and-go with us for a while. I couldn't hear very well and my nerves were shot and we got one room for six dollars a week on Chalmers Avenue.

One Sunday we were walking to church right in downtown Toronto and a plane came flying in low, zoooom! I threw her down on the sidewalk and piled on top of her to protect her. That was from Brighton where the German fighters used to sneak in low, hop over the seawall, and come right up the streets spraying bullets. Nerve-wracking. I loved the town anyway.

So we were married. I was out of one war and into another.

I couldn't find a job. They'd told us in England that there was so much work. Jobs everywhere. Pick and choose. But everywhere I went they'd ask what are you experienced in and I had nothing. Drive a truck. Throw a grenade. It seemed the only thing I was qualified for was to sweep and mop a floor and that was my first taste of the pretty dreadful attitude Canadians had then and would have later of veterans returning. I was most bitter at the time, and I'm probably still bitter about that.

Then there was the Zombie problem that we didn't know much about overseas. I'd see all these big and husky young men, all working, all happy to be making good money and not being in the service and not even thinking that maybe they should be doing something for their country. And me, of course, having been badly wounded and all that and still in rough shape, their attitude didn't sit well with me.

I finally got a job running an elevator at Simpson's warehouse on Mutual

Street at $24.50 a week, which probably was most suited to my talents, and there we were living in this six-dollar-a-week room with no radio, one small bed, one chair, and a hotplate.

We'd go to the deli around the corner and get a big coconut creme pie and two Cokes and to the butcher and get a big steak. We'd cook the steak on the little hotplate and eat the pie and swill it down with Coke and that would be our feast of the week, in our little castle up there on the third floor.

Then, six months later we got a flat, three rooms, wonderful, at thirty dollars a month on Cowan Street and I took all my gratuities, more than a thousand, and we blew it on furniture. It was there we lost our first little girl but we had our second little girl there. We're getting on now. I'd been promoted to thirty dollars a week selling men's furnishings in Simpson's and this is about 1947 and the next year I went over to Eaton's selling appliances and this was '48 when the first post-war vacuum cleaners were coming on in quantity. In one month, I remember, I made $1,100 in commissions selling these new vacuum cleaners. That was just unreal. This was 1948 and people didn't make that kind of money, but in a couple of months it was back to reality again.

Since I had got out I had never been happy in Civvie Street. I could never get along with civilians. The bitterness was there. Caused a lot by Mackenzie King, the Zombie thing, those guys who were conscripted but the government allowed them to stay on in Canada doing absolutely bugger-all while guys their same age were getting killed every day in Italy and France and in the skies and in the Navy. That bitterness will never die for me.

I remember when I got back, down to Niagara Falls, my wife was still a hostess at this YMCA dance and I went to pick her up for the last time and the chap who was running the dance, he came up and put his hand on my shoulder and said "Glad you're back, son." He was no more than five years older than me. He said he'd have been over there, too, but things were wrong with his heart and I told him in front of everybody with some choice four-letter words just exactly what was wrong with his heart. Oh, I embarrassed her.

Another time on Yonge Street a big husky young fellow pushed in front of my wife and I getting on the streetcar and I grabbed him by the collar and hauled him back and I said, "Let white people get on first."

I found it hard to live with civilians in those days, them talking about how tough things were, the rationing, and they were complaining about getting only one egg for breakfast when the English, they never saw an egg in three months.

Then VE-Day. That's when I was working in men's wear at Simpson's at twenty-eight dollars a week and right on the floor there, these young male clerks working beside me were hugging and kissing everybody and dancing around when they heard the news that the war was over and they wouldn't have to go. All the young guys who somehow had wangled out of the Army. It was pretty terrible.

I went home and got a case of beer I had and I went to my neighbor, Vince. He was wounded and back home like me and we celebrated together in our own quiet way. Not out there on the main street, yelling, cheering, and kissing and with all the troops that were with them, the guys who had soft touches in Canada in the depots and barracks and acting like they were heroes when they did everything they could to stay in Canada.

We called them B-Company. They'd be here when we went overseas and they would be here when we got back.

No, I never adapted to civilian life. I'd joined the militia, just because I wanted to sit around one night a week and talk to guys, and then Korea came along but I couldn't get in. I was in a low category, poor hearing and I had about 190 pieces of shrapnel in me, but I got in on a permit call, which meant I wasn't in the Army but I worked for it. Then one day I got talking to this medical officer and he told me to come and see him late in the afternoon and he took the bottle of good scotch I had and he passed me without me even taking off my clothes and that was how I got in the Strathcona Horse, my old regiment.

In '65, after about fifteen years as an instructor, Mr. Hellyer got his fantastic idea of amalgamating the armed forces and I was redundant. I was a sergeant and I noticed that when amalgamation came through there was a sergeant and a corporal doing the job I had done, but I had full pension credits, so I got out.

Thank God I never got to wear the green garbage bags, the uniforms they wear now. Thank God.

"I WAS A BIT OF A PROBLEM"

I came back after fifty-nine months in service. That's only one month short of five years out of a man's life and I wasn't in any frame of mind, let me tell you, to put up with any civilian bullshit. I'd just about had it with civilians. The Halifax variety. I did some time on the old *Assinaboine*, but then they transferred me to the corvette Navy and from then on it was bounce, bounce, bounce all over the North Atlantic. Then those convoys just plodding along and the German lieutenant with his eye at the periscope and boom, there goes another one up, smoke, fire, explosions, or just a boom and she lists and the first time I saw that happen I was stunned that a huge freighter could go down in less than five minutes. I had a lousy war. In Halifax, and honest to God I'm telling you this, there were people there, civilians, who thought we were the enemy.

I get home and here's Victoria, as safe and as sane as ever. What got me, they had Navy around them all during the war and they thought they must have been in the middle of a war zone. My dad's business partner, the first thing he says when I see him again, he says, "We had quite a bit of excitement around here when you were away. The Japs shelled Estevan Point."

I just looked at him and then I said sure, some Jap submarine commander figured he'd give his boys some fresh air so they came up and sunbathed and fired off a few shots at the lighthouse on the point, just to get in some practice. Just testing their sights, I'd say. He didn't like that.

I was a bit of a problem. I got into another humpety-doo at a party that Christmas when a naval officer brought up the same subject, and oh, what a tough time we had here during the war. I said bullshit, and did his nibs know that just a couple of weeks before the war ended a corvette had been torpedoed just off the entrance to Halifax Harbor and a lot of good guys died. Even that sort of thing didn't shut up those assholes.

No, for the first year I wasn't a good boy. I had four jobs in seven months and I couldn't hold one of them. Finally I knew it was no good. My sister and her husband had bought a farm at Duncan and I went up there and stayed a month, chopping wood and fixing fences and digging the garden, putting in plants, feeding their couple of pigs and keeping a watch out for cougar and generally doing nothing.

I remember Christmas. They went to Vancouver on Christmas Day. I'm alone and figuring I'd better fry up some eggs and ham for my dinner and there's a knock on the door. It's the old guy who lived down the lane. An English type. Call him a remittance man, I guess. He comes in visiting and we get talking and I break open my bottle of scotch and, well, he's got one in his game bag he carries. Everywhere he went that old man carried a shotgun, so he's got a bottle in his game bag. We get sipping and talking and he says he'll root around and he comes up with this and that and soon he's got a big dinner going, including the chicken my sister had set aside for me but which I didn't touch. Cooking just isn't in my line. The fire is blazing and we're into the scotch and I let his dog in with ours, so we've got a little family going and soon, after dinner, we're into his bottle and here I am, a little squiffy, going a mile a minute telling him all my troubles.

He listens, and he talks and he says things that make a lot of sense. That I enlisted for more reasons than patriotism and I should consider I had signed a contract with the Canadian government and my dividends would be the benefits I would get from going in the service and taking all that Navy shit. Things like that. He told me a lot. It took a couple of days for me to digest it and then I thought, you know, the old bugger's dead on. I have no right thinking this country owes me a living. I've got no right to think that five years out of my life is five years gone from my life. Know what I mean? I took a lot of shit, but so did tens of thousand of others, who took more than I did.

Hell's bells. We were all in it together. Who was I to feel like I was the only one? I did what everyone else did, fought for my country and I did have a lot of fun. I learned a lot. Not a trade or anything like that. I developed as myself. As a person. Hell, I grew up, but you wouldn't think it the way I've been telling you all this.

This is what the old man pointed out to me and I had to agree. I was only twenty-three. What's twenty-three, I ask you? Nothing. Where would I have been if there hadn't been a war and there still was a Depression? I might be riding the boxcars looking for work on the prairies or I might be a two-bit clerk somewhere with no future.

When my sister came back I'd done all the wood chopping and pig feeding to last me a lifetime and I went over to the Department of Veterans' Affairs and talked with a fellow. Sure, they had something for me. I took a four-month course and really boned up on my high school subjects, physics, math, chemistry, the sciences, and I went to university that fall. I was raring to go, and there I was, in three years, an engineer because I just jumped in second year and took classes in the summer. You could do that then. So I came out as a grad with all the rest, the guys who had signed up for school in '45. No, I didn't get the job I wanted but I got a job and soon I got the job I wanted. I did real fine.

2 SETTING UP HOUSEKEEPING

2 SETTING UP HOUSEKEEPING

During the 1920s housing construction in Canada was uneven; in the ten years of the Depression, it was nonexistent; during the war, only essential housing was permitted. Then suddenly, after VE-Day, everyone wanted a home, or an apartment, or just a place to sleep. The government and private industry worked full blast to satisfy the demand, but it was never enough.

Wives had taken the kids to live with Mom and Dad and now husbands were back home and out scouring neighborhoods for living quarters. Many of the university-student veterans who competed for a room in which to sleep and study wound up with a converted closet. Lucky were the ones who had set up homes before enlisting, or who had a large farmhouse to return to, or who could borrow the family cottage at the lake for a while. Unlucky those who had to endure the mean and sharp-eyed landladies who flourished all over Canada.

Quick to capitalize on the shortage, people renovated their homes to create small, uncomfortable apartments. Or they jerry-built partitions in garages and basements and rented the cubicles for twenty-five dollars a month—an outrageous price at the time. Water was often a problem: just taking a bath could be a luxury. Furniture and appliances were in short supply, and so unscrupulous secondhand dealers gouged returnees eager, or desperate, to set up housekeeping. Many a wife and war bride learned to cook Christmas dinner on a two-burner stove. With so little space and even less money, couples got together

to share what they had for a little party on a Saturday night. They can look
back and laugh now, but the livin' was not easy for vets in those post-war
days.

"A NEW-BRAND KIND OF MONSTER"

Housing was the big worry. No housing had been built during
the Depression. Certainly all the material and labor that went into special
housing during the war didn't have much bearing on what the civilian
population would need after the war. After all, you couldn't expect half
a million veterans and their families to sleep in barracks and eat in mess
halls.

This created a new-brand kind of monster: the landlady. The woman
with a big house and her kids gone, married and away, and she had three
or four rooms to rent and remember the stories in the newspapers:
"Veterans Demand Housing." "Housing Shortage Seen." That certainly gave these monsters the idea that they had a good thing going for them.

There was also another factor, and that was rent control. Rents were
set by what was called the Wartime Housing and Rentals Board and it
set rates, controlled rents. It seemed to the veterans' council I joined
in Winnipeg that this government agency favored the civilian and not
the veteran returning to a wife and a couple of kids. They seemed to
think that if the wife and kids had survived when he was away, then
all was fine and okay. It wasn't. My wife and son had lived in an absolute hovel. It was a garage that had been converted into living quarters
and it was cold in winter.

Another problem was that people with apartments had no reason to
get out and move into better accommodation as they were better off finan-
cially to afford them. The civilians had made good money, saved it,
nothing to spend it on but black-market booze and meat and gas, and
they could afford to build the new homes. Jobs had been plentiful and
wages high. But you had a situation where a man who might have been
a bank manager and his wife who had taken a part-time job during the
war, they were living in a fine and big apartment in a warm brick apartment block and they paid only thirty dollars a month. The situation was
ridiculous, but there was nothing anybody could do about it. The
bureaucrats in Ottawa were now totally in control.

The landladies I mentioned. I hate to say this, but most complaints
that came before our council were about landladies of foreign

extraction. Yes, Ukrainian. Polish. Some German, yes. Oh yes, some German. If their cousins in Europe were losing the war, a lot in Winnipeg were winning it.

I used to trudge all through that area west of the Mall from Portage south to the river looking for something decent. I found places but so mean, ah, so pigstyish, that you couldn't put a family in some of the rooms. I got home late, in September, and all the good places had been taken. It is a long time ago. I can still remember the places where I knocked and see the door open and this flat Slavic stupid face look at me with absolute hostility. I don't know why. She would be taking my good money, about half of my allowance from the government. The rest was for everything else. Food, clothing, carfare, maybe a show or something.

You had to spend thirty-five dollars for two rooms and share the bath. That might include a little kitchen which had been a closet. You imagine that? In those days thirty five bucks was a lot of money. A hamburger was ten cents, a strawberry milkshake was ten cents. A movie, two bits.

The point was this. Housing was a national crisis. The government was building homes for veterans, but it was a program that was continually being screwed up and there was opposition to it. People who might have opened their homes to us for one year, two years, did not, and frankly I do not blame them. After all, these were their homes and we were strangers. That flung us back on the Wartime Housing and Rentals Board, and they were no help. Their main objective was to maintain the status-quo. The thousands of vets sure as blazes were not the status-quo. And that flung us back on the unscrupulous landladies, and there were a lot of them. As I said, mostly ethnic, to use a polite word.

It really was a long time before I got over my hatred of these kinds of people, as you can see I have.

I guess it all boils down to this. Between '39 and VE-Day you were a hero if you wore a uniform. When we came back, there were parades and the mayor said his pretty piece. When they saw that, God forbid, we wanted a decent place to live, that was another matter. That's when the grubby money business started. Then we were just some bums off the street begging for a place to lay our sorry heads.

We finally did all right. My cousin's uncle in Fort Garry let us live in his rec room for a year and we managed, but no thanks to anyone, really. As veterans we weren't expecting to be heroes for ever and a day. We just wanted a fair shake.

Listen to me, those guys who came back in '45 with all sorts of problems, personal, I mean, who needed a fair shake, they did not get it.
They did not, and it is Canada's shame that they did not.

"LET ME TELL YOU ABOUT THAT HOTPLATE"

Regina wasn't much of a town then, and it had one hell of
a housing shortage for veterans you would not believe. There was no
point in looking in the paper. They said the girls in the advertising department gave out the rent-ad phone numbers to their friends before they
even got in the paper. I can believe that. Hell, if I were them I'd have
sold them. Maybe they did. Just maybe. Human nature.

I thought we'd leave the kids, Shirley and Wayne, with the wife's folks
until we found a place in Regina for all of us, but no, she says she's taking everybody and everything with us, but I talk her into dumping the
kids off with my sister in Winnipeg for a week or so until we got settled
and that's the way we did it.

We parked ourselves in a hotel over by the tracks and set up housekeeping with a hotplate for breakfast and such. Let me tell you about that
hotplate. We could have brought one from Kenora but we didn't, and
when we tried to buy one there wasn't one to be found. They didn't
seem to be making them during the war. Anyway. I finally found one.
In a secondhand store. Yep. Maybe the fourth store I went to, and the
guy wanted more for that old one than I figured I could have bought
a brand-new one for. That was the way. Skunk the veteran. The war's
over, so skunk the veteran. You paid what they wanted or you didn't get it.

Now back to the rental business. We couldn't live in that hotel. It
just wasn't right. It was run-down then and I'd hate to think what it
is like now. It would still be there. Those railway hotels in those prairie
towns never burn down. They're made of solid brick. But we were paying seventeen dollars a week and that comes out to nearly eighty dollars
a month and that was high. High as a kite. They allowed housekeeping,
so we didn't have to eat out and that saved a lot. Food was cheap and
you had your ration book, so you could stand outside the liquor store
and sell your beer and whiskey ration ticket for two, maybe three bucks.
Naturally that meant you didn't drink yourself.

Yes, the rent business. I remember one old woman and her son had
chopped up their basement into about four bedrooms with a single
bathroom and a community kitchen. Four families, and she was asking

forty bucks. That would be $160, which would have got you a house then in terrific shape and nine bedrooms and four bathrooms if such a thing existed. The son wouldn't rent to us anyway, even if we'd wanted to. I told him I had been an administration officer in the Army and he said he had been a Zombie. Yes, the bastard said it proudly. A slob, sitting out the war on his duff drinking milk and eating cake and probably robbing the quartermaster stores blind. There were others. None seemed to want kids. Some even wanted to see our marriage licence, which was packed away in one of the boxes or suitcases. It never crossed my mind we'd need the thing.

It went on like this but kept getting worse. It was October coming up fast and that meant a prairie winter and God, I wasn't sleeping nights and not doing my job right by day and we'd been looking for a month.

Finally I said to the wife, I said this. We're going to go over to that district by the Parliament buildings, south of there where the nice people live and every person we meet on the street, if he's raking his lawn we'll stop and ask if he knows where we can rent two rooms or a basement or anything. That Sunday I put on my uniform with my ribbons and Stella wore her best bib and tucker, and about one in the afternoon this sunny Sunday away we go. We look like a fine couple. We were, for that matter. War hero and pretty young wife and I've got a good job and she's a smiling mother. I'm going to cut the suspense right now and tell you that it worked. It didn't that Sunday, but the next day I got a phone call from a woman we hadn't even talked to and she said that she'd been talking to a Mrs. Brownell and she *was* one of the women we'd talked to. Yes, she knew where there was a place for rent. Sheer luck. Her son and daughter-in-law were moving to the coast and their place was for rent. An apartment, a suite in their basement.

I got real excited and asked when, and she said I'd have to talk to her, Mrs. Adams, and that night over we went. I even took a cab. Doing it up brown. We had coffee with she and her husband and talked and yes, I promised I would do all the garden work and taking out the ashes and shoveling the walks and then she showed us the suite in the basement. It even had an outside door. It was perfect. Two bedrooms and a little kitchen and a dining room and living room combined and plenty of space for the kids to play in the basement and in the back yard and she even had a clothes dryer. I remember it. One of those with a big copper pot. I could almost see my wife do a hippety-hop.

Mrs. Adams . . . now there was a wonderful woman for you. She's dead now and so is her husband and I don't know who has that fine house now but just knowing her and James, her husband, made everything worthwhile. I mean coming back and taking all that crap from these low-life families in Regina trying to gouge the last dime out of a war veteran, and then along they come.

The rent was forty a month. Imagine! That draft dodger's mother wanted that for a slum in a basement in the worst part of Regina.

We moved in and that winter I shoveled the snow and swept the walk and took out the ashes and helped Mr. Adams around the house, fixing things, and we kept the kids quiet and she'd make cookies and bring a plate down to us, things like that. Presents for the kids at Christmas. Taking my wife shopping. Introducing her to friends of her daughter-in-law, girls of her own age.

That was the best thing that happened to us. I wish my wife could tell you more but she's gone now. We're divorced. After thirty years of marriage. That's a long time for anybody.

"HE RENTED THE ATTIC"

Of course the time you are asking about was a long time ago. I really can't remember much. I'd been in the Navy 954 days. I remember that. This here is my "Statement of War Service Gratuity" certificate or paper to prove that. A lot of the time on convoy between two of the rottenest towns in the British Empire, St. John's, Newfoundland, and Londonderry in Ireland. The British controlled St. John's and the Yanks were all over 'Derry, and Canadians were considered like they were lepers.

I was discharged in one day in Toronto and my father was there to drive me to London and I got married to my girl two days later and there was no honeymoon. The money I got, not much, would have to go to finding an apartment.

Did I say an apartment? I did, but in those days an apartment meant anyplace with a roof and a place to go to the bathroom. I'd go down to the Free Press building and when the edition came off, you'd grab one from the kid who was selling them at the door and you'd tear open the paper and find out where there was an apartment. I always remember the taxis. There was always fifteen or twenty or more guys swarming around the kid when he came out and you'd grab a paper and run for a taxi. They were lined up, maybe five or so, so you'd jump in and tell him to start driving slowly and you'd choose one ad and if it was a phone, you'd stop him at the nearest drugstore and run in and phone. If it was a street number, you'd tell him to drive like the dickens to that address.

I found out that it didn't matter if it was a phone or an address; it always seemed the place was gone. Never could figure it out then. I know now. Somebody always had advance information. Or when you got there, another taxi or two would be ahead of you. Faster drivers, maybe. I'm telling you, it took us a week to find a place and all this time we were living with my folks and sleeping on a Winnipeg couch in the kitchen, and if you know what I mean, both of us were getting pretty jumpy. The house was full of people, my younger brothers and sisters and there was just no place to go except the park or somewhere like that and I wasn't going to start out our married life that way. But finally, about the fifth night, I guess, we did. It wasn't very good, I can tell you.

Then my father, he worked at a bindery, and one of his buddies told him he'd decided to rent out the attic of his house. It wasn't large but it had stairs up to it and a floor on it and two big windows at either end and somewhere I got a long extension cord and we ran it up through the stairs and you might say, that was our home. It wasn't much. We went out to a secondhand store and bought a bed and dresser and a table and two chairs, and my wife brought in her stuff from the place where she lived, a farm near Thamesville. We had dishes, bedding, knives and stuff, pots. These kind of things. I guess you could call it home, but looking at the place we've got now it was pretty pretty low down. I also bought a two-place electric plate and a big frying pan, the cast-iron kind, and a coffee pot and a few other things. I think the rent was $22.50 a month and a dollar for the electricity. Oh, maybe two dollars. The one bathroom was downstairs and we never liked that. You had to ask if you could take a bath. Anyway, they weren't bad people.

London was a quiet city but a very nice place to live and it had a good library. I wasn't unhappy with our lot and things got a whole lot better, much better when we did latch on to an apartment and then, thank the Lord, we had our own bathroom and a stove you could put a roast into. No, I had no complaints.

You know, though, the thing that always bugged me was those taxi drivers. There they'd be, lined up like a bunch of vultures. They didn't use the meter, not then. They drove you to where you were looking for an apartment or room and then they'd say four dollars. My God, four dollars or three dollars would have taken you a long way in those days. They were gouging the troops, and you better believe it, but you had to fork over, and before the job money started, every last red penny counted.

My old man wasn't mad about it when I told him. He said taxi drivers were always like that. He said when I was away the only way to get a bottle of hooch at night was from a taxi guy at three or four times the price. So, when the guys came back, there they were again, charging maybe three times more, except they were doing it in broad daylight.

"LUCKY TWICE THE SAME DAY"

It was pretty damned hard to find a place to live, and with a wife and two kids nine and seven and no place to live except with her parents in their dinky home, living in their basement, when I heard the vets taken over the Hotel Vancouver, I said I was going down to find out.

Sure enough. There they were. The old hotel was right downtown there, on Georgia, and there were police around but nobody was stopping you from going in and they had a table set up. They had a committee. I went to the table and they asked a lot of questions. War service? Name? Where was I living? Married? Any kids? Where was I working? That sort of thing. Then they said, yes, we've got room.

This was what you would call a sit-in later on. Like the hippies did, but we sure as hell weren't hippies. We were grown men with wives and kids who were back from the war. There was the government sending all these guys with better schooling than us, sending them to university and college and giving them farm loans and money to start businesses. And for us? With wives and kids and sleeping in your in-laws' wet and cold basement, they give us not a damn thing. Nothing.

So the fellow at the desk he takes a sheet and it's got a floor plan on it and he circles this room on the fourth floor and he says, "That's your room," and he gives me a piece of paper and a thumbtack. "Go up there, the door's open. Stick this paper with your name on it on the door." I do this and then I take the suitcase I've got and I plunk it down on the bed. I think, gosh, is this really better? I walk around down in the lobby and talk to guys and they're like me, no place to live decently and they've tried everything like me and they can't find work. Neither can I. I should have mentioned it. What can a guy do who's been a cook and a rifleman and the town is full of cooks who aren't working and the rifle business has been over for a long time? Even the Jap war is over. Nobody's fighting. I can't see me getting a job. Christ knows, I tried but I came back late. Everybody was getting jobs and apartments

when I was still over there cooking for the guys wno didn't have enough
points to come home. I've got the points because a wife and two kids
mean more points, but no, I'm Little Joe the bull cook cleaning up with
a lot of other very unhappy guys.

I'm talking to these vets and they're saying it's not too bad. It's warm
and if you bring your own blankets and bedding and, well, you rustled
in the Army, didn't you? Now you can teach your wife and kids to rus-
tle, too.

I got it all straightened out, how things were going in the hotel, and
they had committees set up and things were moving. Some people in
the newspapers said it was run by a bunch of Commies. I don't think
so. What if they were? It was just the CPR we were talking about. They
deserved what they got. That was railroad property and hell, before the
war I slept in enough of their boxcars and rode them looking for work.
What's wrong with sleeping in their hotel, eh? Nothing as far as I could
see. They weren't using it. It was going to be torn down. When they
did tear it down, you know what they turned it into? A bloody parking
lot. For years and years. Then somebody built a skyscraper on it, but
that was years later.

Okay, I said, and we moved in. Everybody helped each other. I think
my wife took the kids to General Gordon School. She worked in the
hotel doing chores with the women of other vets. Cleaning. Scrubbing.
Looking after things. We didn't break anything. Everybody, I think, was
clean and kept things right and that's the way it went.

No, the police didn't do nothing. What could they do, for Christ's
sake? Club women and children? They just were around and they were
good guys.

The place was nice and warm but I didn't feel right about it. Not at
all. Would you? Here we were, a big lot of guys who had been overseas
and fought for their country and here we were. We were squatters. I don't
think there was one guy in the Hotel Vancouver who wasn't trying to
get out. Like me. We just couldn't live with her folks, and I had
no job. There wasn't TV to look at in them days. I'd of gone nuts just
sitting around thinking of the whole mess, so I just kept looking for
a job.

I got lucky twice in the same day. I was coming on the streetcar over
the Cambie Street Bridge and I see Johnston Terminals at the south end
of the bridge and I hop off and go in. I hadn't tried that place. By God,
there was a foreman in the office complaining he needed two more men
in the warehouse and I'm standing there, waiting to talk to someone,

and I says to the guy he's talking to, I said this, I said, "I'm a vet, a wife and two kids, and I'm squatting in the old hotel and I need a job bad." He says I'm hired, and in ten minutes I'm in the warehouse pushing boxes and furniture around and loading trucks. I don't even know what the pay is and I don't care. It turned out it was okay for me and I can walk to work. That saves me, I think, twenty cents. Hah!

At noon I'm sharing lunch with about five guys. You see, I don't have my lunch. I'm eating part of their lunch. This guys asks me about what is going on and I tell him and he says, hell, I got two rooms and a bathroom in my basement up on Seventeenth Avenue. I just about fall over him asking if I can have it and he says he'll phone his wife and sure enough, he comes back and says sure, I can have it, when do I want to move in?

It's got a bedroom and a living room, which is also the kitchen, and a little bathroom and a shower and it's thirty bucks a month. Hey! Just great. He's a nice guy named Battastoni or Battaloni. Italian. I forget his name. A nice guy.

We'd been in the hotel for five days and, yeah, that was just enough. We were glad to move out. Some people criticized us for being there, in the hotel, but a lot, lot more were on our side. It was a good thing. You see, people in Vancouver, they didn't know about the housing shortage. That's the trouble I found with civilians. They didn't know bugger-all. The war had been a nice time for them and they even had fun bitching about the shortages. Rationing. Now they could see right on the front page of the *News Herald* and *The Sun* and *The Province* that things were tough for the veterans.

I'm not sure when the veterans moved out of the hotel. I guess they stayed until all of them found some sort of place to stay. I think the occupation, the squatting, helped though. That way people said to themselves, hey! we've got a room or two or three we can rent. Why not help out a veteran's family? Of course, they were helping out themselves, too. If everybody got an extra thirty dollars helping vets, every month, that was a nice piece of change in them days. So it helped everybody.

"WHEN I GOT SMARTERISH"

I signed up with the Cape Bretons and I was with them everywhere until I got myself wounded by doing a dumb thing which

would have got me detention if I was back in England, so with the wound
and me now getting a thirty-five percent disability pension, I got back
to old Sydney town a year ahead of the boys and that was something
to see. That Sydney town.

There was prosperity around and all the boys who couldn't have gone
into the Army or them that pulled some strings and such and kept out
and they was all working and overtime, you could say it was coming out
their ears and I don't think the old home town had had it so good.

You're looking at about August or so of '44 and nobody was concerned
the smallest twinkle that the boys in the regiment were dying over there
and they'd have to face those who had got arms or legs blown off, the
ones that would be coming home. There was a fat old Scotsman, he
says the boys from the island have always been able to look out for
themselves. I wondered, do the Germans know that.

There was too much frivolity, to put a word to it. It was like it was
fun, fun, fun. I'd sit in one of the beer parlors with a few of the boys
and we'd drink until they closed the doors and we'd call a taxi and off
we'd go to a blind pig that two of the town policemen's wives ran and
it might be three in the morning before I got home.

This business of all the drinking didn't last too long, as I can tell you.
I'd be getting up to the point where my back teeth was floating with
booze and there were a few times when things would come up which
reminded me of the Army and I'd say something which meant, why
weren't you guys along with us instead of this nice free ride. It didn't
take long to get unpopular and finally I started going to another beer
parlor where I didn't know many people.

This is a long and sad dance of a story, isn't it?

Things wasn't going at all well at home with my mother either, and
that is the honest-to-God truth. The woman had changed since I'd gone
overseas. She'd remarried again and her new husband was a rat. Maybe
I do rats wrong by saying so. Another thing, I did not like somebody not
my father sleeping with my mother, in the same bed, you know. It got
so bad, the stupid arguments over nothing, and me coming home more
than a bit half-pissed, and me not working and laying around, that I just
decided to go. To Halifax. They wanted men in the war factories and
shipyards there and when I'd made up my mind to be off to Halifax I
told my mother when I was eating breakfast that morning that we'd go
to the bank when she was cleaned up and she up and says, like, for what?

I told her I wanted her to draw out the money I'd been sending home
for four years. Three years and eleven months and so many days, accord-

ing to my pay book and I'd been sending twenty dollars a month to her and I knew just about how much because every letter, you see, she'd say how much the account was. The last time she said, I guess it was about eight hundred dollars, so I knew it would be a lot more now.

You just shoulda seen her. She flared up like a mean old rooster and this wasn't my mom, this was a crazy woman, and how she had had a twenty-hour labor with me, and how she had brought me up, and sent me to Sunday school and prayed for me all the time and now I was asking for my money.

Something just told me. I knew. It was that little shit, that Willy of hers. The skulking mean little cur. I shook her and I yelled what I was thinking: did she take out that money for her and Willy? She was cursing and crying and I knew she had, the money was gone and I slammed out that door and down the hill and into the bank and by God, McGregor, the manager, he shuffles his feet around a bit and says, yes, she took it out, she took it out a month ago. I don't have to figure that is just a week before I gets home, me, her son Dugald, with his wounds still aching and fit for nothing in the Army's eyes, and here's my own mother, here she is, a damned thief of my money. There was nothing I could do. She had a right to take it out, and I finally got it out of her, she took it out because that damned Willy of a husband was at her and at her and that was it.

I left home with a suitcase of my clothes and I wore my Army uniform with my colors proudly up there on my chest as if to say, "Screw you, bastards, Dugald McDonald's been there," and I got a job in Halifax at good money in welding, helping two welders, and we were on a bonus system and overtime and I made real good money. Then when the war was over—and as it usually does, Halifax turned mean and sour again with no money around, and there's a mean and ugly city which you can have as far as I'm concerned—I went to Toronto. I got in on the ground floor what with the war veterans not coming back yet and no immigrants for a few years yet and with my savings I got me a secondhand business and I did wonderfully from the start, because a lot of people who didn't have no jobs after the war factories ended were going back home or back to Manitoba and places there and B.C., and I was buying furniture cheap. A table, fifty cents. A chair, ten cents. A good kitchen chair, two bits. You know. Old but still good appliances. Stoves, mostly. Beds. Mattresses. I bought everything. The kid I hired to go around in this truck I bought, $300 for the truck and black-market gas, his dad had an empty barn up at their farm near Markham which was all countryside then and I stored stuff in there and when the veterans started to come back like a flood, I sold, sold, and sold. That table, fifty cents, now five dollars and they were kissing my hands that they could get it at all.

I could tell you about that business. I just had a store out on King Street East and not big, thirty-five feet across and it wouldn't hold much, but I had it coming in the back door and going out the front door and if they knew, over at Eaton's and Simpson's, I know I was selling a hell of a lot more furniture than they was. Ever. Ever and ever. You didn't have to advertise. My truck would be unloading a bunch of my furniture into a house or apartment they'd managed to, by hook or by crook, get a hold of and some other vet would come running up and ask where the truck had come from. For instance I said that table would have sold for five. Then when I got smarterish, I'd talk to these vets and they'd know I was one, with a big bloody scar up in here and I'd find out they might have been an officer, a pilot, a captain, anything, and I would just tack on five or maybe ten dollars onto that stove, the oak chest of drawers. And then, I still think they was getting a very good bargain. Which they was. I don't have to convince me of that. They was.

I read all the time these stories about this Mirvish guy. Honest Ed, and how he done it. He's a smart cookie and if he was me then, he'd of made ten times as much money as me. He has that extra bit of something you need. Even though I was in it for the money, I was still a guy who had been there, a veteran, and I was dealing with veterans all the time, mostly, and I didn't want to dig too deeply into their pocketbooks. This Honest Ed, he's a merchant dealing with people he don't know, so the guy thinks like a merchant and that's where he's got the edge. He doesn't have to be a nice guy, only when he meets them in his store. So he makes more money? So what. Didn't I do good? I got out of it in '49. I made lots of money and I helped people in a jam with no furniture and that makes me happy.

I still got that wound, the scar, and sometimes today when I look around me and see what I got I pat that thing and think that it got me in ahead of everybody and got me started.

My mother? What about her? Oh that. Hell, I forgave her almost as soon as I left home. Wasn't her fault. The guy Willy, the husband, he was taking advantage of her. No, I forgot about it. You can't blame your own mother for things. She's okay. She left him a couple of years later and she's still in her home. Everything's okay in that department. Everything's okay.

"WE TRIED THE SECONDHAND STORES"

I'll tell you where one thing went wrong. With me, anyway. With a lot of fellows. Maybe thousands. It was setting up house again.

I came back to my home town, Hamilton. My wife had lived with her mother and dad outside of Guelph and we hadn't set up housekeeping when I enlisted. We were only married three months before I was called up by the Air Force in October of 1942. There was no reason to set up house when we could live with my folks or hers.

When I got back, a lot of others had come back before me. I had no trouble getting a job because I had had one and I was entitled to go back to it. But we had to have a place to live.

The thing was to find a place to lay our weary heads and that came easily enough through a family connection. An old house and we got the one side of the main floor, which had been split up into a living room and bedroom combined, a kitchen. We used the bathroom on that floor which we shared with a chap and his wife named Crawford. The place was twenty-two dollars a month, which was good, no sweat in that department. But it was empty and we needed a bed, chairs, a table, a set of drawers, lamps, and all the little things. A rug, bookcase. Okay, you know. The cutlery and dishes my wife had from wedding presents and, oh, yes, she had the bedding.

The department stores had pretty well been cleaned out by the veterans getting home earlier than I got home and besides, what we did see was just too damned expensive. Remember, I think I had only about six hundred dollars to play around with. No savings. Just what we had on our backs and in suitcases and so we tried the secondhand stores. This was the problem.

The secondhand dealers were not fools. They knew the war was ending, say from the day, well from D-Day. They had been going around buying up all this stuff and naturally they got it. For a penny. A dime. A dollar. You couldn't put a classified ad in the *Spec* and hope to get household goods; you couldn't go out and look for stuff in the little towns, even if you had a car. No, and this is where the government might have stepped in. You had to go to the secondhand stores and they charged an arm and a leg. Supply and demand. There was this big demand and they had the supply, but I know they let the supply out just enough to keep the demand price high. The rest of their stuff they had stored away. So, prices were very high and a lot of it was junk. Stuff that under any other circumstances you'd turn your nose up at. But in those days, they had you.

It was discouraging because I was working and Marion had to do the hunting and with no car, that made it rougher. When we got a mattress we slept on that, and then came the bed, and then the table, and my little stake was going down and down. Thank God we didn't need a whole house! Anybody who moved into a house, they were in trouble.

It wasn't a crisis. I should tell you that. After what I'd been through, nothing could be a real crisis anymore, but you might say it was annoying. An irritant. I'd think, here we are starting out in life and here are these people trying to make a fast buck on the veterans. You know, Canadians being Canadians and decent and kindly, not wanting to raise a fuss, I don't think anybody ever said anything about it. No letter to the *Spec*, no getting up at some veterans' meeting and shouting about it.

Perhaps I'm making too much of it. But it did stick in my mind right up until now that the thing I was most upset about was paying twenty-five bucks for a table that I know the guy had paid maybe three or five bucks for and there I was, off fighting a war while he was preparing to fleece me when I got back.

"WE RENTED TWO ROOMS, A SHACK"

We had an awful time finding a place but finally we rented two rooms, a shack, and it was thirty dollars a month and the only water was down this rutted road about five hundred yards away. So, when I was at work my wife was in this shack, but she kept her mind occupied and got some very good exercise by carrying pails of water.

The place was no good, so after looking around for a long time we found another two rooms and they were cheaper and even though they were beyond the Calgary city limits there was water—a well, and it was right near.

Our landlady was the cheapest woman in all Calgary, I think. She went around making life miserable and when she wasn't doing that, she was sitting down thinking new ways to make our life miserable. But we had to put up with it.

My wife gave me a new electric razor for Christmas. That was some razor. But when the landlady found out about it she came charging up the stairs and said she was going to charge me twenty-five cents a week for electricity. That would bring the rent to twenty-six dollars a month. Now, she was a religious nut. Holy roller. Pentacostal. The only time she played her radio was at 10:30 every Sunday morning for this special

religious program, eh? I knew this new razor jammed up our radio with
static when I turned it on, so every Sunday I'd wait until 10:30 and then
I'd turn on the razor and put a couple of pillows on top of it and at eleven
o'clock I'd turn it off.

It drove her nuts. She'd try the radio at other times and it worked
fine. When her program came on, loud static and she couldn't hear a
word. She took it in to be fixed, and nothing wrong. She was going nuts.

She never caught on and I did that every Sunday morning until we
left the place and got a warm and nice little apartment in town.

"THINGS WERE HARD TO GET"

In '43, June of, I joined the Air Force and I came back from
England in '45. Lucille fixed up a little apartment in the basement of
a house of a neighbor, full of stuff you could buy almost for nothing,
and we had about fifteen hundred dollars and I went looking for cars.
I'd do it the way I remember men used to sell books during the Depression. You'd go into a town, any old town. Let's say Athens, which was
a few stores, a few businesses and a few houses, and you'd ask around,
read the weekly newspaper, and you'd start knocking doors. Anything
to sell? Furniture. Appliances. Tools. A big business in tools. I bought
hundreds of good ones in a few months. Fifty cents. A dollar. Stuff people had lying around. But mainly I was looking for cars. Trucks, pickups,
stuff that wouldn't even run. I called myself Johnson's Trading Company and say, after a day in Athens or Augusta or Spencerville, just
villages, or as far away as Smiths Falls or Kemptville or even Brockville,
just knocking on doors, door by door, trudging along knocking on doors
with Lucille driving the truck along the street behind me and helping
to carry, you'd be amazed what you'd get. Amazed! Almost for nothing.
People almost offered to pay you to take out their junk, and a lot of
it was not junk, believe me.

I got to know the tricks. People didn't know the value, but I sure knew
what I could sell it for. We bought everything.

We'd do that Monday to Thursday, lugging the stuff back each night
to the old garage we'd rented for fifteen dollars a month, and Friday we'd
work about fifteen hours straight just cleaning stuff up, arranging it, putting prices on it and everything had a sixty percent markup. If I bought
a chair for a dollar, then it went for two bucks.

We had ads in all the local papers, Prescott, Belleville, Smiths Falls,

Carleton Place even, and especially in Ogdensburg across the line, and on Saturday there would be people lining up at 8 A.M. We had hit on something big, you know. Things were hard to get, and we had them, by knocking on doors. Hard work, long hours, too. But we advertised with kind of funny ads, like "We're Not Hogs, But You Can Come and Skin Us Anyway." That sort of thing. Lucille would write them. People came from all over and they thought it was a holiday, bring the kids, and we had a hotdog stand and soft drinks and ice cream, even in winter, and free cookies for the kids and it was a holiday for them. A chance to have some fun.

If you want to believe this, you can, but in '46 money was worth something and people had it, all saved up from the war and good wages and all that, and veterans and their wives looking for bargains. We had bargains. Things they needed to start their new homes. I get a bit excited just thinking about it, and those Americans from around Ogdensburg, they piled across that border. Lord, did they ever. Just shoving money at you.

By about two on a Saturday afternoon the stuff would be gone and I might have put $2,200, $2,500 in my pocket. That would work out to about a clear thousand bucks in my pocket every week when you took off the cost of gas and payments on the truck and the money for the free hotdogs and soda pop and the wages of the kid and Lucille's two sisters, and Saturday night we'd sit in our apartment and count our money.

The money was rolling in like you wouldn't believe, but then it all turned around and blew the other way. By fall there were two others doing it in town and others were doing it in Ogdensburg and Brockville and the word was getting around even further. A chap came down three Saturdays running from Smiths Falls, and he hit us just right the third time. I sure knew what he was up to and when we'd closed down he said he wanted to talk to me. I already had it in my mind what I'd ask for and it didn't take him long to get to the point and I asked $9,000 and he grabbed it, and that didn't include the truck. That was another $1,200. We signed the deal Monday morning and I got his certified check and that was it for us. We just walked away from it.

He shut down for two weeks, no ads in the papers, no publicity, and just to get organized, you see, but the Saturday sale had lost its momentum and he didn't have the swing for it and I heard he did everything wrong and went belly up sometime next spring. The first thing, he cut out the free hotdogs and soda pop to the kids and the free coffee to the parents, and I warned him not to do that. But he was a smart-ass and

I guess he lost his shirt. If you can believe it, in the year we were in business we made more than $27,000, which was more than the prime minister made, I'm sure.

A PLACE FOR THE BRIDE

Gosh, but you sure bring back memories. Things I'd forgotten a long time. Forgotten, I guess, but they were just lying back down there in my memory.

I was living with my folks in Calgary. My dad and two kid brothers, they all worked in the packinghouse there, and I was figuring on getting me a job there and this day a letter comes to the house by a special messenger from the post office and it says for me to get hold of the Red Cross downtown and I knew what it meant. That would be about Jennie. She was the girl I had married about three weeks before the invasion and the ceremony had been in the church in her village south of Birmingham. I'd met her on a leave in '41 and we decided to get married before the invasion in case I didn't come back; then she'd have something, my pension. I'd only been with her five days then and then for a fourteen-day leave in '45 and then the next time, six days, and then I'd been shipped home.

Now, let's see. Yes. I go downtown to the Red Cross and they tell me that Jennie is coming in just about five days and I whistle back to the house and when Dad and the boys come home we have a family pow-wow. Where are we going to bed us down, me and Jennie? There was no room in that little house and we didn't have a sewer because we were out in northwest Calgary where there wasn't any. I'd been bunking down on the floor of the room my brothers slept in and Dad and Mom, they had the other bedroom and here we was, man and wife, and nowheres to sleep or eat or anything like that, and that was because I didn't know when she was coming, at least not so fast. I'd only been home three weeks and here she was, coming. They moved fast with those war brides. I guess it was England not wanting them on their hands, or something.

We have this pow-wow, and the old man does all the pow-wowing and he says we got to get a house for Donny—that's me—and Jennie and fast, and you could see his mind working and he was acting like he was the sergeant instead of me, which I had been. His mind started clicking. I remember that. He wasn't killing hogs now. He was down to the real serious part.

First, he says, we'll take over the lot next door, and that was simple because on our street there was lots that had been taken back by Calgary during the Depression. You could have your pick, and there was about four in a row to the south of us. I said we don't own it and he said nobody owns it but the city, and that ain't anybody. That's just a constitution put down on paper. He meant the rules and regulations of the city, and I could see that.

We needed wood, and there were four of us and he told us, get out and scrounge, and what he meant was, get lumber. Jim and Henry got in their old truck and went one way and I went the other on Mary's bike, and the first thing I see after I passed the grocery is the widow I used to mow her lawns, do her garden, six years ago when I was a kid in high school and I remembered she didn't have a car then. She might not have a car but the big garage was still there. I knocked on her door and she said, well, she invited me in and set to making tea and putting out a plate of cookies and she asked was this a visit or what, and she didn't ask me about overseas or nothing, because the old gal seemed to know I wasn't exactly on a social call.

I put it right straight and clear, that my wife was coming in on Tuesday from England and I had to have a house for her and seeing as she hadn't been using the garage for a long time, maybe she would let me buy it. She didn't bat an eye, that old gal. Not a blink. She just said yes and I said how much and she looked me right in the eye and said, "That can be discussed later, Donny. The thing now is to build that place for you and your bride." She was a real old trooper.

Okay, I thought, we got a garage and what it will cost me? I don't know and I don't care, and I thank her and she says, what else do you need? I said, oh, the usual stuff. You know, you get your mind set on something and it sits on top of that and there's no ass left over to cover anything else. You understand?

I remember clear as day she said, "Just the usual stuff?" and I said, "Yes, Mrs. Dawson, just things we'd need," and then she shooed me out like she used to and I hightailed it back on that bike and told the old man I had Mrs. Dawson's garage. He let out a whoosh! I remember he yelled, "We're holding the aces."

Then he gets on Mary's bike and he goes down to the grocery store and what he did, he started phoning some of the guys at the Burns plant and when he comes home he said he had three guys coming out and two of them had trucks and so, even when we ain't even finished breakfast, the other guys he rounded up had come and it was like he was the sergeant again.

He sent me and Henry and two of the guys over to Mrs. Dawson's place and we started to tear down the garage. I thought at first we were going to move it, but Dad had other plans. No, we were going to tear it down, board by board, and I'm telling you, that lumber was straight and true. The best B.C. stuff. Not a twist in twenty feet. Built like one of your battleships. When we got a pickup load we'd load it and the driver would run it back to the lot next to our house and by this time Dad and Jim and the other guys had cleared the lot, a place the size of a house. They had leveled it off and kind of prettied up the ground with scythes and a few neighbors had wandered over and everyone was pitching in, but that was only part of the problem. Not the working, but materials. We needed more.

This is where the old man came in again. There was a telephone line which had never been strung because there were no houses past our place and he told the boys to get out there about eight poles down, so nobody would notice what we were doing, and to cut four of those poles down and drag them back. I know it was stealing, but let's not discuss that now. They were back in short order, maybe half an hour, dragging the poles behind the truck, and Dad measured them and had them cut square and that was our foundation. As good as you could find under the times it was like then because, you must know, there was no cement to be found for foundation work. Why, you almost had to mortgage your body to get it. But everybody was getting into the spirit of things and guys remembered they had a few nails and there was the nails from the garage and we straightened them and we did manage to buy a few and one neighbor had a henhouse with windows, except the windows didn't have glass and Dad said to give Jim twenty dollars. He and the guy with the truck went to a junkyard and they found glass. The glass was out of a couple of junked Model-As, Durants, old Chevs, don't ask me. They brought back glass. Thicker, but it would do. We used the door from the garage and I think somebody said he knew where he could get flooring cheap and I give him another twenty out of my Army discharge pay and off he went and by God, he came back with a lot of stuff, shorts and longs, odds and ends, and somebody said he sure wished he had that stuff himself.

Here was Dad measuring boards and somebody sawing them and somebody passing them up and two guys nailing them and by nightfall that house was going up. Now, you couldn't exactly call it a house. Say, twenty by thirty, 600 square feet, but that was good, all we'd ever need and we had another month to insulate it and fix it up. What we needed was just about all there.

Somebody made a fire of scraps of lumber and junk and my mother had gone to the store and cleaned them out of wieners and buns and got a jar of mustard and she'd been making meat pies and ordinary pies, like apple, all afternoon, about five of them. Dad accidentally found a couple of jugs of his raspberry wine and about six o'clock that night there we all are sitting around on whatever we could find toasting wieners and having a feast.

Now, this was great, and I was the only one worried. I knew. Oh, I knew. I'd been thinking of Jennie all day and that big house, all stone, the lawns and the gardens, the oldness of it, the furniture, the kind of clothes she had even in the war and I was wondering. How in the blazes is a girl from a home like that going to fit into a shack? You had to face it, the place was still a shack, winter coming on, no toilet—but of course, we would use our biff, the folks' biff—but what would she think and besides, it was bare bones inside. Oh brother!

Then, I remember to this day, I look up and there's Mrs. Dawson and she's standing there and nobody's seen her and she has her cane like she always has and that little white dog and she's walked all the way, those six blocks. From where the good houses were. She's standing there like she maybe wants to be invited in.

I get up and call her name and go over and I ask her if she wants to join us and she nods. Then I did the right thing. I took her around that circle, about twenty people, and I introduced her to each one and I got every name right and I took the chair somebody was sitting on and I put it down for her and she said, she said she'd like a hotdog.

Jesus Christ! About four wives jumped up to the pot to fish one out and Dad is feeling no pain by this time anyway, he asks her if she wants a glass of his wine and she says she'd love one and I catch my mother throw out her wine and dry the glass on her skirt and reach over and pass it on to Dad. That was Mom's wine glass, the best she had.

Wait, this didn't start out this way, this story. This was about Jennie coming over, but I got to tell you about Mrs. Dawson. I don't know what her husband did. She always seemed to be a widow lady. She was little. I didn't know her first name, and I'm coming to that. She wore good dresses and she had a good way about her. She had something to do in Calgary society but she didn't seem to want to move to Mount Royal where they all were. She liked the northwest area. Somebody said her husband had owned a lot of it once, so maybe there's where she got her

money. Oh, she had money. I got to know her when I was talking to
the district supervisor of the *Herald* when I was looking for a paper route
and he told me she was looking for a boy to do her lawns and stuff. I
was seventeen, no boy, but jobs were so tough even a paper route and
the few dollars a month looked good, so I went and got the job. I worked
for her, gardening in summer, you see, and shoveling in winter, putting
on the storm windows, taking them off, cleaning, the heavy work. I did
that for four years until I joined up. I liked to talk to her. She knew
a lot about everything, the world.

Well, there's Mrs Dawson sitting there on that chair with a hotdog
and she's got the glass of wine wedged between her shoes and everybody's
looking at her. I mean, not her kind comes to our kind of party. She
fishes in her purse and you can only hear the fire cracking and she says
something like this: "My name is Mildred Dawson, and I'm a friend of
Donny and because he is welcoming his bride to our neighborhood in
a few days and he has no place to welcome her home—although I see
you have done quite a bit to fix that—I, too, have done my bit and I
have been phoning around and I'll give Donny this list and the things
I have arranged can be picked up Monday morning. If you don't need
some of them, well, then you won't have to pick them up. We all have
to do our best for our returning heroes."

That's made up, but you get the gist of it. That's what she said, a different way. Like in her own words.

Done her bit! Hadn't she given me the garage? Later she just asked
me to donate forty dollars to the Salvation Army, so I got the garage
and the money fed a few bums, so that was a good deal.

Anyway, she left and one of the guys drove her home in the pickup,
and I laughed at that.

The party broke up then and next day the rest of the place was finished,
even though we had to wait a few days for the tarpaper for the roof and
twist a few tails to get three gallons of brown paint for the sides, but
inside it looked good. A sound floor, good big windows, and there was
a living room which was wee and a storage room and a good-sized kitchen and a place where a bathroom could go, although Jennie said it
was her crying room when things got rough that winter with no friends
and all that cold weather outside. It had a nice bedroom with lots of
cupboards and we dug a trench and run water pipes in from the street
and electricity from my dad's house and it was pretty sound. Just about
two day's work, and no more, and that included a gravel walk between

the two houses and one to the road. When our taxi came I wanted to walk my bride down that path and I figured I'd be talking a mile a minute to keep her mind off the shack. But it turned out she knew Canada was a wild and wooly land because of the books she'd read as a kid, so she was expecting anything.

Christ, almost forgot. This is a dandy! That list, the one Mrs. Dawson gave me. I read it when we were having breakfast next morning and here's what she had done. Phoned a lot of her fancy friends and I guess twisted their elegant arms and she lined up stuff for us. A double bed. Kitchen table and chairs. An armoire—that's a big thing that stands against a wall and holds clothes. Real upper crust. Coffee tables. Rugs. Knives, forks, and spoons, plates. The works. About all we wanted for was bedding and sheets and pillows and towels. I mean, when the folks heard me read that list, there was whistles, you better believe me. On Monday I took a neighbor and we went around with the truck and I collected everything I could and that house was jam-packed with stuff in Dad's basement, and you could tell none of it was cheap because it was from the basements of Mrs. Dawson's friends and they didn't buy cheap stuff. Good solid stuff you'd pay a lot for today.

To wind it up, Jennie came and I took a week off from looking for work and we bought a stove and sink and curtains and a big stove for coal and wood for the living room, which was all the house could handle. She'd look the stuff over and put marks on a diagram she'd made of the house and there I'd be, putting down a rug and pushing a chair here and a table there and rearranging things and it didn't take long until everything was just jake.

One day I went down to City Hall and I go into the building-permits place and a guy comes up and I take fifteen minutes telling him what happened, how we were squatting, the why of it, what we'd done. I remember him, a grizzled old guy about fifty and I remember him looking at me and finally he said, "Son, did you do worse in the war?"

Naturally I said sure, a lot worse.

He looked at me, tapped me on the shoulder and said, "Forget it. Wait until we come after you," and he winked. That's the way it was. Everybody was helping you when you got out of the service. They never did come around, not in the two years we lived in that place.

About a month later I took Jennie one Sunday over to see Mrs. Dawson and we had afternoon tea and they hit it off like two old Dutch washerwomen and when Jennie went out to the truck Mrs. Dawson said to me, "Bring her over more, Donny, she's going to brighten up my old age and I know she's going to make you happy. You're a pair of aces, back to back."

What an old sweetheart she was. Dead now, of course. A real gal.

3 HAPPILY EVER AFTER

3 HAPPILY EVER AFTER

We'd be sitting in the living room, in a farmhouse or a suburban bungalow, and after the interview we'd be having tea—carrot cake was big on the prairies in the summer of 1984—and she'd look at him and say, "Did we really do all those things? All that work, that worry . . ."

Sometimes she was the war bride he had brought back from England. Sometimes she was the wife he had left behind to fight for King and Country. And sometimes she was the girl he scarcely remembered from before the war, but who had blossomed while he was away. (Often she remembered him.) After the courtship and the marriage they settled down, probably with almost nothing while he struggled to make a go of the farm, or studied for his university degree, or started his own small business, or tried to find the right job.

They took their lumps. They had their fights along with their joys. They moved, they raised their kids, they worked hard. And they "got ahead," as most of them phrased it. An inch at a time. Then a foot. Then that long step of a yard.

When I left, I'd shake hands and they'd say, "Come back again. Try to come and see us," and I always felt they had such solid, sound marriages. I also felt that I had given them something: a chance to look at each other in a different way before a stranger's gentle questions, and say to themselves, but actually to each other, "What we have is a good thing. We did it the hard way; we did it together."

"ALL PEACHES AND CREAM"

You want a happy story, eh? Okay, just say that Happy Graham
went over happy to be seeing the high spots of Europe and came back
happy that he had survived with only about eighty little pieces of German nuts and bolts in him and that everything went along happily.

My wife was waiting for me after the banners and the parades at the
station and she had been working for the American Air Force, who
seemed to have taken over Edmonton in those days. Why, I think their
basketball team even won the Alberta championship or some such
foolishness, so those boys had really buckled down to winning the war.
My wife had on a fine new coat and dress and I looked pretty sparky
in my Army-style uniform, and in my kit bag I had a lot of little pieces
of silver and gold—bits of this and that that were lying around in Germany and I had picked up.

We hiked off to the McDonald Hotel for our second honeymoon. The
first had been in the same hotel in 1928 and the old Mac hadn't changed
all that much, but we had. We spent three days there, just roaring around
and having a fine time, and then it was time to get down to the business
of making an honest living again.

I had my old trade, construction mechanic, and when I walked into
the shop the boss came out and hugged me and said, "Happy, get out
of those Army duds and get into overalls. I been waiting four years for
you." So that ended the great job hunt we'd been warned about all the
way across Canada by these officers who were to warn us of all the terrible things that waited for us. I was halfway to believing them when I
got off the train. My wife would be living with another man and the
Edmontonians would throw horse manure at me when I walked down
Jasper and I'd find my job taken over by a Zombie.

No, it was all peaches and cream. My wife had found us a nice cozy
apartment and it had rent control on it and she'd spent a year fixing
it up. I'd put my '40 Olds up on blocks when I enlisted in '41, and in
two days I was driving just about the finest car you'll ever see around
Edmonton, me at the wheel, perky in my new duds, which my wife had
bought when I'd been away whenever a bargain came up. Good seamstress
that she was, she'd made me shirts and knitted me a fair range of lively
sweaters and ties and socks. Remember them hand-knit ties of them days?
Real snazzy. Wish I had a few today.

Now I ask you, what could go wrong? I had a fine wife and while she
was no better looking, she wasn't any the worse for wear. My old job

back at a hefty wage boost. Fine apartment. A car, and that car I was offered terrific money for every time I parked it on Jasper. Could have sold it eighteen times. No sirree. That was my baby.

I could have used up my credits and gone to university, because Emily's job was a good one with the telephones, supervisor. It would have got us through, but I was thirty-eight and hey, an old engine basher doesn't need any more education. Grade Nine is enough for any man. I can read and write and five times ten is fifty, isn't it? So, I've got as much real education as any professor.

Back to where we started from. Did I have any problems? I've just told you. None. The war, I enjoyed myself and if Emily did, too, then that's her business. Coming back, the biggest thrill was tearing into a sixteen-ounce rare steak in Montreal where we landed. It was great to be home and everything tickety-boo and just the way I liked it. No, put me down as one of those guys who did well out of the war, but I'll tell you this. If I hadn't gone I would have cleaned up. Some of the stories I heard about this town, what went on. The money some made. I'd have cleaned up.

Who cares? Everything worked out well for me and I think it did for most of the guys in my outfit. At our reunion three years ago I didn't hear anybody bitching too hard. About Trudeau, sure, because he was giving a little squeeze or two where it hurt the most. But not about anything else. Everybody's happy.

"ONLY NINE PEOPLE SHOWED UP"

I'd joined in June of '41 and now it was October of '45 and both wars were over. I had a wife waiting back in England. She became what they called a war bride and she's always resented that. I don't see why. I think she has her reasons, though. She wasn't treated very well when she finally got over in May of '46. Like, I'd introduce her to people in the post office or the general store in town and they'd be looking her up and down and I guess she could hear them thinking, "What has Billy Wilson gone and done, marrying this little girl from England?"

She was as good as half of them and better than the other half, but you know, the local boy who was captain on the town team and played hockey, big star and all that, why couldn't he have married a local girl and not gone halfway around the world to find one? You know, those English girls just waiting to get their clutches on that fine young Canadian airman. Ah hell, you know.

When Jocelyn, my war bride, did come to Canada my aunt thought the thing to do was to throw a bridal shower. She went ahead, issuing invitations and getting the place all fixed up and this puzzled my wife because apparently this was not done in England. But she thought it was nice. I think Aunt Hilda asked about twenty women. Friends of hers and girls who had gone to high school with me. You know, the usual kind of mixture these things have. Well, the big day came and only nine people showed up. They all sent their regrets, but you have to be one big dummy to think in a small town eleven women have something else to do on an afternoon. And especially when they have known about it for two weeks. It was a slap in the face. My Aunt Hilda was smart enough to not tell me who the women were who didn't come, but I had a good idea. I didn't forget that for a long time. Anyway, Jocelyn didn't know this and she thought it was a fine party and she made friends there that she kept for thirty years until we moved to the Okanagan Valley.

It was the smallness of it that bugged me. And what surprised me was their lack of curiosity. Look at the picture. Here's me, a popular kid and from a well-known family, a big farm, and everybody had known and loved my mother, and here I am, back again, taking over with my brother Angus, and I've got Jocelyn, an English girl. You'd think these women and such would have a lot of curiosity about her. Like, what did he see in her, or her in him? No, the gates just shut tight. They wanted no part of someone from a foreign land. England, I mean.

And I thought, Christ Almighty, if they could have seen the house that Jocelyn lived in, what I had taken her away from. It wasn't a castle or even an estate, but it was sure a far cry from the three down–two bedrooms up kind of houses everybody in town lived in. It was a big and old and gracious house and her father was a merchant and when he died he left her and her two sisters enough shares in two steel mills that would have filled a bushel basket. So she should have been judging the women of the town, and not the other way.

Oh well, as they say, all's well that ends well. It did end well. They got off their high horses and within a year we were totally in the social swing of the town and the district and it was all as if it was just a bad joke. It wasn't a big joke at the time. I was furious. Of course, Josie, the little dear, didn't even know what was going on.

"IT WAS FATE"

There is always a bright side in every story and I imagine you've heard a few horror stories, the way some fellows were treated when we came back. Not me. I just sat on my duff on the west coast of Vancouver Island at a little fishing village filled with fishermen and Indians and heavy drinkers. It was called Tofino. I suppose it is still there. Anyway, you've heard of Long Beach. It is famous. That's where we were, guarding those beaches of Long Beach waiting for the Japanese to come over and conquer Canada.

I'll tell you something interesting. If the Japanese Army had landed around Tofino or anywhere on that coast, we would not have had to defeat them. We'd just have let them land and we'd retreat and they'd have died of craziness trying to figure out how to get over to the east coast of the island where Nanaimo and Victoria was. No roads. Just a jungle of bush and muskeg and high mountain ranges. Two of them. I lost two good years of war just watching for the Japanese Navy, which was 3,000 miles away to the west getting the living hell knocked out of them by the Americans.

But the bright side. This is a story I tell when my kids asked, "Daddy, what did you do in the war?" They never asked, naturally.

I joined up in Calgary with the Army and so I got my discharge there and there was a big party at home. My folks didn't drink much, but everybody bought the liquor their ration coupons allowed them to buy, so there was quite a party.

The next day my dad told me to look outside and there was the car. It was the Graham Paige. Remember that one? A block long and gray with dark brown trim. If you had one today, people would stop you in a service station and ask to look under the hood. It was a huge car. A beauty. He handed me the keys and told me it was full of gas and asked why I just didn't take it for the afternoon and go for a spin? That was great. My mother packed me a big lunch and a big thermos of lemonade—I guess they figured it would be nice for me to get away by myself for the day, and I guess I thought that was a good idea, too.

I remember driving down the hill to Twelfth, southwest, and I see this girl cycling up the hill and when I went by her I said, "Why, there's Mary Temple!" Just like that, there was Mary Temple. She'd been with me in high school and I had taken her home a couple of times from school dances, some bowling with the gang, things like that. But I'd thought of her quite a lot during the war.

I swung the car into a side street and backed up and took off after her, and when I got beside her I pulled in front and got out of the car and I guess I said hi or something like that. Boy, was I ever glad to see her. She looked like a million bucks, all of her. She hadn't changed in four years. Not a bit. Same smile. Same blue eyes. Brown hair.

By God, but she was glad to see me, too. We hugged and hugged and laughed and were just like a couple of kids and then I asked her if she wanted to go on a picnic. She'd love it. It turned out she was in nursing and had the day off and so we went. Her house was just up the way and she told her mother she was going for a picnic and we went whooping off.

You'll see why this is my own war story. It is because I was still in uniform. We drove out to Bragg Creek and found a honey of a spot and we had my mom's lunch and then we talked and talked and I'm not sure just how this happened. She can't remember either. I mean, we can't agree how it happened, but that afternoon we got engaged. I said something, like how much I had liked her and how I thought of her all the time I was on that god-forsaken beach, and she said she had always thought of me and we asked each other, I guess, why we hadn't written and maybe I guess we were edging toward each other. And then, whap! I was kissing her and she was kissing me and, well, it is all kind of blurry. But I knew I had loved her a long time and I just had to grow up to realize it, and going down that hill instead of heading out into the country, that was it, there was somebody up there watching us. And that she should be going up that hill, pushing her bike. I mean, what else can you call it but fate?

We got back to Calgary about supper time and we'd already set the date. We couldn't see the point of waiting.

Much argument at her mother's place. Much argument at my place. You can't do this. Can't do that. You're just kids. God, I was twenty-two and so was Mary. We had our way, of course. If we hadn't, we'd have done it at City Hall and Mrs. Temple and my mother were both snobs enough that they wanted it written up in the *Herald*. So that's the way it was. Funny how things work out, isn't it?

"ONLY ONE NIGHT AT THE HOMESTEAD"

I can make this damn short. When my wife got out of that caboose on runners and took one look at my parents' shack, the homestead, I didn't have to take one look at her face. I could tell by the way her body stiffened. It was winter, a hell of a cold day, and we'd just spent four hours in the caboose bumping over those damned northern Alberta roads and trails and here she was, straight off the boat from England and looking at a homesteader's log cabin. Eighteen by twelve feet, two windows and a door, and not much else.

I thought, thank the bloody Lord I didn't tell her it was a palatial farmhouse or that we owned a big ranch. That's what I thought. I had just told her we farmed in Alberta and left it at that.

Margaret came from that lovely farm country in Devon. Her father was a farmer but he was in Egypt, a squadron leader, when we married and so there really was nobody around to ask me, "And Mr. Benson, just what kind of farming do you do in Canada?" Her mother couldn't. She was hopeless—horses, horses, horses, that's all she and her daughters thought about. I knew I wasn't bringing her back to anything remotely resembling the family place in Devon, so I would blather on about the wild roses in the spring and the crisp autumn nights and the sunsets and the terrific partridge hunting and let her imagination run off at the mind.

To me it was home but to her it was a dump, and when you looked at it through her eyes, it *was* a dump. Oh shit! I won't even try and describe it. I'll just say it was pretty bad, and here is this English war bride, in all her finery, her hand-loomed traveling suit and her cloth coat made in Edinburgh and her little fur hat, Russian sable for all I know, and she's standing in the snow outside this cabin and what is she thinking?

That night in the bedroom . . . yeah, the bedroom. Blankets and grain sacks strung around three sides on a line to give us some privacy. That night she tells me in a kind of hard but quiet whisper, but kind of desperate, too, she tells me she's leaving tomorrow and if I don't want to come with her she'll hoof it out alone.

I knew there was nothing I could say when she got in that tone of voice, and I could hear my mother and father whispering away in Norwegian and I knew what they were saying, naturally, but my wife didn't, and what they were saying was, well, what the hell were they going to do with this Englishwoman?

After a while we all went to sleep, I think, and in the morning it was all decided without anybody saying one goddamned thing that she'd go and I'd go with her. Just like that. Breakfast was a happy, laughing time and then Margaret thanked Mom and Dad for having us, and she came out behind the curtains with her bag. I had got the horses out and Dad got the heated stones wrapped and my duds had been packed by my mother, such as they were, and about nine o'clock, well, that was it.

We said good-by and that we'd be back, maybe in the summer, and Dad whapped the team with the reins and we drove away, four hours to the railroad station, and caught the five-o'clock train. That was it.

Looking back, it was just the damndest thing you ever saw. Nobody said anything. The little homestead cabin. The clutter, the mess of traps and wolf and bear and marten, weasel skins. Dad trapped in the winter. The smallness of it all, the little homestead cabin in miles of snow and drifts and bare poplars and no neighbor for two miles, just a place cut out of the bush. And me, dumb cluck of all time, I expected a well-bred English girl to live in it. I sure had rocks in my head those days.

There wasn't a living for one family on that place, let alone two.

Just the way she said it that night, "Ingvard, we together or I alone are leaving this place tomorrow," and I knew she meant it. Ingvard is my name, but little English lady that she was, she called me Geoffrey. More class, she thought. So when she used my *real* name, she meant business!

We went to Edmonton and stayed with my sister for a week and then got an apartment. I got on with the CNR right away because I'd worked with them summers, '41 and '42 when I was going to varsity, and Margaret, ah the cunning one, she got on with the library system. Married women couldn't work then if their husbands had jobs. I don't think it was the law, just the unwritten law. But she said she had been a war refugee, one of those thousands of kids who came out from England, here to Canada, because of the bombing in London. She said she was one of them, lived in Toronto and then moved out West because her only aunt was here and she got a job. I think that lovely English accent did it, really. It was something else again. Right out of royalty, it seemed like.

So, that's how it was. I got back in September of '45. She came out in December. We spent one night at my parent's homestead the first of January and that, my friends, and that, my foes, was how it all happened. There was lots more to tell as the years went by, but that's really just the only good story I've got to tell.

"WON'T YOU COME IN, SIR?"

I've still got it and I've dug it out and here it is and it says that I was honorably discharged from the Canadian Army, Active, and my service was in Canada, the United Kingdom, and Continental Europe and that I was discharged under, and I'll read it, "Routine Order 1029, 5-C-1 by reason of return to civil life on demobilization."

You look at it now and you think, "Routine Order 1029, 5-C-1" and you wonder what that means. It doesn't say that I left a wife and two children and put up with all the crap they could throw at me for four years, nearly four years away from home, and down here it says, "Marks or scars" and it is typed in, "nil" and you want to ask, what about the marks and scars on my personality, in my head. There could have been some.

Just a piece of paper and so old I can hardly read my signature. What I can see sure isn't the kind of signature I write now. It looks like the signature of a kid. I've done a lot of growing up since then, at least judging by my signature. Anyway this piece of paper says I'm entitled to wear the France-Germany Star pinned to my 1939-45 Star, which should prove to anyone that I was over there. But it is just a piece of paper and about all I got from them.

I didn't expect any help when I got back and I didn't get any. I just came home and I'd written my wife not to meet me. We weren't coming home as a regiment but in bits and pieces, tens and fifties, so you know there was not going to be any whoop-to-do and, besides, Fredericton was a long way from Halifax for her to ride to. There was no point in it. I just went through the rigamarole in Halifax, got my bus ticket and hopped aboard, and when I reached Fredericton I hiked home. I wasn't far, just a dozen blocks, and it was a wonderful autumn day and down those streets with all the wonderful tall trees turning colors and that sound I heard was me whistling. Not free, not twenty-one anymore, but still white and so damn glad to be home I did little hops, skips, and jumps like a kid coming home after the last day in school.

Madeleine wasn't sure when I was coming because my phone call from Halifax three days before, I didn't know exactly, but she was always a prepared woman, even as a kid. When I knocked on the door I could hear her running down the stairs from the suite she had rented in this old house. Yes, I could even hear her steps and she yanked open the door and there she was and there I was. We were both four years older but she looked the same, as pretty as ever, with that French look of hers like a lot of those girls around the French villages have, and she smiled and you know what she said?

She said, "Won't you come in, sir? I've been expecting you."

I wonder how many years she'd been practising that line, but she always had a sense of humor and then, naturally, everything was a buzz. Kissing, I guess. Hugging. I guess I was crying. Might as well admit it. I guess she was, too. I guess she showed me around the three rooms, pointing out this and that and what she'd done, but frankly, it was a buzz. Bzzzzzzzt! It just flew by and I couldn't remember a thing. Here I'd been thinking for the past six months that the war was over and I was going home; I'd been thinking how it all would be and she had, too, because she told me and even a day later I couldn't remember what happened. So I still can't. Just bzzzzzzzt!

I think it was that way for a lot of the fellows.

The kids were more of a problem. Ronnie was nine and I hadn't seen him since he was five, and Donnie was just two when I sailed away, so it took a lot of getting to know them, and Ronnie, naturally, wanted me to play the big soldier, the hero. That's all kids were fed on in those days. Newspapers and magazines, the war, heroes and the like. I know I disappointed them. Here I was, just an ordinary man, just like the guy who stared out at them from the picture on the table. Off the paper of the photograph to just flesh and blood, like the owner of the grocery store or the principal of the school.

Ah, I think for most fellows who had a wife and family at home waiting, that first week was probably the best of all, getting to know each other again, soaking in a hot tub using lots of soap, sitting at the table and telling Ronnie not to slurp his milk and Donnie to sit up straight. And after the kids were in bed there you are sitting with your wife and drinking whiskey with hot water and lemon and just lazily telling her some of the things you had done and the room is warm and you both know that in an hour, when you both feel right, that you are going to a nice warm bed.

I guess it was a process of falling in love again, but in a different way because you were falling in love with a real-live family. So much better. Yes.

You might say that I'm a romantic and that this was the way it should have been but wasn't. But with me it was. I know there were fellows I met later in business who had a real hard time of it. Oh, the usual. Looking at their wife when they met again and asking himself, "Who is this woman?" Like, "I'm not married to her, am I?" Remember, there was a lot of that, probably far more than people believe. We were a different society, too, and men that I know, they felt that way but they continued on and I suppose it ruined many lives. You enlist, you fight for your country, you come home, and there is nothing.

I was lucky, of course, but lucky in other ways, too, because everything fell into place for me. By '50 I was doing well, secure, and the war was so far behind me that when my wife and I were talking, something she would say about those four years was all that reminded me that I had been in the most terrible war that mankind had ever fought.

"A LOT OF IFS"

I didn't give a damn when I got out of the Navy. I had seen the *Sioux* go down and I lost a lot of buddies and I had been kicked jackass to breakfast by the Navy and I'd just had it up to here with the fat-cat bunch of bastards that so many Canadians I met had turned into, thanks to the war I fought for them. I just didn't care.

That's the way I felt when I got out. I was drinking far too much, sipping away on home brew in the morning and going to the hotel for beer all afternoon and then to the Legion at night, and this went on for a while. I wasn't looking for a job and my savings and my rehabilitation pay was just about done and I thought, oh shit, I've got to do something. I was tired of fighting the world.

I was a wreck, to put it mildly. My father wouldn't even talk to me. I guess I was breaking my mother's heart. My brother Len beat the hell out of me, and my two sisters wouldn't even bring their friends home when I was around. That bad. If I'd known what a psychiatrist was I might have gone to one. Hell, sure I knew I was in trouble.

I'd always read a lot when I was a kid and when they opened a new library branch in East Toronto I was walking by one afternoon and that was one day I hadn't bought a pint of bootleg hooch from the guy in the Legion who sold it. I walked in and started looking around. I was just passing the time waiting for my two buddies to show up at the beer parlor down the street, because we always met there about one, and I'm pulling out books and flipping them and I hear this voice say, "Can I help you?" I look and there is this young woman and she's friendly and I guess I mumble something and we get talking and she had a brother who was Navy too, and I guess that started it.

I'm sort of dawdling around at five or so, when I figure she gets off work and I sort of run into her, accidentally on purpose, and so there we are again, talking. I get up my courage. You know, I didn't know a damned thing about girls, but she says yes, she'll have coffee. Didn't really know me from a bale of hay, you know, but she's friendly and we go across the street to Jimmie's Restaurant and before you know it the time is seven o'clock and I wasn't even thinking about going to the Legion. We were having a lot of fun.

You got it. She's my wife now. You sort of spoiled my story.

We went for dinner that night to a nice café and I walked her home and I told her all about myself and she said she wanted me to get a job. I said I'd never had a job. Right out of high school and into the Navy, and I didn't know what to do. She said, it's coming up to Christmas so why don't you go down to the post office and be a postie. That job lasted for three weeks, two weeks before and a week after, and I saw her every night and met her folks and she met my mother and in May we got married.

We got a small apartment and I got a job at John Inglis and three nights a week I went to commercial college and worked Saturdays, too, delivering meat for a butcher, and he let me keep the truck Sunday as he knew my folks. That was our honeymoon, rattling around Southern Ontario Saturday night and all Sunday. When I finished, the commercial part, I got a job with a sporting goods wholesaler, Dunlop, a good outfit, and bit by bit we got things together and here we are, both of us coming up to sixty and still happy.

It's not much of a story but I'm just telling you this, or I'm asking you this. What would have happened to me if I had bought that pint of hooch that night and if I had gone to the pub that afternoon and if I hadn't just walked in to that library? A lot of ifs in there, but I guess all of our lives are governed by those little ifs.

"HOW I GOT MARRIED"

First, let me see, I sure gotta tell you how I got in the Army. She's important, you know. My mom and dad and me are sitting down there having breakfast when the door waltzes open, not a thump or a knock, and in comes his cousin, a big man, and he walks up to me and he says, "Jamie, put on yer cap, yer comin' with me," and Jeezus Christ, then I knew what was coming. I was going to get killed.

My dad jumps up and he says, "Johnny, steady, what're you doing to the lad?" and his cousin says, "If he's old enough and big enough to take my kid down to the gravel pit and get her in the family way, he's big enough to join the Army and that's where he's going. Not tomorrow, but right today. I'd kill him myself but they hang people in this country for that, so I'll let the Germans do it."

Oh, he was right, of course, because I had given the old prong to Jennie and she was going to have a baby, but I didn't dare tell my parents or they'd have had a fit. So I just took my cap off the peg and put it on and walked out, telling my mom, and she's got this daft look on her face, I tells her I'll be back.

The cousin is the recruiting sergeant for the district, all the places around this town in Nova Scotia, and he marches me down the street and in and he grabs up some papers and scribbles a bit and shoves them at me and tells me to sign. No, there was no way out of it. I'd told her I was no way going to marry her and I'd met another girl, and so her father was going to let the Germans do me in. That was the start.

Now, I won't say I wouldn't have married the girl. If I'd stayed in the town I would have had to. They wouldn't have let me live in it if I had not married her. That was the way it was done in those days.

I should say my father never said a word. Just get the hell out of me house and this town. That's the way it was. So there I was in the Army, me, just seventeen, with half the Macdonalds and Mcdonalds and McDonalds and MacDonalds in Nova Scotia and I went across the Pond and England and through Europe and I saw enough of those rotten people to last me my life, and I got a broken leg when a DR [dispatch rider] went out of control and slammed me, and a bullet fired by a Jerry at the Rhine. Funny, you saw the prisoners and their wounded and dead but you never saw the guys who shot you.

It is a fine day when I come home with my kit bag stuffed full of the dumbest souvenirs you ever saw. Others was picking up valuable stuff and there I was collecting junk. Watches that didn't work and cameras that wouldn't click. I walked in the kitchen door and my mother and father are sitting at that same awful table and my old mum, she hugs me and cries. My father looks at me and says, "Jennie's still at her father's house. Go down the road and see your bairn. She's still waiting for you."

Well, let me tell you, that tore it. I went to her house and saw me son and Jennie and three weeks later there was a wedding in that wee town and believe me, nobody said no at the banns.

I want to say one thing. I didn't ask for nothing. Anything, I mean. I did my honor toward Jennie and when people see us in church on Sunday morning, I know what they are thinking. They're thinking, "What a fine couple." Do you reckon why? Because that's what I think myself.

"THE BEST THING THAT EVER HAPPENED TO ME"

I joined the Air Force in Calgary on July 14, 1941, and I didn't have to because I had a loving wife and a wonderful four-year-old son, but I had been through the Great Depression on a farm in southern Saskatchewan and I don't have to tell you how rough things really were. When I walked into that recruiting office in downtown Calgary I hadn't even told my wife what I was going to do.

When I got home that night and told her, she was shocked. Here we were, me twenty-five, and Hyacinthe twenty-three, and here I was going away, and God knows where. God knows where was England within eight months and three and a half long years of it, and just letters and me with a wife and a nine-year-old son to come back to and to start again, and starting again meant this. It meant the competition with thousands of other vets and, mind you, I was twenty-nine by the time I was discharged. Besides the vets, there was the competition from the high schoolers who had grown into men in those years and had one hell of a lot of those jobs that we needed desperately. Our jobs weren't there.

When I came back we found we still loved each other and I vowed then and there, forever, I would work my guts out, my fingers to the bone to make life better for her and Dougie. It didn't work out that way. My intentions were of the best, but you know what they say about good intentions. Good Lord, that was me all over.

There were jobs, but fifty cents an hour was about all I could find and I'd picked up a back injury that wasn't bad enough to get me out of the Air Force but it was bad enough that I just couldn't handle heavy work. I had no skills.

Do you think some people develop a kind of smell of fear, like they say dogs can smell if you are afraid of them? I started to think that was me because when I'd go into a store, a building, or a factory and ask for work, I just had this feeling that the person I talked to smelled fear. Maybe it was the wish to get a job so bad that I smelled that way. I used to ask Hyacinthe if I smelled funny and she'd wrinkle up her nose and say I smelled good. To her, maybe, but I wondered. I just could not get a job and what rankled me was that I knew that they were hiring. So I talked to a government job counselor about it at the Unemployment Center and he told me maybe I should grow a mustache. I said why, for Pete's sake? He said maybe that when they were looking through the applications when a job came up, the fellow who did the hiring would say, "Hey, I remember him, he's the guy with the mustache." It sounded nutty to me because nobody wore mustaches or beards then, and if that was all the help these guys could offer me, like grow a mustache, I guess they couldn't do much for me.

There was also a drinking habit I'd picked up. It was hard not to drink in England. Why? For the simple reason there was nothing else to do, and besides, that was where the fun was, the friendship, the people you could meet and talk to, and if you want to put it another way, the girls you could meet. And now I was home, in a small apartment in the run-down area with a wife and a boy and afraid that another one would come along because we were staunch members of the church. It was so easy to go downtown at nine in the morning and walk around.

There was still money because I had my pay for service from the Air Force but it was dwindling away, but no matter, somehow just like I was a steel filing and the Palliser was a magnet, about eleven every morning I'd find myself going down those five steps to the basement level and going into the beer parlor. And there I'd sit. There were other guys there like me. It was like a club. The old fat waiter with the limp, he knew everyone. Called us by our first names and that was something. Somebody who had a tiny bit of authority recognized you and was friendly and there was all these guys, and we'd sit around and talk about England and the war and the bull was piled high and when it was time to go, when the money was gone, well, it was gone. Maybe three bucks. A lot of beer. A lot. Thirty glasses, and I'd go home plastered and that went on and on and on and bloody well on, and one night about supper time when I got home it was all over. Nothing was changed about the little place, just the clothes gone. Empty. Hyacinthe and the boy had gone. Her note said it wasn't ever going to work out the way I was carrying on, and she didn't mean carrying on with women. Those days were behind me. She meant the drinking and the mickey I'd sometimes buy for Sunday and so on. Her father and brother had driven in from East End and had taken her home and that was it. She didn't even write "love" or ask that I write her.

Best thing that ever happened to me. I got mad and I went to the grog shop, which was still open, and I bought a quart of rye and I went to the Chinese restaurant down the street and I counted my money and I ordered about seven dishes of the most expensive stuff they had and it came to about six dollars. I ate and drank and ate and drank, and I made an absolute pig of myself on Chinese food and whiskey. Then I went home and finished off what was left. About four ounces, five, three. That's when I blacked out, the first time. All that whiskey. Wow!

Next morning I got up and there was this pad on the table and I could see that I had written on it and what I had written was this. I wrote, "I will never have another drink again, so help me God."

And I never did. Even at a wedding I wouldn't sip the wine at the toast to the bride, and that was at my own son's wedding twenty years later.

I got a job. I walked into it. I went to the church and talked to the priest in his house. I told him everything, and I'd always thought he was a cynical red-haired draft-dodging son of a bitch, but he was sympathetic. He made a phone call. He wrote the name of a company, a trucking company, and handed it to me and wished me luck. Know what I did? I took a cab way out the McLeod Trail. I was going to show this guy who might have a job for me that I'd still had some get-up-and-go in me. Did I get the job? I sure did. Forty cents an hour. They put me on the grease rack and the cleaning steam hose, the lousiest job in the shop. Forty times eight, three-twenty times six, and you're looking at around twenty-seven dollars a week, and times four and you've got about one-ten a month and that was heaven. In those days it was. Hard work and out in the cold a lot, too, but boy, that money looked good. One-ten. We laugh at it now. No-talent guys with union seniority make that in a day, easily. But then it was something.

A tip from a shop mechanic named Bill Chalmers led me to a job in a big laundry, night work and fifty cents an hour, and I didn't care. I had no wife and son anymore, so I worked like a robot. I didn't want to think. In four months I was taken on permanently and I got up to foreman on the shift and that made better pay and I thought, maybe I'll try again. I took a much bigger apartment in a better district and furnished it. Eaton's. On time. I used my rehabilitation grant, and paid the rest on time and they gave vets ten percent off on buys anyway, and I set that place up real nice and then I went down to East End. I borrowed a friend's car and drove all night and walked into her folk's farmhouse as though nothing had happened. She took one look at me and we both started to bawl and her old man said to her mother, "Well, I guess there's not a damn thing we can do about this turn of events." That was it.

Next morning we're steaming back to Calgary and when she and Dougie see the apartment and the way I've got it laid out and food in the icebox and cakes and cookies and ice cream and steaks and you know, the works, well, that did it. We've never been separated since.

"MATTIE'S GIFT OF GAB"

The only good thing that happened to me was I brought back what they called in those days a war bride. I can't remember but I think I read that 40,000 Canadians married English girls. That seems awful high but that's what I read.

I was a nothing before a war. Just a mechanic in a garage at Barrie. Anyway, when I was nineteen and old enough I joined the Air Force to get away from all that and the eight bucks a month I was getting to learn the art of pumping gas and patching inner tubes.

I came back in '45, still a nothing, still qualified to pump gas and fix tires as my job had been with armaments and there isn't much of a call for repairing heavy-calibre machine guns in peacetime.

But I had a wife. She was a going concern. In London she'd run her parents' fish-and-chip shop in the winter and in the holiday season she ran the one that they had in Blackpool. That's where I met her. "Fish and chips, please, miss." I was stationed just an hour away and the electric tram was running, so I could get out there most evenings and it was great. Soon I was in a white hat and big apron tossing those chips or cutting them or flouring the fish, and all that.

Mattie could hardly wait to get to Canada. It was the pot at the end of the rainbow as far as she was concerned. She was going to open a fish-and-chip shop and by golly, a month after she got to Toronto in, oh, say March of '45, sure and begorrah, she had put down a payment, signed a lease, and when the season opened there she was, frying and cooking, the grease splattering, and wrapping the chips and fish in the *Star* newspaper. Clacking away a mile a minute at the crowds in Blackpool-style English and raking in the money hand over fist. I had got back in June so I dug in; getting the supplies and seeing the garbarge was cleared up and making the stand neat and tidy, those were my jobs. I was just the guy around the kitchen, so to speak. She even raised the prices ten cents on each, the fish, the chips, and the fish and chips, twenty cents, and I said she'd never get away with it. Oh yes, oh yes, she did. Nobody noticed, even. That made the profit so much more that we couldn't believe it. Our fish was no bigger and our chips no longer and thicker. It was just Mattie's gift of the gab, Blackpool style. She could sure spin off a lingo. She was a caution, let me tell you. I laugh every time I think of that summer. That was the year when the war ended and everyone was having a good time. Money to spend like it was water. A merry old time, if I do say so.

We did that the next year, too, and the next and she worked in a café as a cook on the off-season and I worked slinging beer. We had a cozy little two-room affair of an apartment on Jarvis, but in the fourth summer she was pregnant and you can't work in a chip stand on your feet from noon until midnight when you're carrying a baby. We didn't sell out. We had nothing to sell, you see. It was a concession you rented from May 24 to September 6. The city got one quarter of your profits and you kept the rest. The deal. It was a good one.

We made a lot of money those three summers. Those dimes and quarters sure add up. You bet they do. I think people who thought, oh, our stand, Mattie and Harry's Ye Olde Chip Eatery, we called it, they thought we were slaving our hearts out for peanuts. If they were peanuts, they were the biggest I ever saw. It was a good business and I know because I asked and found out that the two young fellows who bid on and got that location the year we quit didn't make many peanuts. They didn't have the angle to do it. They thought they were selling fish and chips. Hah! We were selling fish and chips and Mattie's special ketchup she worked up. Buy tomato paste wholesale and mix it with vinegar and sauce and make it real tart and it made the chips better. Then, they didn't have Mattie's gift of the gab, her little jokes, her comments, and they weren't selling the fun we both had running that little stand. That's what brought them back, too, a couple of happy people working their guts out and having fun at it.

I think that's the secret of a good business. If you can't have fun at it and laugh at yourselves once in a while, then why do it?

No, I heard a lot of moaning and groaning when I was slinging beer in the tavern, all these veterans sitting around swilling the stuff and bitching and all this. Not me. I'd tell them to cheer up and go out and get a job which gave them a few laughs. That's the secret. A few laughs.

"I DID NOT HAVE TO JOIN UP"

I joined the Air Force in November of 1940 and within one year I was a pilot, an officer. The reason I had joined up was because in our town, which I won't name even at this late date, there was no work in sight that winter and I had a wife and a one-year-old child to support.

What I'm saying is, with a wife and baby I did not have to join up, but we talked it over and, remember, we had no ideas whether it was going to be a long or a short war. In other words, I enlisted because I would be able to send enough money back to my wife for food and the rent for our small house. The rent was fifteen dollars a month. I joined the Air Force because it was a job and part of my salary would support my wife and child.

I was in England and then attached to a British squadron in Egypt in the Western Desert. I got mail infrequently from home and one letter said she had had a child. A boy. She was a very practical woman, Mary, and that's a practical name if ever there was one. She wrote that the father had agreed to pay fifteen dollars a month for the boy's support, that she was not living with him, but she did not think she could manage with two children if she went to Winnipeg to live. I'm perhaps telling this more coldbloodedly, if that is the word, than you might expect. I wrote and told her that I understood and that she could stay in the town or move, whatever she wished, but perhaps the town was best. My parents farmed near there and my mother wrote that they would help, and they did. Enormously. I don't think Mary could have survived without it. Her parents would have nothing to do with her, or with my own parents for that matter. Her letters said the townspeople were kind. I've often thought that the people on the prairies, they have a reputation for being intolerant. That is not true. They are a lot more broadminded than city people.

The war moved up to Italy and I was posted to England again, with Canadians this time, and did crew training. A landing accident finished me for flying. The pilot overshot the runway and wound up in a farmer's yard. Just the pilot and myself got out. Three months in hospital and then I was shipped home and this was late in '44.

I was discharged and went back to the town. I was the first veteran to return and the council wanted to put on a dinner for me. Maybe I was just the excuse for a dinner, but do you think I could think of a way to get out of it? No. I made excuse after excuse, but none of them washed. Never the real excuse. My wife and I would be guests of honor and there would be everyone we had known since we were kids, everyone there and everyone knowing there was a little boy at home who wasn't mine. That's what was getting to me.

I think the word was sifting around the town about what I was doing, these excuses, and an old lawyer called me into his office. He had known me since I was a button and known Mary since she was a button, and he called me in and said, "Now what about this dinner? The town wants to do it for you. You're a hero, and look at all those medals and that DFC and now, Bud, what's all this about?"

The upshot was, he told me the town loved Mary and loved the kids and what is done is done and then he said, "He was a fine man, and now he's dead."

I knew he was talking about Mary's lover and I asked how he knew he was dead and the old lawyer told me, and get this, listen, he said the man had been an officer trainee, to be a pilot, the Air Force, and he had met Mary at a dance the town put on for the boys at the station. The station was only a few miles away. Mary had come to see this lawyer when she knew she was pregnant and he had given her advice. She had told him the chap's name, from a Winnipeg family, and he had kept tabs on him somehow and about six months ago he had been killed over Germany. I broke down, cried, like a baby. I still don't know why. Relief maybe.

When I got myself together I went over to the mayor's office and told the town secretary to put on the party, make it a big one, invite everybody, and just let it ride down the track sixty miles an hour. They did. Everybody was there and everybody had one hell of a time and I was the hero of the night with all the chicken and mashed potatoes and pumpkin pie I could eat and Mary was the hero's wife and we had a fine time. Even her parents came. I guess they could not hold back any longer. Three years and not seeing their daughter and she lived only a few miles away. Anyway.

That night Mary and I talked it over in bed for the first time. She told me everything that I now knew and how it had happened and why it had happened. While she had liked him, she said he looked a lot like me, blond hair then, blue eyes still, and that he wore the same color of uniform that I did and that he told the same kind of jokes. I'm not going to tell you what she was trying to tell me, and succeeding. You'd have to be pretty stupid not to figure it out.

There's not much point in going into it any further. We spent the winter in the town while I swotted up hard on the last year of high school which I had anyway, but the Veterans' Affairs counselor had told me first-year university, Arts, was just an extension of high school, so it would make the task ahead much easier. In August we moved to Winnipeg and after two weeks we found what Mary called the perfect apartment with the perfect landlady. I should say it was the upper floor of a house with the bathroom on the main floor, but the landlady was perfect, loved Mary, loved the kiddies, and tolerated me, which was the best I could hope for.

We had tough times but in '49 I was up there with the rest in my black gown and my mortarboard hat and, well, I guess here I am. A Mr. Chips. A teacher. Out of U. of M. into a town school after my teachers' crash course. A few months. Then in September, all those expectant faces looking at me. And me? Well, I wanted to get on a good level with them, so I introduced myself and asked them to ask me questions and this one kid at the back of the room shot up his hand and asked, "What's it like to shoot down a German?"

"SHE DIDN'T LIKE ENGLAND ANYMORE"

The hard part, I think, was for the war brides. My wife was one. We were married at Cheam in April of '44 and then there was D-Day on June 6 and I was D-Day Plus Two, which meant I was in on the fighting all the way into Germany. I got off with a busted ankle and a few pieces of shrapnel just a week before the end of the war.

I had seen my wife for only four days at Christmas in '44, and then I was in hospital in Holland for three weeks after the Bren gun carrier was hit and I went up the gangplank of the *Nieuw Amsterdam* on crutches and Eleanor was to follow me later.

The upshot was they gave her three days to pack, say good-by and be at Southampton for her ship, and she arrived in Canada just a couple of weeks behind me, and the way things worked out, she had somehow leapfrogged me and got to Vancouver first.

When I arrived that was the biggest shock of my life. There she was. I just couldn't figure it out, but it was okay and we all went to Scott's Café for a back-home dinner, everything, and the place hadn't changed. The same waitresses, even. Friendly and motherly and, I might add, quite a bit more friendly and motherly than my own mother. She didn't know what to think. She actually didn't do much thinking. Her little engine ran on prejudice, and she was staunchly Scottish and Eleanor was very English.

Dad had sensed what was going on in the two days Eleanor had been at the house and he suggested, and he wasn't a very subtle man, he suggested to me while we were paying the bill that maybe we'd like to spend the night in the Georgia. I'd been thinking of something along those lines and that one was on target.

So he drove us around the corner to the Georgia, the dear old Georgia, and we spent that night there, a Saturday, June 20, and I never forget a date. We spent the next afternoon down in the park feeding the ducks and walking and talking. There's a place where you can leave the park and walk up Comox to Denman Street. Well, there in a huge old house was a sign, "For Rent," and we went in and there was this huge front room just to the left of the door. It would have been the dining room, and the pantry affair was a little kitchen, very tiny, and it had hot-and-cold, which was great, although the bathroom itself was down the hall. It was five dollars a week and we just grabbed it. Five dollars a week, still in wartime and furnished. We couldn't believe it. The rest of the tenants were nurses from St. Paul's Hospital.

We moved in next day and I still remember our first shopping trip. Dennett's Meat Market was just around the corner and Eleanor bought two spring lamb chops and I thought, oh God, she still thinks she's in England where you bought a bit of this, a bit of that in another shop.

Anyway, we settled in and life was grand that summer. Vancouver was lovely and we hooked up with my school chums and their wives and girlfriends. Walking in the park. Picnics, renting the old lapstrake dinghies with the one-lung Briggs and Stratton gas engines and doing some fishing and cooking the Rock cod on the little stove.

About a month after we settled in on this honeymoon I met a very kind man who was moving to Toronto and he kindly said he had a three-ton truck for sale and he kindly said I could buy it for $1,800, and as that was nearly all our savings and everything, it cleaned us out—but I was going to start a huge trucking line. One, I did not know that the truck had been used for four years hauling gravel on airport construction and I did not know that it was ready to lie down and die at any moment. I did not know that every veteran who had wheeled a 600 CWT around during the war was doing the same thing, buying a truck and starting the biggest trucking company in Canada.

The luck of the draw—and I mean on the first job the contractor actually drew lots—my name came up and I know it sounds unbelievable now but I think the truck and driver got $2.10 an hour. Something ridiculous. Before I could go broke working at an honest living, the truck expired and I sold it to a mechanic for $800. There was nothing else I could do. I was in the wrong business, and so there went about four years of re-establishment credits just like that.

Don't think I was the only one taken. There was a big horde of shysters out there just waiting for the veterans to come home and every damned one of them had a scheme. It was called transferring the money in the veterans' pockets into their own. They were everywhere, and I suspect

that every one had been a Zombie or a draft dodger or had shot himself
in the toe and got out with an honorable discharge.

But Eleanor and I survived. I still had the $800 left and I got a job
in Flavelle's mill, hard work but the pay was good, and we moved out
of the Comox address and out to Port Moody. A house. The rent was
thirty dollars a month and the sawdust heating was one real, proper,
number-one bastard of a furnace, but we were doing fine.

I mean, I thought we were doing fine. Then one day Eleanor announced
she was going back to England. Why, for God's sakes? Aren't you happy
here? I'd heard of this kind of thing, but I didn't think it could happen
here, right in my own house. No, she wanted to go home and she didn't
know how long she'd be and her father had sent her money, and that
sure as hell was something I hadn't known about. Little kittens walking
around on little soft paws, that's what was going on. I blew up, but anyway
she went, and I was pretty bitter and did a lot of drinking in the Port
Moody Arms and I thought, well, maybe it's all for the best.

Then comes the letter. Oh, she'd been writing all right, but this was
the letter. She didn't like England anymore. She missed Canada. She
missed her wee house. She missed me. It appeared I came third, after
Canada and house. But I wrote come back, come back, and before the
letter could have got as far as Montreal the phone rang one night and
it was her, Eleanor, phoning from Montreal. She'd hopped on a ship
maybe just a few days after mailing the letter and now she was on her
way home.

She hadn't liked England. It was becoming full of rotten people. I mean
it. That's what she said. There was still rationing and it was like wartime. All smoky and nothing to buy in the shops and besides, she missed
me.

So that was it. That's about all, the one thing of importance that happened to me after I came back. My wife hated Canada, went to England,
and hated it more than Canada and she came back and we raised a family
and everything has been hunky-dory ever since. Peaches and cream, every
day.

"MY LITTLE ENGLISH GIRL"

I'm not sure if the events of so long ago are really the true
memories of today. Don't we tend to gild the lily, flossy things up, make
everything better or worse than it was, depending on how everything
turned out for us in later years?

In my case there seems to have been little friction. I had been a teacher and after the basic and advanced training in British Columbia I was sent to England and wound up in intelligence. It was a drudge job and even the most flamboyant imagination could never convince anyone, let alone myself, that I was contributing to the war effort in any way.

I came home and my common sense told me I would be a much more successful teacher if I went to university and got a degree, and as that was open to us, I took it. My wife came over from Manchester in December of '45, so we had a nice Christmas together, giving her a chance to see how Canadians celebrated it.

Jean was what they called a war bride and the first year was hard on her as we lived in two rooms upstairs in a house. It was hard, yes, but many of the married vets at U.B.C. were having it hard. Some were living in places much worse than we were. At least we had access to a bathroom and a dear sweet little old gal for a landlady.

I studied and Jean kept the two rooms immaculate and prepared good-to-excellent meals on the little thingamabob we called a stove, two burners and a tiny oven, big enough to take a roasted pigeon, I would say.

Jean should be telling you this. Here she was, a girl of nineteen just out from Manchester, coming out to Vancouver, a totally different environment. She was one bewildered little lass for a while. I suppose in a way it was almost like she was being reborn again, amid all these strange and loud-talking Canadians. Four of us renting a boat and going fishing for a day and no fish peddler coming to the door at eight in the morning singing out his bargains. The ceremony of the mickey. Do you know, we'd have another couple over to our tiny rooms on a Saturday and there would be a mickey. Twelve ounces of rye. Four of us. Three ounces each. We'd have dinner and play bridge and have a bed-time snack and the four of us would manage to consume that whole twelve ounces. All by ourselves! Fun. Laughter. God, what a lark!

Oh, I forgot. Our little old landlady would go out to her picture show every Saturday night. That's why our place was so popular and why the other couples always brought the mickey of rye. We had a bathroom! It was hers but we shared it and when she left, the minute the door shut, Jean was down there filling up her bathtub full, hot and full, and first the wife would get in and paddle around and soap and bubble-bath it up and then out would go that water and then her husband would nip down and flounder around like a whale. The old lady never caught on. Well, maybe she did but I did enough repairs around the house that we more than repaid her for her water. But you see, people would come over for dinner, bringing their share, naturally, and the mickey, and they'd get a loverly, loverly free hot bath. It was the only real one they probably had. Most of the places they rented, I suppose, had showers or nothing at all. A spit bath by the kitchen sink, you know.

Oh, university was a lively place. Chock full of veterans, of course, everywhere you looked. The professors and lecturers were harassed and today I'm not sure we got an education of a very high calibre—not under those conditions. But not surprisingly, an astonishing number of the veterans who graduated, they reached places of high rank. Well, you know, we got our degrees and went off into the world. I can't say my degree did me good, but it gave me a breather, a gap between war and making a living again.

I was thirty when I graduated and I think that if Jean was alive today she would agree that those fours years at U.B.C. were the great adventure of our lives together. We were young and in love and eager to reach out at life and hold it and what seemed like adversity at any one time could be made into a bit of a joke with a hug and a kiss and the thought that we were together. My little English girl and me.

"I FELL IN LOVE WITH MY WIFE"

When I got out my wife met me at the railway station and she had the democrat and the old nag and there didn't seem much to say to each other.

It had been nearly four years and I guess the reason I had joined the Army was we weren't getting along too well and the whole thing had just sort of carried over, you know, and our letters hadn't been all that too frequent, just about how things were going around the farm and the kids. My letters, well, I guess I was never one to put it all down and there was the censor to think about, and besides, what I had been doing over there in England and the Continent, I figure she could read in the Edmonton *Journal.*

I asked about the kids and how they were doing and Helen said they were doing fine, both at school and four years older, and that the farm was still there. I wished I could have hitched a ride, and I was thinking mean thoughts about her not being too bright and why didn't she get our neighbor Joe or someone close by or in town to take her in one of their cars. But no, the upshot was, it was a long ride with the buggy and I guess you could say things got off to a bad start there and then.

I remember, though, it was sure a nice day. The countryside was nice and even though all the crops weren't in, you could see they'd had a good year. But it wasn't a good start for us. She was jumpy and so was I.

At the Fort [Assinaboine] we stopped at the store and we filled up the back of the democrat with food and groceries and I bought candy and stuff for the kids, and even in that store in that little town it sure had a lot of the good eating things of life I hadn't seen for a long time. I remember saying that Canadians at home didn't seem to have had such a hard time of it, and she looked at me and said something like, "You'll never know." At the town bootlegger I bought a pint of his white lightning.

I talked to a few people in the store who knew me, but I didn't get any rousing welcome. I didn't expect it but I didn't expect one guy to say he hadn't seen me around for a few years and where had I been. I said where the hell did he think I'd been, and was I wearing this uniform just for the hell of it? He laughed then and I said forget it.

Driving to Holmes Crossing, I asked Helen about the other guys and she said she thought most of them were back, and that Amos Stevens and a few others had been killed. I thought if all those guys had got back earlier, then there wasn't going to be many jobs around, and when I told Helen this she said we wouldn't be around too much longer anyway, so why bother. This was the first she had said anything about plans, so I kept my mouth shut and that was that for a while.

We got more friendly-like as the miles went by and I made a few of the little jokes we had had before and that loosened her up and she told me Billy and Marianne didn't have to walk the three miles to school in winter because a neighbor picked them up when he drove his kids there, and I thought that was fine. She said she had boarded the school teacher for two years and when I asked why, she let me have it. She said she and the kids had had such a tough time of it that neighbors close to the school had felt so sorry for her and the kids that they told the teacher they couldn't take her, and so Helen got that thirty bucks a month. I said good, then the teacher would be company for her, and she said, "Yeah, you could say that." Something along those lines.

When we got to the place, nothing had changed. I mean, I didn't expect it to have changed. The house looked the same. It needed paint, but then again, when I was working the place as a farmer there hadn't been any money for paint either, so why now? The barn looked in good shape and I could see part of the eighteen acres I had cleared, a square foot at a time—four or five acres a year and that was working hard. You have no idea how hard that was.

The house was neat and she had the teacher again and what with my pay that I sent home, and what she got from renting out the land, a third of the crop if the guy was honest with her, and selling some butter in town, trading it for food and such, I guess she got by. Nothing fancy. Not at all. But she got by.

All in all, the place looked in good shape and she'd built up the cattle and thank God she'd taken the advice I'd given in a lot of letters, and that was to get advice from one of the old-time farmers over near Barr-head who had cattle and they'd tell her what to keep and what to sell and forget about a milking herd. She'd done that and there was a bunch of sixteen good-looking steers and older cows and that looked like a good start, what with the three hogs and the chickens, and the bush had always been full of berry bushes and there was plenty of fish still there in the Athabaska River. The good old Athabaska. I'd thought of drifting down her a hundred times while I'd been away.

The kids wouldn't be home for an hour or so and Helen made two cups of coffee and she sat me down at the table and this is what she told me. We were selling. She had got hold of a real estate man in Barr-head and he was driving out in two or three days. We would take the money and go to the Okanagan Valley. She was tired of cold and snow. I told her I had hitchhiked and rode the rails through there in the winter of '33 and it was cold and there was snow there, too. She said that didn't matter. She wanted a place where she could go out in her garden, reach up and pick a few peaches and have a peach pie hot out of the oven when her man came home from work. Something like that. She talked on and I don't think I heard a word that woman said. But I was think-ing along these lines: six hundred for my getting-out pay and a thousand for the quarter section, and the cattle might bring six hundred and an auction might bring in two-fifty and, well, I'm just making these figures up for you now, but then I figured it might come out to seventeen or eighteen hundred bucks and I was pretty close to it.

I guess I just came in on the tail end of her talk to me and there she was handing over a bankbook to me and it was open at a page and there was the last entry, $360.75. I remember those numbers today as clearly as if it was then. She told me how she'd saved by doing sewing and she'd had the butter money when there was not any for flour and sugar, and the teacher brought in quite a bit and, well, goddamn it to hell, there she was living alone with those two kids growing up, out on that miserable

stick farm at the end of the road and working like a man around those
cattle and sewing at night for some storekeeper's fat wife in the Fort and
all these things. And I was out there in the war having a pretty good
time of it as long as some bugger who was not quite as scared as I was
wasn't pulling a lanyard on an artillery gun and trying to blow the hell
out of me. I thought then and there, here's a woman who's done all
this for me and my kids and our future, and I'll tell you this and you're
the first man I've ever told this to. At that moment I fell in love with
my wife. I hadn't been in love with her before and I'm not all that sure
she was in love with me. After all, Billy hadn't exactly come along a
nice thirteen months after we got married. He came along five months
after. But enough of that. I'm telling you, when all this business of how
she got through the war kind of exploded in my head I looked at her
and smiled and she said, "Quick, we can have some time for ourselves
before they get home," meaning the teacher and the kids, and we scooted
like bunny rabbits up the stairs and into bed, and wow! My, oh my! A
hundred times better than the first time when we were just dumb kids
of nineteen and seventeen. Ten times better than ever before. We were
in love.

When they came home we were sitting at the kitchen table giggling
like a couple of teen-agers and were taking sips out of our glasses of that
white lightning and doing some figuring and I didn't have to put on
an act to say a happy hello to my kids. They were my kids and they
looked wonderful. I gave them candy and some souvenirs I'd lugged all
the way home from Germany, little dolls and such, and a German Army pistol with the mechanism broken so it wouldn't fire. That was for
Billy.

That's really about all I remember about coming home, you know.
Nothing big about it. A guy who didn't know what he was coming home
to and whambo-zambo, it all fitted into place.

If this is the kind of story you're looking for, then you've got it on
a platter, for free.

"A LITTLE KID SISTER NAMED MEG"

It's a short story.

I didn't do much thinking about what I was going to do when I got
back to dear old Canada. When you're an artillery spotter, up front of
everybody and with nobody to cuddle but your buddy and he's just as

shit-scared as you are and worrying if your wire is going to snap or your field telephone is going to wonk out, you're not thinking too much about anything but hoping you stay alive.

Anyway, it's over and even though I've got the points, there's a lot of cleaning up to do. If we had of been in Germany I would have bitched like hell because I wasn't going to help them bastards clean up the mess, but I was in Holland and it's a nice country with nice people, so I didn't mind staying behind.

Then I'm home. October 17. Remember it like my own birthday, June 14. I'm not one of these guys who can put things down on paper but it was one of those Manitoba days in autumn. There is nothing like it. I guess it's the air. I can't describe it but you know what I mean. I got some new clothes and stuff and was learning table manners again and not saying "Pass the fucking butter" when I was having dinner with the folks, and things like that.

One Sunday my sister Shirley comes over for dinner with her husband and kid and we're talking, you know, back and forth, and I'm asking what happened to So-and-So and she'd tell me. Like they say, there was bad news and good news.

My sister asks, "Have you looked up Stewie Williams yet?" I thought, Christ, one of my good friends at high school and I'd forgotten all about good old Stewie. Shirley says he's back and they still live on the same street in the same old house and he's just kicking around like me and so why don't I just drop over after dinner? Only three streets away, don't you remember? Sure I remembered.

After dinner I have a drink and a smoke with my dad and Shirley's husband and she pops her head in the room and asks wasn't I to go over and see Stewie? They don't have a phone, but we don't either, so that makes things kind of even, wouldn't you say?

I go over. It is a November night. Clear, kind of cold. I remember that. The house is still there. Well, there's me, up on the verandah and I knock and the door opens and this girl is there. I can't see her too well because naturally the hall light is behind her, but I figured right then and there that she was something pretty special. I figured Shirley had forgot to tell me that old Stewie had got himself hitched up. Anyway, I ask for him and she says he's gone down to the corner to get a pack of smokes and I said who I was, an old buddy of Stewie's, and she said, oh yes, Ron, I've heard him talk of you, and won't you come in and wait? He'll be glad to see you, and so on and so forth, and so there we are sitting in the little living room off the hall and I'm thinking, I'm twenty-four and Stewie's twenty-four and this girl can't be more than eighteen, nineteen at the very most, and I thought, old Stewie's picking 'em pretty young, ain't he?

She sure was pretty. She was beautiful and she was dressed like a million bucks and we're talking, back and forth, this and that, you know, and I'm sizing her up and I look, kind of sneakily, at her left hand and she hasn't got a ring on the ring finger, so she isn't married.

She had told me her name when we was at the door, her name was Meg, just Meg, and I thought, Meg, Meg, Meg? Hmmmmmmmm? I remembered Stewie had a little kid sister named Margaret but there was no Meg around, no Meg hiding behind the woodpile.

Finally I came out with it. I asked who she was.

She smiled that beautiful smile and said, "Why, I'm Stewie's sister. Meg. You'd remember me as Margaret Ann. I didn't like those names, so I changed it to Meg. Do you like that better?" Then she laughed and said, "You didn't like me at all when I was a kid."

Well, Jesus Christ our Saviour! As I'm sitting here now, I'm telling you I almost fell through the floor. Of course. Of course. But I had been gone four years and she had been a little kid of fourteen. What guy of twenty looks at a little kid of fourteen?

Well, I think I said something like Jesus Christ! Jesus Christ!

And there she was, sitting on that sofa with her blonde hair and her frilly white blouse and that little skirt and just grinning at me and I'm babbling something like, My God, you were just a little kid with scabs on your knees from falling down when you were roller-skating, and wanting to come out on hikes with Stewie and me, and getting us cold water when we were playing ball over on the diamond, and always getting in the way. That kind of thing.

We went on talking and it was beginning to surprise me just how much I had remembered about her, although I had never thought about her all those four years. And no, she wasn't eighteen. She told me she was nineteen. She worked in an insurance office and was learning to water-ski, something I'd never heard of. Everybody does it now, but that was back in 1945. She loved sports and so did I, and movies and so did I, and the outdoors and animals and cooking and so did I. Do you like? Yes. Do you hate? Yes.

This went on and on and when I looked at my watch it was 9:30 and I asked where was Stewie and his mom and dad. That was pretty late to be out on a Sunday night.

I remember her exact words. She said, "They've gone over to Grandmother's for dinner. They'll be back at ten."

Just like that. I fell into the trap.

I asked what about her. Why didn't she go, too? A family Sunday dinner.

She smiled, a big smile, a huge one, and she giggled and said, "Oh, I didn't go. I stayed home waiting for you, Ronnie."

I'm telling you, that tore it. A plot. A trap. I jumped up and she met me halfway and I hugged her and I told her. That Shirley and she, Meg, she must have been in cahoots, so that she'd be alone and when I knocked on the door she'd invite me in.

I hadn't been kissing many girls in my life, and especially in the past four years, but I gave her one she'd remember for a long time, and when her family came home at ten, right on the button, there we were, sitting on the sofa. Know what we were doing? Holding hands and grinning.

So, that's it. That's the story. I gave her the engagement ring on Christmas Eve and we got married on March 2 and that was it. I guess you'd say we lived happily ever after. There was never any doubt. I wanted a girl and a boy. Meg wanted a girl and a boy. We got a boy and a girl. We're happy. We love each other. We're sitting pretty. Who should have it so good?

4 BROKEN HEARTS, BROKEN DREAMS

4 BROKEN HEARTS, BROKEN DREAMS

They met at a dance where the prettiest girls in town were asked to be hostesses. He was a dashing Air Force fellow with new sergeant's stripes and she was vivacious and, well, she guessed she was patriotic and anyway, wasn't it wartime? And so they married, and a month later he was gone, overseas.

There were thousands of those quickie marriages, which could not survive the years of separation or the reality of being man and wife in earnest. They split. They didn't hate each other. They just didn't know each other. Or, more likely, there was someone else . . .

Some men never came back to the brides they married in such a hurry. Other couples stayed together—"for the sake of the kids," as they told each other and themselves. And years later, when the nest was empty, there was nothing to keep them together anymore.

I once worked with a fellow who had been sent to jail for beating up his wife when he returned and found she had two children he had not fathered. No one thought of him as a criminal. It had just been one of those wartime things.

Remember the "Dear John" letters? The girl back home wrote that she was going to marry a man with a solid job in an insurance company and, "I'm sorry, Johnny, but it will work out best for both of us." He probably said, "Oh, to hell with it," and went on with the job of winning the war. Sure it hurt, but in the long run, she was right: it did work out for the best.

"THE UNHOLY BONDS OF MATRIMONY"

I have no way of knowing how many of those wartime marriages just went down the tubes when the troops got back, but if my own observations mean anything, I think a lot did.

Take just two of my buddies. Johnny and Red. They had what was then called wartime marriages. They both met girls when they were in uniform, and in those days you pretty well knew when you were going to be shipped overseas. Both Johnny and Red married on their embarkation furloughs. The way things had been in the Depression, you sometimes waited two or three years before you got married to your girl. Then, all of a sudden, the whole thing had to be done in a hurry and Johnny and Red, why they hardly knew the girls. It was a kind of madness, this marrying and pledging to be true to each other and in a way I'm sure the girls thought it very romantic stuff.

So, we're away three years and because we're all in the service corps we were pretty much in the same area, as most Canadians were in England, and we kept in touch. Leave together in London when we could arrange it. Letters. Johnny and Red were together and I was with another outfit. But we managed.

I knew their marriages were rocky. Just by what they said. Acted. Horsed around in London. That kind of thing. Once Red said to me, "Well, if she's doing it, then so can I."

Let's put it another way. They were married and their wives were getting their allowances but these two guys weren't in love. Whatever it was when they got married, I wouldn't call it love. I suppose they liked the idea of being in love and being married, but what they were wasn't that.

When I got back in February of '46 both Johnny and Red were back, and had been for some time. I think being married gave you quite a few more points. I had nothing to do and a few days after I get home I phone Red's home to ask his mother where he lived and Red answers the phone. We talk, and he says he really can't talk, so let's meet that night at the beer parlor by the CN station. I go in there and Red's sitting there and after the usual bit of business, talking about getting home, he just out and says that he and his wife are getting a divorce.

I was dumb enough to ask why and he said nothing's why. It was just that they didn't have one damn thing to say to each other and they didn't have anything to say in their letters. He said he wrote his out of duty. I guess she did, too. I knew her slightly, she was a nice kid.

From a good family, I mean. But they'd done this marriage thing when they were too young and they didn't know too much about each other and, as Red said, every soldier wants a girl to write home to. Anyway, he told me they were going to get a divorce because she had a boyfriend and wanted to get married. I guess Red cared a little about her and he wanted to help her.

I don't know how divorce worked in those days, but it was rough. I know that adultery was the main thing. Of course, it was faked. All evidence was faked and that's where I came in, although I didn't know it that night. That came later. I think seven years in the insane asylum could get a divorce for the other person. That was it, I think. It sure looked like the government didn't want people to get divorced, even if they were very unhappy and one of them was in love with someone else. You just could not go to a lawyer like you can now and say, "I want a divorce," and the lawyer asks why and you say, "Because my wife won't cook my bacon and eggs the way I like 'em." It was different then. Marriage was fine, but divorce was a disgrace. When I was divorced in '67, my mother said it was the first in our family. She thought it would bring disgrace on all of us and, hell, she didn't even go to church. That was the way it was.

So, as I see it, there was an awful lot of unhappy couples after the war and things were just too complicated to do it or too expensive or the wife had a little loaf of bread in the oven or they already had one kid and they would decide to keep together through thick and thin. Look, I don't *think* there were a lot. I *know* there were a lot. I know a lot of my friends when I joined the Legion, why do you think they were sitting there night after night letting the stew get cold and dry? Because they just didn't want to go home and too proud, too dumb, too broke, to say to her, "Hey, we've tried it and it isn't working and it won't so let's pack it up, eh?" Maybe these guys did. Maybe it was the woman who said no, we'll stay together. That to me is some kind of hell that God did not invent and it was the guys who made the laws who were responsible. I don't think God would take responsibility for that kind of lousy business. He didn't like sinners but these people were honest-to-God nice and decent people caught in the unholy bonds of matrimony, and boy were they tight.

Then about a week later Red phones me at my mother's house and he says, hey, let's have a bit of a party, and he says Johnny is coming. Great! Good old Johnny. Ain't seen him in a coon's age. Bring him on.

It's a Saturday afternoon we meet about a week later. We shoot the bull around, the good old days, and what we're going to do once we get settled and that kind of thing, and then we get around to talking about life, love, and how tough it is. I'm getting a little tanked but I still remember and at the dinner-time closing call we pile into a taxi and scoot down to Chinatown to load up. Johnny says he's paying.

Now here is the beautiful part of it. They've got together on the phone. They say, and I'd say it was Red, he said, look, our friend Ken is free, white and twenty-three and doesn't give a damn, so let's hook him in to being our corespondents. It must have something to have been along those lines. For your young readers I'll explain that a corespondent was the person the private detective found when he opened the door of the hotel room and found him in the room with the wife or husband of the person who was getting the divorce. In other words it was a setup.

I sat there quite stunned when they told me this plan, or maybe I was too busy eating my pork chow mein and fried rice, but I said sure. Why not? I had nothing to lose and if it would help my old buddies out, I'd do it. The only thing I wouldn't do was to testify in court, but I didn't say that then.

To this day I don't know if I was breaking the law, but if I was, so were Red and Jill, his wife. The lawyer didn't mention that little point when the three of us met with the lawyer and the private detective. He looked like a guy who had paid the city ten bucks and they'd given him a licence to play private detective.

Two nights later, Jill and I register as man and wife at a hotel and we've got no luggage. The lawyer said no luggage. She takes off her blouse and I take off my shirt and she sits on the bed and I sit on a chair and in twenty minutes there's a knock. I open the door and there's the detective and a Chinese bellboy and they walk in and the detective asks me my name and Jill her name and he writes them down and that is it. I mean, that is all. We dress and go into the beer parlor and have a beer or two and she gets on the bus and goes home.

I did the same thing for Johnny a week later. Exactly the same thing.

And they both got their divorces and the girls were happy and they were free after a year's waiting period. I thought that was unfair. They got their names in the paper, though. I don't know why but the papers used to publish divorces. In fine type. I saw mine, too. Oh yes, the bad guy was named, too. I didn't give a hoot. Everybody knew it was all a big sham anyway. The government knew it was and so did the judges and, of course, the only ones who made the money were the lawyers, who made the big bucks, and the men and women who acted as professional corespondents.

Now, what I'm getting around to is this. How many sailors, airmen, and Army fellows or their wives went through that little bit of razzle-dazzle? I'm going to make a bet and say it was one hell of a lot more than you'd suspect. I know that soon after the war divorces went zoom, sky-high. Some of those guys who got divorced after the war, they just didn't talk about it. It was just that way. Now, if you asked them if they were divorced they'd have to think and say, "Oh, yes, sure, back in '46. I'd all but forgotten." Something like that. It was all so long ago.

"NO GOOD FROM THE START"

I remember, I was sitting in a small restaurant in Montreal having about the fifth meal of the day. We'd got off the ship that morning and they'd given us the day off to just walk around in and stomp down hard on that beloved Canadian ground again and I was eating so much because the grub on the ship had been so bad. Seven bad days of storm and that long with grub you could not eat. I mean it. If the couple of thousand guys hadn't been coming home they would have mutinied. Thrown the cooks overboard in mid-Atlantic.

I'm eating this big meal of good Canadian meat and potatoes and vegetables and there is this couple at the table next to me and suddenly I hear him say, "When we're finished here I'm gonna walk out that door and I don't want to ever hear from you or see you again," and she said, "Same here. When you walk out that door it will be a breath of bad air that has gone and, as far as I'm concerned, this whole thing was just no good from the start."

Not those exact words, mind you, but I remember that sergeant getting up and walking over to the cashier and paying and I watched and he walked out of that café without even looking back. I'm not sure why I should remember that so well, but I did, and I remember asking myself, is this the way it is with a lot of them? You understand? The sergeant coming back. Maybe on the same ship as me, for all I know. Meeting his wife and all the thinking they each had done, how bad their marriage was, you know, and him taking her to supper and telling her, let's get the damned thing over with now, good and forever.

I wonder if he was surprised when she agreed like that, right off the bat?

That would have been the time to ask her just what had happened. I guess she probably had a real story to tell. But you just didn't do things like that, but I remember looking at her when she was getting ready to go. I don't know if you can really tell what a person is thinking just by the look on the face, but I can tell you this. She looked like a woman who had a real load off her mind.

You know, maybe that was the way to do it. Get it over with fast.

I'm quite sure it was one of those wartime marriages. They get married in an all-fired hurry and then a few days together and then he's gone for three, four years and they both knew, almost from the start, I guess, that there was nothing there for either of them.

This story has nothing to do with *me* coming home, but I've often wondered how many other times when the guys came home that the same kind of thing happened.

"DEAR JOHN"

The government set up the position of rehabilitation officer in several cities even before the war had ended in Europe, and by the end of May I was geared up to handle anything that came my way. I had not been overseas, but as a clergyman I certainly could understand the problems that would come across my desk. I expected the worst. I didn't get all that many because many of these men were, I believe, too ingrown with themselves after all those years to come and spill their problems to a chaplain.

Many of the cases I did get, however, mostly referrals, were what are known as Dear John letters. The soldier, airman, sailor receives a letter from his sweetheart, the girl he plans to marry, the girl to whom he is engaged. Oh, those letters, some kept for months, even two or three years. The letters said, "I'm sorry, John, but I have thought it over a great deal and I don't think we should get married." What she meant, naturally, was that she was marrying another man. Sometimes, you know, the other man turned out to be the soldier's brother or cousin or the best friend who chose not to go to war but into war production.

It was difficult, yes, but these were grown men. They may have been only twenty-one, some of them, but after what they had been through, yes, I'd say even the twenty-one-year-olds were grown men. They could take it, but I was rather a court of last resort.

Mind you, they weren't in shock. They had had plenty of time to think it over and accept it. I'm not too sure that some weren't even relieved. That is wrong; they were relieved but there still is something in every one of us that says, it might have been, or it could still be, or, at the other end of the scale, I have been harmed, someone I trusted has betrayed me, and I want revenge. "Revenge" is too strong. I want justice.

I had a set speech, like the old clergyman I am, but I could vary it. I would say, "It is over, it is done with, she is married or she is going to be married and you have that bright horizon out there which is your future. Walk out of this office and walk toward that horizon. On the way you will meet someone who will be all that you ever wanted. She will be looking for you and though you do not know it right now, she is the one you have been looking for, too."

If that sounds trite, too pat, forgive me, but it worked surprisingly well. And why did it work? Because every one of those men who had come to me or had been referred to me, that is what they wanted to hear. I was a captain. I was a chaplain. All their lives they had gone to church when they were young. Their families were religious and ministers were respected. That's the way the world was in those days. There I was, the symbol of the church, all that was wise and good and bountiful. I know this sounds ridiculous in 1985 but we are talking about 1945.

They wanted someone to say it. They would nod their heads. Yes, they were thinking, there is only the future. It is for the best.

I'd give them my card and shake their hand and walk them out to the door and I'll tell you this, I did get letters from many of those fellows. A few would just write "Thanks, padre" or something like that. Others wrote from long distances and distances of time, perhaps two years later, on how they had done, what they were doing, and surprising to no one, especially me, they did meet that girl as they walked toward that horizon. That's the way it was in those days.

"THE WORST SAD STORY OF THE LOT"

There's one thing I'll always remember. Like it might have made a movie some time, or somebody could write a story about it. Even after forty years you remember something like this.

There was this business of the veterans coming back from Hong Kong where they'd been prisoners of the Japs. Remember that? Okay. Remember that one of the battalions or regiments was the Winnipeg Grenadiers? So all the boys in that were from Winnipeg and around here.

So this is the summer of '46 and it's a nice morning and the guys who survived, they're coming back and the arrival is at the CNR station, Union Station. I'm outside in my cab with a lot of others and there's one hell of a lot of confusion. Then this soldier comes out and he makes a beeline for my cab and jumps into the back with his bag and right off I can see he's pretty upset. You know.

I ask him where and he says Middlechurch and that's quite a way north of town, out where the big dairy is—a long way in those days. We start out and I'm a pretty talky guy, but somehow I can see this guy will start the conversation if there's one to be started. He does, soon. Saying his wife wasn't there to meet him and I think, oh-oh, this guy's been in a Jap prison camp all those years and, my God, now he's home and she's not there at the station. Everybody knew they were coming. All the papers and the radio had it. You know, this is a pretty big day and the mayor is there. A band. Flags outside the station. I think something is wrong. I'm not going to say I had been overseas for three years and this and that and maybe she didn't want to face him after all those years. The crowd. That kind of thing. I still thought it was kind of funny, though.

That's all he says about that and then he's asking what it is like in Winnipeg. You know, jobs. The people. What was in the papers about the Grenadiers. Coming home, that is. I tell him and soon we're out in the country and he says something like, "Is it this far out?" I know then he doesn't know the city.

We get there and there's a little store and he gets out and goes in, comes back, and then he gives me directions. It's just a little white house. I remember that. I let him off and he pays me and I swing away and head back and when I get into town I stop at a little café for a sandwich. When that's done I go over to the Green Briar Inn and I have a beer and then I phone the office, asking if there is a fare out this way. There is. I guess you can see what's coming. I'm to go out to Middlechurch. The address is a little white house by the elevator. Well, I know that house. So back I go.

This same soldier is waiting for me on the road. He's just standing there and he gets in and this time he gets in the front seat. He does not say a word. The poor guy, he just points back toward the city and I look at him and he's crying. He's just a young fellow. Oh, I'd say twenty-two, twenty-three, around there.

We're sailing along and he's not saying a thing, just looking straight ahead, and then he asks me if I can get him a bottle. I say sure, what does he want? He says a mickey, a mickey of rye will do. It is still hard stuff to get and I've got four wrapped in a rug in the trunk of the cab, and when we get down by the station I pull around and dig one out and, big-hearted me, I only charge him six bucks. Most of us charged eight, but I feel sorry for this kid. Then he asks for a hotel where he can go and we're coming up to the McLaren right there on Main Street, and by this time it is getting through to me that this is a kid who is in some very sad trouble and I know what it is. At least I think I know. Holy smokes, a guy would have to be a dummy not to figure it out.

But I still feel upset about it. In this business, or then when I was in it, you haul a lot of people around all the time and you hear a lot of sad stories and sob stories and I think, it looks like this kid has got the worst sad story of the lot and he's not even talking about it.

There's nothing you can do. You'd like to do something. At least say something. Just maybe give him a punch in the shoulder and say, "Hey, buddy, it might not look so good now, but it can't be all that bad." Something along those lines.

No, I couldn't even do that, and so I just swung up in front and let him off and he paid me and thanked me. He just lugged his duffel bag into the hotel and that was it.

You know, and here's the other part of it. I felt, oh, I should have told him my number, so if he phoned for a car he could have got me and I might of helped him. I didn't, though. But for the next couple of weeks when I was cruising around or on a fare I'd be looking at the street seeing if he was still around, but I never saw him again.

Now, as I said, I hauled a lot of people around in those days, a lot of them, and heard a lot of stories. Cabbies sometimes are like priests, I guess. But of all the fares I had, a lot, that's the only one I remember. I remember that kid very, very well.

THE SECRET ENGAGEMENT

I was in the motor pool at Petawawa. There were a few of us, CWAC drivers, and while it wasn't exciting around there, just a training camp, it was exciting for me driving officers all over Ontario, to Ottawa and Toronto and all over. And then it came to an end. The war was over and the men were coming back and they didn't want us.

I was discharged at Mewata Stadium and went home to Red Deer to wait for my Johnny to come back from Europe. This was in August of 1945, I'd say. I'd been secretly engaged to Johnny Turnbull—that's not his real last name but it is like it—and he'd always written me that our engagement must be kept secret. Very secret. Not my mother, not my best friend. Just us. All his letters had been very strong on this, so nobody knew.

One day Mother and I are walking downtown and who should we meet but Mrs. Turnbull, the mother whose name is also fictitious. Our parents are old friends and she greets me with kisses and then she turns to the girl beside her and says to me, "And you must meet Johnny's wife. She just got over from Britain a week ago and Johnny's due back next month." Well, I know what my face must have been like, but I hope it wasn't. I was stunned.

A couple of days later I phone his wife and ask her out for lunch. We'll go for a drive and I'll show her the city and then we'll have lunch at the hotel. That was fine, she said she'd love to. She was a really nice girl and we became very good friends.

Anyway, I found out from her about Johnny. She was just dying to talk. Everybody had to know what a gallant soldier he was. What a wonderful beau he had been. How kind and generous he was. How happy they had been. And how long had they been married? Two years. And in those two years he had been sending me these wonderful love letters and telling me "now you mustn't tell a soul. Not a soul." "Just you and me." The rat.

In the long run I married and have been happy the rest of my life.

"I SMELLED A RAT"

I guess the thing I remember about coming home was fairly typical for fellows in my situation. Dear John letters. You know, "Dear John, I hope you won't take this too badly, but I've met a wonderful man and I'm not sure how it happened, but we have fallen in love and I'm going to get married to him. I hope we can still be friends and I hope when you get back home you find a wonderful girl who will make you very happy," et cetera, et cetera.

The funny thing is, you know, I didn't get any Dear John letter. The V-Mail letters just kept coming, but they weren't like they had been. They were friendly letters. I smelled a rat right there. Before she had been writing love letters, two or more a week and numbering them so I could read them in the proper order. I think I know when it all changed between us. You see, we had been sweethearts at high school and I worked for a year after school and we went together still and then I joined up in early '44. After learning drill until it was coming out of my ears and firing ten shots on the rifle range and other nonsense, I was on a troop train for Nova Scotia. Then it was England for a couple of weeks, about three, and then into a battalion and that was where the real learning of a soldier began.

Anyway, this night we're in a little village, in a cellar of the biggest house, and the guns booming away behind us and we've got a big sheet of tin sitting on top of a stack of bricks in each corner and we've got a big fire underneath and we're having a great time cooking goodies. The lieutenant had sent out a party and they kicked into a store and came back with arm-loads of goodies, wonderful German stuff. The storekeeper had gone and hidden this stuff in his basement, but there's no scavenger like a Canadian soldier and they found it and we were eating it.

Then the sergeant opens the mail sack and the stuff starts to go around and there were three letters for me, from my mother, my sister, and Frances, and naturally I read her letter first. She described a wonderful party she'd been at, and I don't know if she realized she was doing it but maybe she did, but there was a couple of references to a guy she'd met. Okay, she met a guy, so what? When I looked back at it later, that was the first of the friendly letters.

I got hit the next morning, the left leg and in the belly, and before I knew it I was back in England and three months later, hospital and convalescence. Okay, but the war was winding down and who needs a guy who had taken one in the belly? I was lucky to be alive. Then it was a ship back, Quebec City, a night on the town and lights everywhere and Molson's beer and I'm on a train back to the Peg.

I should mention that when my mail caught up to me in hospital there were several letters from her, but they were getting friendlier and friendlier. You'd think she was writing to her brother.

After the worst train ride I'd ever had in my life I was back in Fort Osborne Barracks phoning my mother, telling her I'd be out next day, and that afternoon there I am getting out of a taxi in front of the old house and my mother is at the door, crying, of course.

The old man didn't think he should take the day off at the elevator firm he worked with and the kid brother was at school, so it was just her and me and we had a long, long chat. Then she walked over to the mantelpiece and took a clipping and said, "I didn't think I should send you this, not while you were in hospital."

There it was, from a newspaper, about two inches long, saying that Fran was going to marry this guy on such and such a date. That date was a month ago. She was married. I even recognized the guy's name. A wealthy family, a lot of dough, and I thought, if he's married to Fran, then he sure as hell would have been old enough to be in the service, but I let it pass. Too many sons of those kinds of families were getting deferments. You could almost say it amounted to a scandal.

I told my mother not to worry. I had figured something was up with those friendly letters, but I was disappointed in Fran that she didn't have the guts to write me a Dear John. In my letters I hadn't indicated my gut shot was serious. Just that I'd caught one. So she couldn't have figured I was going to die. She knew I was back because I'd written her saying I was coming, and I wondered what the little gal was thinking.

So that was my homecoming. A life ahead of me, so to speak, and I get the pins knocked out from underneath me crack off the back.

I didn't even try to find her phone number or address to write a letter. If I had I would have been too much of a nice guy and I would have wished her all the happiness in the world. So I just let it lie there.

Now comes part two. I'm walking down Portage one afternoon, just wandering around, wondering what the hell I'm going to do with the rest of that life the doctors had saved for me. And bang, right out of a store walks her, the gal whose letters I had waited for all those months and still had in my duffel at home. It was a shock, I'll tell you. She was as beautiful as ever. She smiled but it wasn't much of a smile and she gave me a quick kiss on the lips. Not the kind of kiss I'd been thinking about for a long time. We kind of made small talk.

I asked her if she wanted a coffee. She said yes. We sat in a booth making small talk and then she started talking, making little false starts, like "I know I should have written you . . ." and she'd stop and "I tried to write about how it happened once but . . ." and "I don't know why, but I just couldn't . . ." and things like that. She couldn't get it out.

I guess I did the only thing I could and I said, "Never mind, Fran, we did have good times and I'm sure it is all for the best, the way it worked out," and then I asked, "Fran, are you happy?"

She looked down at her wedding ring, one big diamond and a lot of little ones around it, and she took it, actually yanked it off her finger and looked at it. My heart just about stopped. There was a small mirror on the wall in each booth, and she took the ring and savagely gouged it into the glass and she wrote "No."

Then she burst into tears, sobbed and sobbed, and grabbed my hand and kissed it, kissed it hard, sobbing all the time, and then she mumbled something I guess was "Good-by" and ran out of the restaurant.

Well, that tore it. Family or no family, I wasn't going to stay around a town where the girl I loved loved me but she was a bride to somebody else, some goddamned draft dodger. And since she was a Catholic I assumed she had married a Catholic and, in those days, very few people got divorced and Catholics, well, it was almost unheard of.

I paid the cashier and wondered what she would think when the waitress told her one of us had scratched a big, deep "No" in the mirror.

Two days later I was on a bus heading for Vancouver. I met a girl who nursed there and we started going out. Finally I just asked her to marry me and she said yes, just like that. We never made a whole lot of money but we lived well. A nice house in Dunbar district, both kids put through university, and time just went by and I looked at what we had put away and was surprised when it was all counted up that I could retire. So I did. That's all.

You asked me about the girl with the diamond ring. Sure, I still think of her. After all, she was my first love. You don't ever, ever forget that. But I don't think of her that way. I think of her as a wonderful person who is now dead—I don't know that—but a person who was part of my life at a very important time. That's all. I love my wife.

NO ONE MET HER AT THE STATION

There was a girl got off the CPR passenger at Sicamous this day and when I'd finished putting the day's offloading into the baggage room I looked and there she was, still standing there with a couple of suitcases. She was obviously looking for someone.

I went up and talked to her. She was Polish. She was a war bride. Her name was—well, it doesn't matter as how would I remember a name after all that time? But she'd married her Canadian soldier and the Red Cross had got her this far and there was no soldier to meet her. I'd lived in the town for a while and there was no family named Whittier there—that was the name she'd married into. Her name was on her documents and she did have a marriage certificate and she had married a guy named Whittier.

She told me she'd escaped from Poland and got into France and then over to England and for three or four years she'd worked in the fields.

She spoke of harvesting sugar beets and working on farms, and I'd been in an artillery unit in Devon for eight months, so I knew the part of the country she was talking about.

The documents? Oh sure. She had all of them, she was legitimate. A war bride, no doubt of that, eh? It was just that here she was, in a little town a hell of a long way from anywhere and she didn't speak English well and she was waiting for some guy named Whittier to pick her up.

We had the provincial police then and the corporal took charge and I left it at that, but a few weeks later I asked him what had happened to her. Nothing happened to her. He'd got in touch with Vancouver and Victoria and they'd chased down the Red Cross and, yes, Sicamous was where she was supposed to go, but nobody could find anything about a soldier named Whittier. There must have been quite a few Whittiers in the Canadian Army, but for some reason he hadn't told her enough about himself to give them any real clues. You'd think he'd have his regimental number and other identification on her documents, but apparently no.

The corporal had put her up in the old railroad hotel there for a few days and the local Red Cross looked after her, but it was hopeless, he said, so the Red Cross finally told them to ship her on to Vancouver and they'd see what they could do.

Yes, that's the end of the story. But it is a story. I've often wondered, now here is a girl of maybe twenty-two, married to a fast-talking Canadian—and believe me it happened often, I'm sure—and sent out to Canada to be with her husband. And there is no husband. She's alone. Doesn't speak English all that well. Whatever became of her, I don't know.

But I know one thing: that girl was telling the truth. I don't think she could have fooled all the authorities she'd have to go through. No, she couldn't have. She was 100 percent legit and her husband, as far as I'm concerned, was 100 percent an illegitimate bastard. I wonder how many other girls got stuck that way?

"SHE HAD HER SUITCASES AT THE UNION STATION"

I wonder if we ever really thought that seriously about what we were doing? Here we were in England, waiting for D-Day and battle, and every leave we were whopping off to some city or town to see the girlfriend and in some cases the wife, and sometimes even the kid.

There was a deadly war on and these crazy Canadians were acting like it was normal to court a girl, marry her, and give her a baby. No thought for the future. Like, wasn't it great to be a husband! Ha!

I was discharged in Toronto in October of '45 and Maureen had been shipped over with a bunch of war brides in late May. As though England couldn't wait to get rid of them. There she was, in Brampton, which was a small town, with my folks and my sister and she was a girl who had lived all her life in Manchester. Among the coke and the steel mills and the smoke, but I'll say this, her parents had a lot more money than mine did. Her father wasn't a clerk in a store. Not by a long shot.

Maureen met me at Union Station in Toronto that morning and by this time it was about seventeen months since we'd seen each other. That is a long time, my friend. People can change and we both did. I had been D-Day Plus Four, so you know what that means. It was infatuation, sure. A lonely soldier, me, and the Canadian uniform, the sergeant's stripes, that sort of thing. I guess we were in love. Anyway, it was a long time ago.

We went to a hotel for the night and I knew something was wrong. We didn't respond to each other, and I'm sure you know what I mean. I could tell she didn't like poor little Brampton town and I felt she didn't like my folks and she had to room with that crazy sister of mine.

We just sat up all night, me smoking and sipping from a bottle I had picked up and she sitting in the chair and knowing we weren't going to bed together and waiting for six in the morning or whenever the first restaurant opened. Finally she broke down and told me she was going back to England. In fact, she had her suitcases at the Union Station. She was booked on a ship from Montreal that was leaving in three or four days.

That's my story. I guess you want to hear more. I was a gentleman. I said fine, if that was her decision, and I added, I'm sure, that I hoped it would all work out for her and would she be going back to her parents' place and would she write me saying she had got home okay and did she have enough money? I don't know what I could have done about that. I sure didn't have enough for an ocean fare, but she said she had enough for her ticket and a bit left over to stay in Montreal and that seemed to be it. We had breakfast in the station and her train left in the morning and I let her go. Without a fight. Without a sob, really. I just knew she was right. It wasn't right for us, and it would have gotten worse and worse and worse. So kill it now. I saw her off with her two bags at the train gate and she kissed me and wished me luck and

I gave her a bit of a hug and I watched my wife walk away up the ramp. That was it. I felt sorry for both of us, but I felt free.

I went home and told my parents what had happened and they had the good sense to say nothing at all. In '53, one more than the seven years needed, I charged my wife with desertion and got a divorce and my lawyer sent the notification and court order to her and that was it.

Chapter over, signed and sealed.

"THANKS FOR NOTHING"

Did I come home to the bosom of a warm and loving family? Nope. I had an experience I'll bet not one other Canadian vet had. I still remember it. She was living with her mother and the letters I'd been getting from her were few and far between and not all that kindly, but I still figured I had a wife and a kid.

Sure, I still had a wife and a kid but when I didn't see anyone I knew when I got off the train I thought, oh-oh, something is funny. I was sure she had got my telegram, so I decided I'd get out there quickly and I took a cab out to the house.

I had a wife all right, and when she opened the door I walked in and there was a guy sitting in a big easy chair in his shirtsleeves. I guess I thought something like, "If he's the postman he's sure taking things for granted around here."

I wasn't a kid. I was twenty-six and even if I'd only been good enough for ground crew and not a bomber pilot and getting my legs shot off, I could still figure what was going on. But I wanted her to tell me. Anyways, she did have guts enough to stand up and say this guy was named Ben and he lived with her and her mother and my kid . . . *That* got me. My kid! This bastard living in this house and he just wasn't around to replace light bulbs and mow the lawn. He was living with my wife, and my kid was there, about ready to come home from school.

Remember, all this was new to me. I was pretty vulnerable. I didn't expect a big homecoming with all the family waiting, because it was just her and the kid and her mother and I didn't have any family except cousins in Alberta, so I remember just standing there and thinking, I should have known this. Her letters, about once a month, didn't show she had any feeling for me. I guess our marriage was bust in emotion and reality even before I joined up and I guess, no, I *know*, that was probably the reason I joined the Air Force. Didn't a man with a wife and kid, wasn't he exempt from war service? I think so.

I'm not describing this very well but it was more than forty years ago and you blot out the bad things, but I didn't blow my stack, beat up the guy and her. I thought, oh well, it wouldn't have worked anyway. She's done it for me. All I have to do is turn around and walk out of the house and I did and I said, "Good-by, Helen," and got in my shot because I said, "Thanks for nothing." When I got out I thought, you know, there was a lot of things I could have told her, told her off, but we had nothing but a suite in an old apartment when I enlisted and she couldn't have added to it on her own. She had nothing and I had nothing and that was it.

I waited down at the corner where the little fellow would come home from school and I tried to think of what he'd looked like at four years old and what he'd look like now that he was eight. A bunch of kids came along rough-housing down the street, kicking the dead leaves, and I tried to pick out my son and, you know, he could have been any one of them. All the same age, the same size, the same sweaters and pants.

That was the hardest part. I mean it is to me now. I could have called out "Bobby Windsor" and I'm sure one of those kids would have stopped and come over, but I didn't. All this was too sudden. When I was standing there I had been thinking, maybe she has been turning him against me all those years and if he knew who I was he'd turn and hightail it home.

I took the easy way out. I didn't say anything. Just turned away and went to the liquor store and bought a bottle of cheap rye and then I got a cheap room—I think it was seven bucks a week. That should tell you something.

I remember it clearly. I went up to the Army and Navy and I bought a pair of light pants, casual pants, and a sports shirt and a pair of brown shoes and a light jacket and some socks and I went back and had a good scrubdown in the shower and got dressed and lay down and put my feet on the bed. Read the newspaper and sipped that rye, and sipped it and sipped it and it was doing nothing for me. And I had a few more snorts and, by God, I remember thinking, this man is sober. I hadn't had Chinese food for about three years and I hiked off down to a Chinese joint with my bottle and I ordered about five dishes. A dish might be five or six bucks now but for a long time after the war you could get prawns with black bean and garlic sauce for ninety cents and that was top of the menu, eh? When I ordered, the waiter asked me how many people were coming and I stuck up my finger, one, and his eyes popped. But you know what? He brought it all and a glass and a jug of water and I dug in and ate and ate and then I ate some more and I finished that pile of grub and finished the bottle and I was drunk by now. It was the finest meal and drunk I've ever been on and I went back to the hotel and I lay down and I slept, from about seven o'clock right up the hours and down again to seven next morning, and I got up and I remember saying to myself, "I'm free. I'm bloody well free."

"SHE DIDN'T RECOGNIZE ME"

When the ship tied up in Halifax for the last time, which would be about October at the end of the war, I said I'd take my discharge train ticket to a town called Brampton, which is in Ontario, because there was a girl named Alice I'd met in London and she was a CWAC and that was her home town.

I'd met her at one of those servicemen's lounges in London and we hit it off right away and we spent several days together. We were both on leave. We hit it off like two lovesick pigeons and that was the last time I saw her, but we wrote. Two letters a week each way, but we never got together, not again, the Army being the Army and me being at sea so much. The thing is, those letters the last year were pretty hot and heavy, if you know what I mean.

I know there is no such thing as a contract in these things but the idea, or at least what I *thought* she meant, and what I *knew* I meant, was that we'd get married. You'll remember, most of the women got out as soon as they could get them out. The government didn't want much part of them after the war, or so I'm told. She was back in Brampton, so that was where I headed with thoughts of a wedding in my head. This dumb old gray head of mine, I still shake it when I think of it.

I think it was late in the evening when I got there from Toronto and I put my gear in a hotel room and went out for a couple of beers and next morning, no, about noon, I walked over to the store where she worked. I didn't phone because I wanted to surprise her. Well, I didn't surprise her. You know what happened?

You could call it a small department store, and there I am prowling the aisles, being all wavy-navy and just waiting for her to sign me aboard into her heart and there she was. Cute as I remembered her but her hair done real different from the way she had it in the picture I had of her.

She was chatting with another clerk and I walked up and stood there and smiled, a big grin on my dumb face, and she looked at me and said, "Hello, Navy, can I help you?"

I thought she was kidding, but she wasn't. She didn't recognize me. *She actually didn't recognize me.* How's that for trumping your partner's ace? I just stood there. I can't honestly remember what was going through my mind, me standing there all wavy-navy and welcome the hero home bit and remember London, remember the hotel outside of Windsor, remember those walks, remember all your letters signed SWAK and do you remember me, your sailor lover? No, I didn't say anything like that. I said something dumb like, like, your last few letters said you were working in this store and so I came to see you.

She got it then. Wow! She turned to her friend and told her she was booking off half an hour early for lunch. We went down the street, not talking, and she steered me into this little café and she's saying hello there, hi, hello, nice morning, isn't it? to people in the café and we go back to a booth and sit and she grabs my hand and says something like, "Jack, listen, I've got something to tell you."

You've got it. Right on the nail. She told me that when she got back home in June she had met someone she liked and now she was going to marry him.

I believe I asked her about all the letters and the lovey-dovey. I must have because she told me she had written them because she thought I was lonely. Well, sure, sure I was lonely and afraid at times, but why? Then I thought, oh hell, she was just being friendly and I was being a sap for thinking there was more.

This story has a good ending. It's just part, a tiny part of my life. It's not really too much about what happened after the war, but I figure it is part of it and that's why I'm telling you. I did the right thing. I told her that I was happy for her and that it was all right. I asked her when the wedding was and where it was and then we walked back to the store and we said good-by and that was it. I caught the bus back to Toronto.

Now here is the bit. On the way home to Calgary I read the last dozen or so letters and I thought, yep, the lady is right. They were friendly letters, not anything serious, although a lot of the earlier ones were, and I thought that I had better try to read between the lines. Maybe she was trying to let me down. No, there was nothing like that. Nothing about another guy, but what the hell. If I had been her I would have done something about that but, you know, women think differently and she maybe figured I'd just go away. Or not come to see her.

Remember, I was doing some thinking and reading those letters and I thought, darn it, I didn't love her either. It was just five days together between two kids in London in an exciting time and those letters probably were as much fun for her to write as the ones I wrote her. Yes, we did get carried away somewhat, but not that much. I liked her for writing to me and those letters did mean something to me at the time, because I was an orphan and lived with an uncle and aunt on the farm and they didn't really give a hoot. That was about the only mail I was getting in wavy-navy.

Looking back, it was a good deal all round. We kind of comforted each other through letters, but the war was over and that was it. I took those letters, the batch I'd picked up in Portsmouth and the last ones at Halifax and I went out between the cars and I tore them up, one by one, across, then across again, and I let them fly out onto the track.

I wasn't bitter, and when the day came for her wedding I sent her and her husband a present. Something small. I forget what. But it was something they could both use in their new apartment or house. I thought I did the graceful thing.

That's my story. It is not about how I prospered in the post-war life but when you hear of some of the horror stories of this kind of thing, the ones that turned out very badly, maybe this one will show you that not all, maybe more than you think, maybe they turned out fine for everybody.

"WE WERE FAR TOO DIFFERENT"

The first thing a lot of us did was get married. I still don't know why. You went with a girl, and she promised to write and you wrote her and you lived and died waiting for her letters. My wife wrote every day and not one of them was torpedoed. I got 939 letters from her and she numbered every one and you lived and died for those letters and you fell in love with her through those letters, because that was all you had over there.

Guys used to read those letters twenty times over, and if my wife had known that she'd have made them more interesting. You couldn't say things that would make the censor's face blush red but she could, but they were just what she did each day. For about two and a half years. "I got up in the morning, I had my breakfast, I went to work," et cetera and et cetera.

Then you came back and there she was waiting, and I know I thought, oh God, this is it. I've got to marry this girl.

I did. The number of marriages after the war was astounding. If you could look back at the old newspapers, you'd see. The florists and the photographers must have made a fortune.

And then it was settling down. My wife had found a small place for us, not much either. One room in the attic of this house and we shared a bathroom with another couple and the family, and I went out to work and on Sunday we'd walk around neighborhoods in Toronto trying to find a better place.

No money, no fun, and she just wasn't the girl I'd known in high school in Stratford, but Stratford didn't have the University of Toronto and I was going to get that degree, come hell, high water, and Mitch Hepburn, as we used to say.

We floundered along for another year and both of us knew we had made a mistake. In those days divorce was an awful word. It was a terrible thing, but damn it all, we still liked each other just like we had at high school—but married, no, not for us.

At Christmas of the second year, which would be 1946, we went home for Christmas and we talked it over with her parents and my parents and they were surprisingly sympathetic. You know, it was best that we had found out when we were young and there were no children.

Phyllis came back to Toronto with me and we packed up her belongings and took a cab to the bus station, and I remember we sat in the little coffee shop there and had doughnuts and coffee and held hands and we were crying a little. I know I was crying inside, not outside. I heard the call for the bus and that was it, I guess. She got on and I went along the bus to the window she was at and I smiled and said, "I love you" with my mouth and she did the same thing and then I walked away. That was it.

I've thought a thousand times if it would have worked but, no, it wouldn't have. We were far, too far different, and the times I thought of her I think it was in relation to the times when the jeep came up with the mail and the corporal would hand it out and I'd get three or four letters, with 612, 613, and 614 ringed in red ink, and they'd be from her and I'd think, well, I can go on for a few more days.

That's the way it was.

The first love is a terrible and wonderful thing, isn't it?

"THE LOW-WATER MARK"

I spent Christmas Eve and Christmas Day and the next day in a hotel room in Toronto with a couple of bottles of hooch and that's because when I got home two days before and got down to Guelph I found I had two kids that weren't mine.

I'm not kidding. I got off that bus and took a taxi to where my wife was living and there she is, in this old apartment. She's got one kid about three and another about two and you know, I was so stupid I thought she was baby-sitting them for her sister or some neighbor. Something like that. I'm not kidding you, mister. I just couldn't think this was happening.

If you're thinking the three-year-old could have been mine, then forget it. It wasn't. I was in England when somebody laid down the keel for that one and as for the smaller one, forget it. The poor little beggars. You know, I can still feel some sorrow for them. Just two little tykes and who is this big man in the blue Air Force uniform looking at us?

It only took a few minutes. She couldn't fool me. These two kids were calling her Mommy. They acted exactly as if she was their mother. Oh no, no, she didn't deny it. How could the bitch? She just said yes, they are mine, and like any woman who ever walked this earth, I suppose, she said that I was having a lot of nookie . . . Hah! There's a word you don't hear anymore: nookie. She said I was having a lot of nookie with those English girls and she had a right to have some fun, too. Well, obviously she did.

I didn't stay long. That was my homecoming. It was my going-away coming, too. I hadn't loved her. Hell, it was one of those quickie marriages. A lot of them around—too many. Married in a rush and away the guy goes. I know this, they sure played old Merry Bob with things after the war when the guys started coming back.

But don't get me wrong, mister. I don't want to say I'm blaming the wives all that much. Just as much . . . maybe more was the blame of the guy, or they should have taken the blame fifty-fifty. You've gotta look at it this ways. They were funny times, eh? People did a lot of funny things. The marriage business was one of them.

Anyway, that was the low-water mark for me. Low tide. I gave her fifty bucks and told her to buy a Christmas present for each of the kids and I got out of that house. Just like that. I wasn't there more than twenty-five, thirty minutes and this was about noon and I just got out on the road and hitched and in pretty jigtime I was in Toronto. Right downtown.

I got a room in that big hotel next to the Union Station. They tore it down not so long ago.

I bought a bottle of rye at the liquor store and because I didn't have another coupon I bought a bottle from a taxi driver. I sat in that room and I drank both bottles. No, I didn't get drunk, but I was drinking steady, reading, looking out the window, a couple more drinks, out to the station for a snack, for smokes, and I did a lot of thinking.

Sure, I can remember what I thought. I thought, maybe I should go back and take over those kids. That's how dumb I was. I was twenty-three. Then, should I get a divorce? Let me tell you, mister. Divorce was a dirty word in my family. My cousin Geraldine in Alberta got a divorce from a guy who beat her up all the time and my own mother wouldn't speak her name. I'm not kidding! And she'd only met her maybe four times! That's the way it was in them days, especially with Presbyterians.

So that was my first Christmas back home.

Ah, it wasn't so bad. I had a nice quiet drunk and I guess, well, it's a long time ago, but I seem to remember feeling quite good about it all. I felt, I guess, like a lift was taken off my back. I didn't really know her and I didn't love her and I think she felt the same way.

I didn't do anything about it and then about four or five years later I get this letter. She's divorcing me. I don't have to do anything. The guy she wants to marry is going to do the business of arranging it, paying for it, and do I mind. Mind? Hell's bells with feathers stuck on! I write no, go ahead and good luck. I wasn't glad for her. I didn't give a damn about her. I was glad for those kids of hers, though. The only time I seen them they were such cute little tykes.

What I'm saying is this: not everything was all peaches and cream for guys who came home from that business in Europe.

"A NO-WIN SITUATION"

I joined the Army in Calgary and was transferred from infantry to the armoured corps. In October of 1942 I got married in Glasgow and we had one child, a boy, Walter. That finishes with that part of it.

In December of '44 I was in Europe with the armoured corps and I received word that my wife and son were being sent to Canada. The front was pretty static then, so I got four days' leave to go back to see my wife and son and we had two days together. She was a pretty bewildered Scottish lassie, I'll say that, but she still wanted to go.

One thing that puzzled me was this. The war was still raging. The Germans were still tough as hell, but more important, out there in the Atlantic they were still sinking a lot of Allied shipping. We both know now that the area around Halifax and Newfoundland had a lot of U-boats hunting. But if the Canadian government in all its wisdom decided to send the war brides over to Canada, then they must have had special knowledge as to protection and everything it entailed. I wondered, but I went along with it. A Canadian Army soldier wasn't expected to think.

I got home in August of '45. No special considerations for me, even though I had a Scottish war bride and a child waiting for me, and I knew from her letters she was very unhappy. I told my captain this and I told the chaplain several times but, no, I would serve out my allotted time, so to speak.

My grandfather's home was on the outskirts of town. It had been pretty crammed in that little house, four adults and a baby coming up to two years of age, and the night I arrived Maggie and I took a long walk out east away from town and had a long talk. She wanted to go back to Glasgow, but me being me, I just did not take her seriously.

I told her that we'd move to Edmonton and get a little house and I'd go to university and become an engineer and we'd live happily ever after. A new life, that sort of thing. She calmed down a bit because if there is one thing the Scots can understand, it is the value of a good education. Hell, Scottish engineers built half of Canada, I'd say.

So, we moved to Edmonton and it was worse. Here I was straining my mental guts out along with hundreds of other vets who hadn't cracked a book for four, five, ten years and Maggie and the kid were cooped up all day in two tiny rooms in a dump of a house which just wasn't right for either of us. That was all we could get. Men would have killed to get what we had. Yes, housing was that bad and worse, and the landladies! Well, all I can say is this. In Edmonton they must have been a special breed and they attended night school classes to learn how to be meaner than they were. You could say it was an anti-veteran attitude although they loved the last dollar they could squeeze out of us. But we had it good compared to some of my classmates. Some of them were living in garages with an electric cord strung out from the house and the landlady would pull the plug at eleven at night. No, I am not kidding. I know these things happened.

Prices were high and the stink of the landlady's cabbage and other Ukrainian foods cooking came up into our rooms and oh, it would take an hour to list all that went on and here I was. There I was. An ex-sergeant, a pretty tough guy in the service, and I couldn't do one damn thing because the law was on her side. As I said, I still consider that Edmonton was a town that did not like ex-servicemen. They did not like ex-servicemen's wives or their kids. All they liked was our money.

There wasn't any point in walking the streets on weekends looking for a place for rent. There just wasn't any in that winter after the war. Oh, there were, and here is something that will shake you. During the war there were a lot of Americans in Edmonton. Being Americans they received higher pay than Canadian servicemen got, and many of them were officers and they had lived out rather than staying in barracks, and the people who had rented to the Americans and now had vacancies, they still wanted the high rents the happy-go-lucky nonwarriors had paid. Of course, that was out. Oh, I'm sure they eventually rented these places, but to civilians. Not the warriors.

Our domestic situation was getting worse. How could it go any other way? It was a no-win situation. I had not promised her the sun and the moon, but I had not said it would be like this. She was whining and crying all the time and wee Wallie was picking it up from her. I had my studies and they were not easy for me, believe me. So it was edgy. It was worse.

She could have given me another chance, but she didn't. One day in spring just after I had finished the exams and had landed a surveying job and what's more, I had a good line on a nice basement suite in a nice area. You see, a lot of my class were flunking out or quitting. I think about thirty percent of my class, the vets, I mean, about thirty percent gave up the ghost that spring. Jobs were easy to get and things were opening up and they just said, why all this work, three more years of it and what's at the end of it? Well, what was at the end, as they could see, were thousands of new engineers across Canada coming out all at once and looking for good jobs. That's another story, of course.

What I didn't know was that certain letters had been going back and forth across to Scotland and that her parents had told her to come home for a holiday. They had booked her passage for the middle of May, two weeks away. And I didn't know a thing about it. I was at the point that I didn't know if I really cared all that much, but it was one hell of a shock. No, I didn't yell and scream or protest or throw punches. I just accepted the situation. After all, it was just going to be two months— but I had a feeling I was wrong.

I saw them off, wee Wallie and Maggie, and I got a phone call from

Halifax saying they were sailing next day and I didn't see them again for fourteen years. That's when I screwed up my courage to go to Scotland. We were divorced by then and both married again and we had a nice meeting. Tea in a tea shop on Princes Street. Edinburgh. She lived in Edinburgh then. We had a few laughs and no tears and we both decided she had made the right decision. Wee Wallie was at a school near Inverness the day that I phoned her—you see, I hadn't told her I was coming—so I didn't see the boy, but that didn't shake me. I knew I would someday and in '67 he came to Montreal for Expo and I flew down and we had a good four days together.

Now what is the moral of all this? I really don't know. I suppose I could say that it was a wartime marriage which didn't work out which worked out better than a lot I have heard of. That's about it. Not lucky, not unlucky, but just a period of my life that happened.

"WE DID THE RIGHT THING"

The best thing to do is tell it the way it was.

We got married just three days before I had to head back to Shilo. Shilo, Manitoba. I was on my embarkation leave, which gave me ten days in Victoria, and her mother had arranged the wedding for three days before I left, so that gave us Thursday and Friday together and then, there I was, off to fight the foe. I'm sure her old lady arranged it that way. Just two nights and you didn't fool around on your embarkation leave. You had to be there when your draft pulled out.

That was two days to get to know each other the way a man and woman have to do it. Not enough. Ah, it was just hopeless. That was in '42.

I did my time, so to speak. An artillery outfit doesn't go through what the lads in the infantry have to put up with, and I came through it all. I got back to Victoria at the end of August of the last year. I was in good shape, maybe thirty pounds heavier but speaking of heavy, that's what I guess my heart was. I knew I didn't love her, and just because she'd been the girl in the high school class I'd dated and who wrote me letters and who, incidentally, whom I had married, that was not enough.

We didn't meet in Victoria. I'd phoned her from the Lakehead and told her when the train was arriving in Vancouver and asked her to meet me there. I remember, eh, there were hums and haws and well, maybe, but I said she had to be there and all the time the train was rolling through the mountains I was thinking, how will I tell her? What will I tell her? Maybe I should have thought, what will she tell me, eh?

Looking back I should have said, "Look, Estelle, there's a girl who was in the CWAC who I met when I was in England and she's back in Toronto now and I've talked to her just four days ago at the station and I love her and she loves me and I don't love you and I'm sure you don't love me and we both know this is no good and never will be, so why don't we just whack it off right now and you go your way and I'll go mine and I'll get the divorce?" Something like that. A long sentence, I know, but I would have been honest with her and myself, eh?

There was a lot of confusion at the station, but I found her. She was just standing there. Oh, she'd seen me, no doubt of that. She knew me. I hadn't changed. I think she was just thinking, "Well, there is my husband. It's been three years. Should I go through with it?"

Then I walked over and she said, "Welcome home, Bob," and gave me a hug and then I knew. You know these things. There's a little radio inside you at times like that and this little voice broadcasts to you, "Okay, buddy, she doesn't want you any more than you want her." You know?

That made it easy. We became good friends, then and there.

I took her into the station restaurant and we ordered coffee and when it came we had finished the "How are you?"'s and all that and I remember, to this day, I started in and I didn't apologize. I just told her there was this girl from Toronto who had been in the Canadian Army in London and that she was far away and Bonnie was very close and well, we had fallen in love and we wanted to get married.

This is all like yesterday. Like that day. She really was a fine person. She smiled and dug into her purse and took out a little bit of cotton batten and opened it and took out a diamond ring and she said it was her wedding ring. She wanted to marry a naval officer who was on duty in Victoria and he had bought her this ring to give her confidence when she met me, when she told me she wanted to be married but to someone else.

Maybe, I don't know, but maybe I was a little disappointed. I hope I wasn't. That would have been male ego. Maybe I wanted it to be a little bit tearful or maybe a lot of tears, but it wasn't. So there we sat. I can see that restaurant now. A high-ceilinged place, big as a church. There were all these couples at other tables, some with little kids, the troops who had been on the train with me and their first reunions and holding hands and crying, jabbering away a mile a minute and there was Estelle and I looking at each other. I know I got a twinge of the heart wondering how it might have been if it hadn't been for the bloody war and the Army.

But it was business, too, and while we did hold hands as we talked, it was how we could both be free. She wasn't the kind of girl who would ever live common law. What a phrase! What the hell does it actually mean? Fortunately, it was not too hard. We decided to get the marriage annulled. We could both lie on that score and the dates of marriage and my furlough ending would back us up. In those days you needed things like that. Three days, in other words, was not enough. Excitement, shyness, not enough skill, being afraid, and you put it all together and it was enough.

It was not as hard as I thought but it was complicated and it did take some arranging, but I got the divorce. That's about it. I think we were the lucky ones. There was no child, there was no complication, time and age were in our favor, and another factor was that her father and my father each had a certain amount of pull.

That's about it. A few phone calls to get certain details in a hurry, and then it went through. Nobody knew. Three weeks later I got a clipping from the Victoria newspaper announcing the details of her wedding.

You know, I've talked to others who were in the same boat. Some of those guys are still living with the girls they married at the drop of a hat, eh? Kids came, grew up, moved out of the nest, married, and had kids of their own, and they're still married to that girl they were or thought they were in love with. They've told me it was rough at the start and I have no doubt of that, but I know, oh how I know, we did the right thing.

5   TO FARM OR
NOT TO FARM

5 TO FARM OR NOT TO FARM

I personally know many veterans who went back to the farm to show the old man how he had been messing up things for the past thirty years. They discovered that Dad had learned a lot in the few years they had been away. I've also met a considerable number of businessmen and professionals who claimed that after the war they wanted to go farming. They didn't, of course, although today some stride around their five-acre hobby farms, faithful dog at heel.

Many farm boys went off to university after the war, only to return to the land. Others just came straight home to take over the family farm, or buy one of their own. For the men who had dreamed, during the grinding years of war, about owning that piece of farmland, the Veterans' Land Act was a wonderful scheme, although many complained about the endless red tape. But it worked. A vet could buy, with a generous government grant, a quarter or half-section of land and through years of hard work he could make it. All he needed was an understanding and hard-working wife, an understanding banker, an understanding God pulling the right weather levers, and lots of plain old luck.

If he gave it his best shot but the odds were against him, he could head for the town or the city, the coast or the oilfields, where he was bound to be luckier.

"IT WAS JUST MY AGE"

When I tell people today that I'm ninety and that I was in the last war they won't be able to put their hats on straight from thinking that how could he be. Me.

The thing is this, about half the people in this country just don't know anything about the war because they are all too young. If it was 1954 today instead of 1984 then they would, but I don't think they'd care any more than do the young people today. Remembrance Day seems to have gone out the window. Nobody cares. There are more of us old duffers marching to the memorial across from the City Hall than there are people watching. I don't say that is wrong; that's the way it is. People forget or they don't know and I guess we forget like they do. Except for that one day when we form up and the kids' band plays and there we are, a bunch of old men picking up the step, arms swinging and our heads high and it was just like so long ago. Of course, I was in the First World War, too.

I was in the Veterans' Guard in World War Two. Now, nobody even knows what that is. I don't know how many were in it, but it was the older fellows who were too old to go overseas, so they formed this Veterans' Guard and we had all sort of duties. Guarding, mostly. Bridges. Gates of barracks. Gates of war plants. Some did instructing and driving. All these jobs that the girls did, too, in the service, the kind which an able-bodied man would have to do if we weren't around. I was at Lethbridge at the end of the war where the big prisoner camp was. Thousands. Germans from North Africa. I'm not sure to this day why they brought them from North Africa to Lethbridge and The Hat. Those were some camps. Big new hospital. Good food. The same as our own boys got in Canada but sure as shoot not the same as our poor boys got in those Stalag camps in Germany. Not by a long shot. My boy was in one of them. A flyer. Lethbridge was the camp where a bunch of the tough-nut boys, the Nazis, hanged two of their own for not being strong for Hitler, and then the Canadian government took four of them fellows out and hanged them. Oh, they had Canadian lawyers, sure, and a Canadian judge, but they hanged them. Good riddance. Bad rubbish they were.

I got out in October of '45 with all the rest. They had the Soldiers' Settlement Plan in the first war and this time they had the Veterans' Land Act, which was the best thing I ever saw. The best. Just the best. If a young fellow had the guts and the determination and the right kind of wife, he could get a farm. It was a very good deal. I thought it over because here was my chance to be my own man. I'd been handyman, cook, swamper, storekeeper, school janitor, well driller, a lot of things before the war, but I wanted to be a farmer.

Anyway, I get my discharge in Lethbridge because I got no wife by this time and the chap who talked to me said he didn't think my application would get passed because I was fifty then. Fifty wasn't old to me but it was to him. He was about thirty, I guess. Anyway, the way it went, he said I should go up to Edmonton where there was more land and maybe they'd see it the other way there. But they didn't. I was fifty. I had no farm experience. Imagine living all through Alberta all those years before the war and they said no farm experience. I'd worked on lots of farms. What they meant, I guess, is that I didn't know anything about, well, figuring books and selling cattle and talking to the banker and all that. I can tell you this. I don't think many of the young fellows who got a quarter or a half knew much about that. No, it was just my age. I was an old codger in their eyes.

I thought of going to B.C. and seeing if I could get some land in the Okanagan Valley and grow apples, and if I'd done that I'd be sitting pretty today. Not sitting in this lodge with all these old people, watching each other die. Waiting for the Legion to visit with some magazines. I could be in the Ok Valley watching my apples grow and then selling them to the tourists who whiz by. I know, I've watched them. They sell right by the road and make good money.

This lodge is fine, the food is good and there are some nice people in it from all over the place and there is lots to do if you want to, but there are, I would say, just too many old people in it.

If I had got a farm in B.C. I would have something to leave my boy and his kids, but here I got nothing. All those years after the war I was always working for somebody else and that is just no good. You don't save any money. Oh, you can save, but not much, but when you own a place then you make a lot more money when you sell because the value is always going up and up.

I have no bitterness because the government wouldn't let me get a farm. The only thing that makes me mad is that in that little book they gave us when we got discharged, it said that we could have a farm. There was no maybe about it. I could be sitting in my little white house on my orchard in the Ok Valley watching my apples grow right now.

"A ROTTEN THING TO DO"

In the summer of '40, with the war just starting to get going with the defeat of France, and Britain in Europe, my dad knew that my time was coming and I'd be called up. Knowing a bit about how things worked, he gave me a quarter section. We went into town and the lawyer transferred the land over to me and in that way I was on the books as a farmer and not just my dad's son and nothing more than a hired man.

When I was called up in March of '41, all I had to say was that I owned land and was a farmer and I wouldn't have had to go. Farmers were important in those days and that is how so many sons of people of foreign extraction missed being drafted. The rest ran off into the bush and hid, eh? But I didn't. I didn't tell them I owned land and so I went into the Army and my dad was furious. He'd lost a hired man he didn't have to pay.

All through the war—and I got married to an English girl named Ellen, Yorkshire gal, by the way—all through the war I got letters saying how well my land was going, the big crops, and I knew that they were getting good prices for wheat and I'd say to Ellen that everything looked rosy.

She came back on a bride ship and then on a bride train and the folks met her and took her to the farm. I got back on the eighteenth of November, '45, and there was the usual party, friends, neighbors, food, dancing, and so it went and then it was down to work again.

Yep, you guessed it. I went back as a farmhand and Ellen helped my mother in the kitchen, just like she was a hired girl brought in for the harvesting. You know why? Because apart from the money I had coming from the government, I didn't own a thing. I'd given Dad my power of attorney because if I got killed or some emergency came up, some dispute over the taxes on my land or a fence-line argument, Dad said he had to have that power of attorney. Dumb kid that I was, I said sure. So what he had done just six months before I came back, he had sold that land of mine using the power of attorney. He sold that land to the very same lawyer who had drawn up the deed by which Dad had given me the land.

What happened next you won't believe. He had sold that land for $1,000 and it was worth three or four times that much, and in three months the lawyer had sold it back to him for $1,250. So the lawyer got $250 for drawing up a few papers and Dad got my land back.

Oh yes, I still call him Dad. I don't know why.

He was still mad at me for signing up in the Army. He was going to show me. I was going to have to start off from scratch the way he had.

It was a rotten thing to do to your own son who'd joined up to serve his country. The old man was mad and he'd been mad all those years because of that.

I told him, so you've got the land back and you aren't going to pay me the thousands of dollars of wheat that land grew. I said, on a rental basis from me to you, I should get one-third of that. No way.

He expected me to stay and work, but as soon as I could get a few affairs in order and another lawyer had told me I was out of luck, Ellen and I left. I said good-by to my mother and I just drove away while the old man was working in the barn and that was that, I'm afriad. If he'd do that to me once, he'd do it again.

We went over into South Saskatchewan and I got a quarter through the VLA and I can tell you we had tougher times than we deserved but we made out. We did well. We got on our feet and we prospered in the good years we had. It was good country anyway. It was mixed farming, so we couldn't take trips in the winter like other folk, but we enjoyed our life.

Sure, I made up with Dad. It was Ellen and my mother that got it fixed up. Myself, I couldn't have cared less, but they thought it was best. We visit now, but that's about all. I don't really think a man like that really deserved a son.

"HOW I WOUND UP AS A FARMER"

I got to be a trapper after the war when I got out because of my big mouth putting this dumb brain of mine into motion. It happen-ed like this.

All those years, standing around in the south of England waiting for those guys in London to decide when we were going to go after the Ger-mans in France, I'd always be talking to Englishmen, mostly old guys who'd stand around sucking on a pipe and grunting "Grrzzz" when they meant yes or no or maybe, and when a new face came in the barkeep, Jennie, she'd point at me and say, "Thizzz lad 'ere, 'e'zz a Canuck. Sezz 'e's a trapper in Canada. Hunts for wolf skins, the like o' that."

Well, you see, when all the other guys were going to London to get laid on Shaftesbury Avenue and the like, I just stuck around the coun-tryside on my leave. Cheaper that way, country folk buying me drinks and inviting me for tea and dinner, and there was usually a bed for me at "Time, gentlemen" time. Besides, it was far cheaper and I liked just leaning against a bar in one of their wee pubs down a lane and talking to the English farm folk.

I guess that me being from Canada, they expected me to be a hunter or a trapper and so I just obliged them. A line, you could say. Just innocent, to be sure, but by the time I'd been doing this for a couple of years and thinking about it when we was in France and then Holland and Germany, why, I did believe I was a trapper, and that was it.

So when I got out in August of the last year of the war, I went home to see the folks and then I got on a train and before I knew it I was in Edmonton and asking around. A fellow in a store said if I wanted to find people who were trappers I was to go to one of those beer parlors down at the end of Jasper, past the McDonald Hotel, and that's where I headed myself.

There were stores around there with windows full of stuff for trapping but I couldn't really get an idea about what trapping was like from just looking in the windows. So I went inside one and got talking to an old fellow. He knew the ropes, all right. I'll say that. A little old guy, but I guess he'd sold a million dollars' worth of stuff for trapping, living in the bush. Supplies, you know. He had this store, and she was just a-bulging. I was lucky to meet that old guy, Saul. Everybody seemed to know Saul and when he sized me up for what I was, a greenhorn, he told me to stick around and that I did. In about an hour a guy comes in and he has a hangover down to his bootlaces, shaking all to beat hell, and this Saul calls me over and says, "That's the man for you. Take him around the corner to the beer parlor and feed him his lunch," and he introduces me to this old guy, about fifty-five, I'd say. And we go over to the pub and it had just opened and I order four beers and he just drinks three of them fast and in a minute I can see the stuff working through him because soon he gets perky and what did I want?

I didn't bullshit him. I said I wanted to be a trapper. I'd dreamed of being a trapper. Saul said he was one of the best in the business and I wanted to know about it. He looked at me and said, "Ever eaten muskrat, for five days in a row? Think you could?"

I said sure, and I told him I'd lived on Army food for four years and he laughed and this is what he told me. First, he said, he wouldn't even be talking to me like this but that Saul had told him I seemed like a nice fellow and the second thing he told me, a person doesn't go out in the bush and start trapping. He said I was an apprentice, like being on a railroad. I thought that was fair, especially as all I knew about the bush was snowshoeing along some trails in winter in the Laurentians.

We talked for hours and we both got drunk and had about five bucks' worth of Chinese food while we watched four guys fighting and about ten cops trying to break them up. I remember that, and that's about all. I must have gone to my room but I remembered enough that this Rocky, as Saul had called him, this Rocky said I should meet him the next day. Same place. That hotel.

This time he was all business. He remembered things I didn't. Sure, if I had enough money he'd take me with him, but it was going to be hard work because he was going up into the country northwest of Rocky Mountain House. The Baptiste River, around there. He said he'd trapped it up to seven years ago until it got too poor, but now he figured she'd be just built up again with fur, and his old cabin and his line cabins would still be there and, well, he had a lot of traps cached and tools and stuff, so it wouldn't take as much to outfit. He asked how much money I had and I said $600. His eyes kind of blinked, as even after the good war days that was a lot to have. I mean, right there in the pocket, all yours. I actually had another $200 I had put away and my clothing allowance, but I didn't tell him that. He said it would be enough. He said we should leave about the end of September and that would give us time to fix up the cabins and clean out the traplines and do the work we needed doing. Oh, he had a long list of things he needed buying, stringing them off right off the top of his head. He said for me to go and get the money.

Of course he was into the beer again, talking a blue streak, and when he went to the can I hustled across the street to this guy's place, the fur buyer, and I told him that I was supposed to give $600 to the trapper, this Rocky, and he said sure, that's fine. He said you're a greenhorn, so you pay most of the freight; he teaches you and you get a third of the crop the first year. He said, "Rocky sells to me, so I know that's the way he works. He always has. You're in absolutely good hands." He said the word, ab-so-lute-ly. I think the way that wise old geezer said it convinced me.

I went back and Rocky didn't even ask me where I'd gone. For all he seemed to care, I could have buggered off, but when he saw me he said to go get him the money. I guess he could tell by my dumb face. He said leave the money with him and come back in a month, go out and get a job harvesting for a month and toughen up and then come back. So I went up to Westlock that very day. My God, to think of it now. I put an awful lot of trust in that man. I really did.

The first few days nearly killed me, but I stuck it and was making nine bucks a day for damn hard work, working on two farms, one further north where the threshing was later, working seven days a week, sunshine, good threshing weather all the way. I came back down at the end of September with three hundred bucks and went to see the fur buyer and you better believe it, mister, I was a little shaky about my deal. Maybe Rocky had buggered off himself. He hadn't answered the two letters I'd sent him. It didn't matter, though. He came along right on schedule and said we were leaving in three days and he took me to a secondhand store to get my clothes, what I'd need, and Saul, the fur buyer, I guess he didn't like that because he sold only new, but I guess he figured he'd make up the difference in profit in the furs we brought back.

About a hundred and fifty bucks did the trick for my clothes and I didn't have to buy a rifle or stuff like that. He had those. A 30.30 Winchester and a .22 repeater, and he went to a secondhand bookstore and asked the guy for about five dollars' worth of books and we got a big sack of pocketbooks. The guy had these sacks all ready, just for guys like that. I guess he knew what he was doing. They lasted us all winter. The old guy was quite a reader, Western stories and mysteries.

We took the train to Rocky Mountain House and then a truck with our stuff as far as the road went, up to the northwest, and when we couldn't go no further we spent a week packing our stuff in and on our first trip there was the cabin. The squirrels and mice had got in and things were pretty well beat up and it stunk, but it was in good shape, I guess. How would I know? He said it was in good shape, so I believed him. It was another four weeks or so before good deep snow was on the ground and in that time he took me over his five lines, one for each day, no work Saturday or Sunday. That turned out to be when we worked on the furs and got meat. Deer and the like. We also cut out five more lines and that would be for me after we went into Edmonton at Christmas for a piss-up. When we got back, he said I knew enough about trapping, oh, a little, but enough. He said that I'd work those lines and if either of us got caught in a blizzard I'd sleep in the little shelters we made. Rough, and just enough to keep you out of the cold and in the warm.

It worked fine. When we did his five lines first, he said there was lots of fur around, more than he'd seen when he first went into that country years before and no competition, and especially those "fucking Jean Baptistes" as he put it, meaning French Canadian trappers. He hated them. That made two of us.

We did good November and December, like except when we went out for Christmas for a few days, and at the General Delivery there was three letters waiting for me. From a girl, the oldest daughter of the farmer

I'd worked for up north of Westlock, and I'd written her before I'd left for the bush. Her first letter said she was happy that I'd written her and the second wondered why I hadn't written and the third said she wondered why I hadn't written her again and was I sick or something. That made me feel good and I wrote her a long letter back and said I'd write her again when I came back again. When I did get back in the spring there were five letters waiting for me at the fur buyer's store where I'd said to mail them, so I guess you know how it all turned out.

That winter we did good. Real good. Old Rocky was pleased as punch and so was I and old Saul was just laughing his eyes out when we pulled up in early April with that load of fur in the back under a canvas of fur and when all was said and done we had $7,000 in furs, wolf, marten, weasel, fox, bear—four of them brown bears we got the first couple of days we were out—and beaver we got in the spring when they was legal and they was in top condition. I think we got a better price because Rocky said to the old guy he was thinking of taking the lot to the raw fur auction in Vancouver or Winnipeg, and I think that notched up the price. Anyway, Rocky said so.

But there was this girl up on her father's farm and when I'd got cleaned up and new clothes and a haircut, I hightailed it up there. I phoned the store in town and they sent a kid out in a car with the message that I was coming and she was there to meet the train, her and her mother. It was just a short time, oh, maybe a week, and we was engaged and soon we got married and went to Jasper for four days on the train and when we got back, well, there was a bit of a problem. I went around to find Rocky and I found out he'd had his big drunk and had gone down to Banff for a couple of months to do some guiding, packing for Brewster's, the tourist outfit. What I wanted to tell him, or ask him, I mean, was could I bring the wife along next winter. She'd be chief cook and bottle-washer and I'd build a room alongside the cabin and we'd sleep there. I got a letter back in about a month and he said no, a woman was a quarrelsome thing in the bush, no matter how good a cook she was, and so on. He told me to meet him in Calgary on such and such a day, which was near then. We went down and he met the wife but he wasn't going to change his mind and so he said, we'd better split up, boy, because this wouldn't work, and he said, you'd have made a good trapper. I laughed at that. He didn't say I was a good trapper. I would, could have been a good one.

Then you know what that old bugger did? He pulled out a checkbook and wrote out a check for $500, in Jennie's name, and said it was a wedding present. I thought that was damn nice of him, then. I said "then." I found out a few days later when we was knocking about Edmonton buying things for our new house, because I wasn't going out in the bush on my own, I stopped in to see Saul and he asked if when I'd seen Rocky had he given me my share of the money. I said yes, my third of the seven thousand or so, and he said no, the rest. What rest? He said that there was a deal in those days that when he bought a winter's catch he estimated what he could get for them at the sale and if it was more, then he and the trapper split the difference which I thought was fair, and I guess it don't happen anymore. Not in these days. No, I'll bet not. I asked how much was the extra. He said a thousand and so dollars and I just laughed.

That old bugger. That five hundred he'd given Jennie was mine anyway.

'Course, when you look it from another way, he didn't have to give it to me at all, figuring I'd never find out. But he did, and he gets the benefit of the doubt from me. To give it to Jennie though, as a nice big wedding present, that kind of took the cake.

The upshot was, the place we were going to buy to live in when we weren't out in the bush, we just told the real estate man we didn't want it and we went back to the farm and that $3,000 less maybe three hundred and Rocky's five hundred gave us a good little nest egg, and I went farming with her old man and lived in a little house on the farm and that's it, I guess.

That's how I got out of the Army, trapping, because I'd been bullshitting about trapping with those old English farmers and before I knew it, I wound up as a farmer myself and did pretty darned good.

Don't you always think, a lot of times things work out for the best even if you go a long ways roundabout getting to it?

"NOBODY EVER WORKED HARDER"

There wasn't too much choice. I came home and the government was opening up a big section way northeast of Edmonton and I figured if I waited, there would be nothing left to file on. I filed badly, without looking around.

People think that the days of homesteading were back around 1900 to, say, the First World War. Wrong. They had a Soldiers' Re-Settlement Plan after that war and then they opened up sections after the last war. The same thing, though: ten bucks to file and you picked your quarter section. Then you worked your fat little butt down to skin and bone clearing it. They had land-clearing outfits by then, but there weren't enough vets in an area to bring a big one in. We did it the hard way. Axe. Pick and peavey. Two horses and dynamite. Chains. Plow. You lost gallons of sweat and the horses died of swamp fever. A kind of malaria. From the mosquitoes. A log house, twelve by ten, and crawl through the door.

If you were lucky you married a girl you loved and who loved you. Some of us just asked the first girl who looked good and laughed a lot. I know I did. After that first year I needed someone with me who was a laugher. Only this one laughed too much. She drove me nuts. It was better than nobody, though. Bachelors who came in hardly lasted more than a year. They'd just walk away. Credits gone. Just worn out. Walked away, sometimes without even saying good-by.

That was what it was like. I was lucky. The wife and I stuck it out for three years. That was to prove it. I'd lost all hope of ever making anything out of it. You just didn't have the money to make it go. My hope was, once I got the ownership papers I'd sell it. It did have a fair-to-middlin' shack on it then and I sold it all—forty acres broke and in timothy hay, the shack, a barn, two horses, and some equipment for $1,500—and when we walked away it was the hardest thing I ever did. Three and a half years of my best years and I had a thousand bucks in hand, another five hundred coming to me which I got five years later, by the way. Two suitcases and a few boxes and sacks and there was me and my wife starting out with hardly nothing. Sitting by the side of the road waiting for the mailman to take us down to Barrhead so we could catch the bus and take us out of that country.

I remember sitting in the bus and driving down the road and seeing all them nice farms. Everything looked so nice. It was autumn of '49 and winter was coming on and every farm looked prepared for it, all cleaned and cleared off and ready for the curling season to start, and I said to my wife, "How come we couldn't make it?"

I remember her saying, "I don't know, Bunny. Nobody ever worked harder than you did."

There you have it. I tried and I didn't make it and we went to Edmonton and I got on with the oil rigs and we made it that way. I guess I just wasn't cut out to make it by myself. There's a million guys like that. There should be some test you can take that tells you you'll never make it as a farmer although you would love to be one. Oh hell, they still were good days. Even when I knew I was losing, I guess we were kind of happy.

"NOTHING EXCITING ABOUT FARMING"

It is easy now as we sit here and look back down through those years, coming back with a dream I had had for four years in England and Europe, a dream of a farm of my own.

I got it, my wife and I got it through a great deal of hard work, and a tremendous amount of worrying, nights when I didn't sleep and my wife not sleeping because she knew why I was not sleeping, knowing I was thinking how we were going to make this place work, how we were going to make it go and, at times, how we were going to hang onto it.

All that is past now. One just does not think about it. Oh, there are times. Say we are driving back from town and I turn off the highway and coming down the gravel road and realizing when we reach the yard turn-off that for the past two miles I have been driving past my own land—and then I sometimes think how hard it all was to come by. It is then, I think, that I have a great affection for my wife and a great pride in ourselves for doing it, making it happen.

I joined the Army in '41 and I got back in '46. The Department of Veterans' Affairs was pretty active in those days and I went to see them because under the Veterans' Land Act I could claim credits. It was about that time when a lot of worn-out farmers were wanting to get off the land and their sons coming back from the war and, well, I don't think all that many were all that keen to go farming. They'd been away, seen a lot, did a lot, and they figured there were other fish to fry.

I won't go into it but there was one hell of a lot of paperwork, but I finally bought a quarter section two miles north of here, and the agreement was I'd work that place, which wasn't enough to make a living on, of course, and help Dad with his three quarters and live here on the home place and use his equipment, and we'd see how it all worked out.

I just couldn't say enough for those government men. You hear stories, guys beefing that the men put into these VLA jobs were retired civil servants and officers coming out who needed a cushy job, and I've got no doubts whatsoever that this happened and the veterans had to deal with people who knew absolutely nothing about land and farming. Thank God that didn't happen to me. There was one chap named Kennedy in Edmonton who was an absolute prince. He knew his business and he knew men and he made things a lot easier for anybody.

I got my land and my grant and I observed all the terms of our contract and paid my yearly bill and, thanks on top of all that, there were good crops. And then along came Leduc and there was good work during the winter on the oil rigs, and when the time came, I was able to take over from Dad and he moved to Red Deer, he and Mom.

There's nothing exciting about farming. That's just in novels. It is a lot of hard work during the hard-work times and keeping busy in the other times, and getting in some curling at the club and serving on the school board and going out to Rocky Mountain House or McBride for a moose in the fall and seeing your kids are brought up right and going to funerals and christenings and weddings and, well, just keeping your darned nose clean and paying your income tax, if you can figure it out, and trying to be a good husband, father, and Canadian. That's about it.

We've got a good farm here now. Hailed out once, so I think we're ahead of the law of averages. Prices go in cycles and you've got good years and bad ones and we've always had good crops, but the reason I'm saying all this is that I wanted to give some credit to the Veterans' Land Act. You see, when I got back I had no money—maybe a thousand dollars, which wasn't enough to sniff at when it comes to buying land, but with the VLA's help I got my foot in the door. With my dad's help I was able to cut expenses, and by working like the very devil I was able to buy more and more land—a 160 here, a 160 there, and I was deep in debt. Sure I was. Sure. But I could hang in and when I was in too tough I could go to Alex, the bank manager, and say, "Look, Alex, here's my situation." I don't think I could do it now with the young pups they've got in these branch banks now. Some of the stories you hear, they're right out of horror movies.

I worked hard, darned hard, but it was the VLA that gave me the step up. I think they helped a lot of young guys like me right out of the service.

Today? Well, I'll tell you. Even with five . . . no, ten Veterans' Land Acts, there is no way a young man like myself then—and I was a husky and eager twenty-three—there is no way a young man today can get started on a farm on his own and if he does, then he deserves to have his head read. That is the tragedy of the West. No small farms, and the big get bigger and when they get too big they run into a couple of bad years and then the banks move in and that is the end of the big farmer. That is the second tragedy of Western Canada today.

"VIABLE! SCHMIABLE!"

Eddie and I came from the same part of the Carrot River district and we knew each other, but just like two people would meet at a dance.

In fact, I didn't know he'd joined the Army until I met him when I was on a weekend leave at the recreational center in Winnipeg, the one they set up in the Eaton's store, which I think they used to call the Annex.

We were surprised to see each other and we danced and ate doughnuts and drank a lot of coffee, and then he walked me home to the YWCA where I was staying, and we were sure surprised that night to find we both were in Camp Shilo. I was driving the station wagon for the officers' mess and he was a corporal, an infantry instructor.

We saw each other a lot after that and one night we were sitting in the Red Cross Cottage having coffee and he asked me to marry him, and I sure did say yes in a hurry. We were married two months later in Carrot River. We had our furloughs, so that worked out to an eleven-day honeymoon. We wore our Army uniforms, of course. After all, we both were in the Army.

That was in April of '45 and the war was nearly over and the government had a policy of discharging CWACs when they got married, so about a month later I got out and went home to my folks at Carrot River. You could not find a place to live in Brandon, what with all the other Army and Air Force wives from stations and camps around, and besides, home was better. In June Eddie was discharged on a deal that said that men who had done farmwork before they joined up could get out to go back farming for the war effort.

We both wanted a farm, naturally being born on the farm, but Eddie had not much money and I didn't either and farm prices were high, so we decided to homestead on Eddie's Veterans' Land Act money.

I can't remember to this day what decided us, but I guess it was that it was too tough to open up new land around Carrot River and it was supposed to have the biggest mosquitoes in all of Canada and the coldest winter and I'm sure that's a fact. We read that the government of Alberta was opening up land north and west of a place called Pigeon Lake, so that spring—and that was in '46—we decided to drive out there and look. It was kind of a second honeymoon after both of us working hard all winter in town.

We made the trip in my father's old car and the government agent showed us land on a map and we had to find it. It was pretty well poplar scrub, and Eddie took a shovel and dug holes to test the soil and he thought it was pretty good so we put in our application for the half-section, which was only about four thousand dollars. Not a thing on it, a mud road for four and a half miles to it, and the nearest store was at Calmar in winter, although the lake did have a kind of store in summer for the summer cottagers. It was dreary when we moved in in July, and that was before our grant was approved.

Nobody should have had the life we lived for the next year. We had bought a granary, which was fourteen feet by twelve feet, in Calmar; it was to be a place to live until we built a house and Eddie hired a rubber-tired tractor to haul it with what stuff we'd brought out and had shipped from Carrot River. It had rained that week and it took us two days to get that shack on its skids over the mud road. It was a caution, and when we got it to the land he just parked the tractor about a hundred feet off the road, just nowhere in particular, and he said that would be our barnyard. God, when I think of it! How green we were, even though we were born and raised on farms. Eddie could have pulled that granary another four hundred yards to near where there was a little slough, a swamp, but he didn't. He was just too darn fed up, or maybe he thought that tractor didn't have enough in it to go another foot. If he had, I wouldn't have had to haul my water four hundred yards two pails at a time.

We couldn't drink the water, as you have probably figured out, but we dug a hole about three feet across and five feet deep and every morning there was enough seepage in it for about eight or ten pails of water. How tadpoles found their way into it I'll never know, but there they were by August, the end of it. We didn't care. Eddie would say, if you see dead tadpoles, stop using the water. There were no dead tadpoles. They just disappeared. Oh well, the water wasn't bad.

Naturally we couldn't do anything that year but kind of fix things up, and while I was trying to do something with the garage as a home, Eddie went picking roots and rocks for a farmer not far away and it was a dollar an hour and the noon meal. He used to come back every night so mad, and he'd say, "I'm picking rocks for the goddamned Bohunk at a hundred cents an hour in this African sun and he's one of the bastards that ran away and hid in the bush every time they sent the cops out to find him to put him in the Army." That was true, as other neighbors told us, and this farmer and a lot of others with those kind of names, they did it and they call themselves good Canadians. Eddie and me was never in the shooting part of the war and actually had it pretty good, but at least Eddie had signed up to kill Germans. He just never did.

Oh yes, the house. The shack. The granary. We hung two blankets across one end so that would be our bedroom—and why we did I don't know as we were the only people in it, but I guess I thought it was a bit of ladylikeness. Maybe it made up for not having a window. It had a door. Eddie cut out one and for a couple of months we hung a blanket over that and that gave us privacy from the grizzly bears and tigers and lions that were always around at night. You read about things like this, but we actually had a skunk living under the place. We had a Winnipeg couch that opened out into a bed, and four chairs we picked up for two bits each, or was it two bits for the four? Such a long time ago. What is it, forty years? I had a good old cookstove which we bought for two dollars. It would be worth a fortune now. People in the city go for those things now, but I could bake anything, cook anything, on that old black and chrome thing. An Empress. I loved the thing. For months our stuff from Carrot River was still in the boxes we'd shipped it in, and four of them made a table, one piled on another at each side, and then a sheet of plywood on top. We had three kerosene lamps.

How we lasted that winter I don't know. The deadfall Eddie hauled didn't last too long, even though we were using it half and half with green poplar Eddie had cut on the place, and no matter how much hay and marsh grass we piled against the walls and hammered it flat with flattened-out cardboard cartons it didn't matter. A bear about two years old and fat as a sow helped us through till Christmas because Eddie got it with one shot. That gave him the idea to go trapping but by Christmas he really had nothing to speak of, just a few skins, and I didn't know how to work them.

And remember, we were still squatting on government land and we didn't have an acre broken and the Veterans' Land Act business hadn't come through. The agent or whatever in Edmonton, he wrote us and said he was just too busy looking up and judging what he called viable locations. Migosh, I didn't even know what that word meant. "Viable." I looked it up in the dictionary when we next went in to Calmar and it said something that could or might be worthwhile. In other words our land was not worthwhile. Eddie and I sat there in that beer parlor there and he started to get drunk and so was I, I guess, and he'd now and again shout, "Viable!" It got so the bartender thought it was Eddie's way of ordering four more beers, and Eddie said that word a lot of times that afternoon.

By the time the neighbor who had driven us in to Calmar gets us out of there and we pick up our groceries at the store where I'd left the order and Eddie wants more booze, see? So he gets another case and about six miles down the road he tells the farmer to stop and he runs into a farm and there's an old Bohunk there who sells home-made whiskey and Eddie comes out with a pint of this stuff. I guess that was the last of his money for the day. Otherwise I'm sure he would have bought a gallon.

The neighbor's never been in our shack because his place is four miles further back by the main road, but he just drives us home because we got groceries and when he sees that shack, inside of it, I'm sure he's pretty surprised. I remember he said, "Shit!" and then apologized and he asked if he could sit down and the three of us are drinking beer and this Mr. Armitage, he starts asking questions: what we got, how much money, how much experience, our plans. Finally he slams his bottle down on that plywood and he says, "You can't, you cannot put in a full winter in this. We'll find you dead the first cold snap. Do you know, some days, when it warms up, the temperature can go as high as forty below zero?" That's one of the things that worried me, how to get firewood and water and, I guess, how to stop from freezing to death. I was sober because Eddie had been drinking three of the four of those glasses he'd been ordering. I got the whole message from the farmer and when he heard that we were just squatting anyway, he hit the roof. It even sobered up Eddie to a point where he could give a straight answer. That nice Mr. Armitage give us holy hell in a nice way, saying we'd be dead by freezing before February.

You want to hear more? Okay. Next morning Eddie, he's got this hangover that fills the granary, and he says to me, "Myrt, to hell with it. We're getting out." We were gone by noon, and by four we were in a hotel room in Edmonton. We left everything sitting there; we only took our clothes and a few little things I liked and Eddie's rifle and tools. We left the rest to the gophers and we never thought about farming again. "Viable!" Schmiable! What a dumb word. You'd never know what it meant from the sound of it, would you?

"THAT FARM WAS MADE FOR US"

I was bitter the way the Canadian government handled me in 1945 when the war ended and I'm still bitter.

First, you know my name is Bodnarchuk. It is Ukrainian. My parents, Nicholas and Sophia, came from the Western Ukraine in 1903. You're familiar with the description, the men in the sheepskin coats. That meant Ukrainians. Nicholas and Sophia and four of their kids. Six were born in Canada. I was the tenth, last. That was in 1914. Got those dates?

My father filed on a homestead about seventy miles northeast of Edmonton and that wasn't where most of the people from our part of Russia went. He felt it would be best for the family if they settled where English and Americans were taking up land and it was a good idea. I've met some of those other kids like me, born at that time and grown men to-day. You wouldn't believe it. They were born in Canada but they still have Russian accents. You'd think they just got off the boat five years ago.

Everything went into the pot to buy more land. This is the way things went. Good. By this time the family had a section and a quarter for hay and pasture. Dad was on the school board. My two teacher sisters had married but two more were teachers by then. We were kind of a teacher family.

Then we get the Depression. I don't think it was really the drought and the hoppers that got us—we always got crops—but it was the banks. Three of those quarters were still under mortgage to the Bank of Montreal and while we had wheat to sell the price was just not good enough. We had money coming in, but it wasn't enough to pay the interest after feeding the family. Then Dad died. A burst appendicitis which we didn't know. He lay there and wouldn't let anybody call the doctor. When my brother Alex got up enough courage to go to a neighbor it was too late. He just died. There was nobody to look after things. My mother knew nothing about finances and banks. So by 1935 we had lost the farm and we moved into Edmonton. I should say, it wasn't until about 1942 that anybody farmed that section again. That's the way it was.

Okay, why am I bitter? This way. From '35 to '41 I worked as a hired man. From the time I was fifteen and a man, I worked around the district, summer and winter. Then I join up. I think it's time I go. I'm going to be called up anyway. I thought it was best that I go. I was overseas for three years and I saw it all. Then I come back. On the ship there was an officer telling us what we could get when we were discharged. You could get to go to college. You could learn to be a welder at a technical school. But I pricked up my ears when I heard you could become a farmer and that was all I ever cared about. Just the soil. Things growing. Feeling good wheat slipping through your fingers when you put your hand up to the spout. Even throwing a fork of cowshit weighing half a ton. That's what I wanted. That farm.

I got home to Edmonton and I went right away with my wife and we started to look for a place to stay. She had the money she saved and I had the money, twenty a month, I'd sent her and with my $600 or so gratuities and my clothing allowance, we were fixed. So we talk it over. I buy two bottles of wine and we have our first meal in our new home and we talk. We got about two thousand dollars and I've got this

Canadian government booklet and I'm reading it to her. It doesn't say much. Just that I can get a farm.

Next morning, and this is about October, we head east and it didn't take long. We were looking at buildings as much as land and size. I had this list the real estate man had given me and the third farm we came to, that looked like it. We met the farmer and he was going to the Okanagan. To pick fruit and fish, he said. We spent all that day with him. The real estate man didn't do a lick.

Didn't work out. Remember my name? That's right, Bodnarchuk. The "chuk" is what you want to think about. Think of a dumb Bohunk eating a chunk of cucumber with black bread and drinking cheap wine. That's me. Except I had been a sergeant for the last two years of the war, I had two wound stripes, and I had refused a commission in the field. Not many sergeants are offered that. I only know of four in all the time I was overseas.

Off we go to the Veterans' Affairs. I've got everything I could possibly need. Everything. Papers, documents, and all I think I have to do is tell them where the farm is. They'll go out and assess it and I sign the papers.

I won't go into all this in too much detail. It is still painful. I was interviewed by what they called a development officer, a man who was trained to do the job. He was an Englishman. A fucking Englishman. An officer who had been stationed in Canada with the Canadian Army and had got discharged in Canada. Here he was, some Little Lord Fauntleroy and he's asking me all sorts of stupid questions when it is easy to see he doesn't know a one-way from a cow's arse. He knew nothing, and besides, he was against me because of my name. What's wrong with Bodnarchuk? You can die in battle with the name Bodnarchuk in your pay book just as easy as if your name is Smith or Jones. His was Little Lord Fauntleroy.

He wanted to know what farming experience I had and I said twelve years as a full-time hired man and I'd done everything. And here is this guy, this Englishman, even taking a job away from a Canadian. He is putting "Mr. Bodnarchuk" in front of every sentence and making it sound like a dirty name and his questions were so goddamned silly I wanted to reach over the desk and smash that silly look off his face.

I had every qualification. I had done everything that any farmer does, and I'd done it a dozen dozen times. I had the war service. I had the money to pay the tenth of my grant, the share the government said we had to pay. I had a wife to help me. Flora's a farm girl. I had no kids to slow us down the first two or three years. I was young. Goddamn it!

I was healthy. I ate nails for breakfast. You know what was wrong? My name was Bodnarchuk. If it had been Bodnar then it would have been okay. That's a Swede name, and Swedes are okay. They've got blond hair. But no, I was a Hunky. There it was, a Hunky.

They turned me down. It was this bastard that turned me down. His report said I was not suitable for farming. It said I did not have the practical experience. Sure, maybe I couldn't drive a tractor because there were no tractors on the farms I worked on before the war. Just horses, good farm horses. But I could learn to drive a tractor as good as any man in twenty minutes. Nope, that was it. And there wasn't even an appeal.

I said to hell with it. I went to my mom and I said I want $5,000. She said when? When. I said now. She'd been taking in boarders all during the war and made good money because a lot of those Americans, they didn't want to stay in barracks and Mom had this big house and about five bedrooms. Hell of a cook. She had a waiting list for these Americans and she also did catering at the officers' mess for parties and special events. She had a real good business going. Five thousand dollars, just like that, for her soldier son was nothing.

We bought the farm cash. The third one we looked at. Mom was happy to get three and a half percent like the government did. She didn't care. Her kids would get it anyway, and we worked out a deal that if she died before I'd paid it off, I'd pay the balance into the estate. Just a nice business deal.

No, Flora and me, we never looked back. That farm was made for us. We did well from the start. Never a bad year. Good crops, good prices. Fine, no complaints, but I wanted to tell you about that goddamned Englishman. I wonder how many guys with "chuk" on their names he stuck it to. Plenty, I'd bet.

"I NEVER LOOKED BACK"

I was a pretty nervy young bugger and I worked in the shipyard in North Vancouver in '41 and '42 and I made good money as a welder and I saved it. Boy, did I save! I didn't get involved in any of those crap games on the North Vancouver ferry on pay nights. A fifteen-minute run and I've seen guys lose their whole check in five minutes.

We were building Victories, which was the Canadian equivalent of the American Liberty ships—you know, those freighters that used to split in two. Hah! None of ours did. I could have worked the war there but I decided in January of '43 that I'd join the Navy and see the world, and before I signed on I took my savings and I put $5,000 on a twenty-seven-acre farm near Abbotsford. It had a stream running through the north end. Then I rented it to a family for fifty bucks a month and said good-by.

I came back in April of '46 and there is my farm and I'm now in the business of getting the family out of the house. I want it.

Now mind you, this was good land. Good, good land. The best, and the people hadn't cropped it. All they wanted was a house and a garage and the wife kept chickens and they had a couple of Shetlands for their kids. The old man was a vice-principal at the school. They just wanted a house where their kids could run around like little Indians, I guess.

I didn't get them out until June because of the school year, but I bumped their rent to sixty-five dollars and I lived, boarded in Abbotsford, which was just a tiny town then. Hell, I think it was a village. Once the Mennonites really started to take over, that's when things boomed. They didn't fight in the war, you see, and a whole pile came out from Manitoba during the war and picked off the good pieces. But that's not what I was going to say. They've got their religion and I've got mine. They've got their patriotism, which seems to be for themselves and their church, and I've got mine, which is for good old Canada.

Anyway, I go down to the town hall, the village hall, or whatever and it's about my property, some kind of drainage-ditch problem that the municipality has got to figure out. We're talking and the clerk pulls out the map and he says something like, "Oh, this property, a lot of people are interested in this piece." Okay, it's a good chunk of land with four good roads around it and close to the highway, so on and so forth, but I ask why people are interested. I tell him nobody has come up and asked me what I want for it.

He looks at me funny and he says that this property is going to be on the land sale coming up. The what sale? The land sale. And then I find out.

When I bought it I plunked down $5,000 in $100 bills and the lawyer had put it through the land titles office and the place was mine, lock, stock, and barrel. Everything—house, barn, hen runs, fences, the creek, and the squirrels in the trees. Now he's telling me this?

It seems that there was two years of taxes on the place, and somehow my sale had gone through without them being paid. Then I'm in the Navy three years and I don't get the notices. That stupid school teacher,

I guess. So it's five years and now the place is on the tax roll, ready to go for unpaid taxes, and I'm only finding out about it now. I ask what the taxes are and he says about seven hundred dollars, which sounded right to me and I could have written a check there and then, but I don't because he tells me not to. He says go to the auction, watch the bids being opened, just stay at the back in a corner and watch what happens. Mind, I'm not risking a thing because from the day of the tax sale I've got one full year to pay off and redeem the place.

Half the farmers in the district know the land is up for tax sale, and they want it. The clerk says he'll hold off my property until the rest of the bids have been opened and sure enough, the community hall has got this big crowd and I sneak in about two hours after the sale starts and my number comes up. Like, I was the last. The clerk reads off the rigamarole, the legal description, and then he says something like, "Well, folks, we've got a real bun fight here today," or something, but you don't get any laughs out of those Mennonite farmers and market gardeners. They've come to do business.

There are about twelve bids, and all are at the tax price. Oh, more than $700. Say, $747.78. You know how taxes are. Never clean-cut. Then the clerk says it's auction time and remember, I bought that land for $5,000 just three and a half years before. Away we go, as Jackie Gleason used to say.

Yes, I know it's crazy but the bidding starts at $700 plus and it jumps right off to $3,000 and then $3,200 and the $4,000 and there is no way. I think that land is worth $8,000 or so. By the time I stop thinking that price, it's up to $9,000 and then $10,000 and I think, these sod-busting Holy Rollers are here to buy. All the money they've made, all the high prices they got for their pork that was shipped to Britain, all the money they made in milk and eggs and corn and rye—they've got it all in their little old blue bankbooks and now they all are going for my land.

Finally it hits $14,250 and it's going, going and anyone else, no, and gone, and then I walk up to the front and I take out my bankbook and I said something like, "The war's over, you fellows," and I write out a check for the back taxes right there in front of them. I've had my fun, and I know now what the land is worth. Just what that town clerk told me to do: just try 'em out. I did and it worked. Everybody goes away and it's just about five o'clock and the clerk shuts her down and I invite him over to the Abbotsford for a beer and we're sitting there and all these farmers and their sons are sitting around, just looking at me. Boy, did they hate me! I'd made damned fools of them all.

Then one of these Old Jacobs comes over to the table and he wants to talk. I tell him I'm busy but I'll be home that night after supper, so if he wants to come over, sure, let him come. That night he does, him and his three sons, and I tell him what I have worked out.

I want $18,000. It's crazy, you know, but he's the guy who has the farm next to me, about five times bigger than mine, and you know how those Russians are. Land crazy. Buy it all up, buy, buy, and buy. I say I want $10,000 cash tomorrow and I want to hold the first mortgage of $8,000 at nine percent, which is high, and there's no pay-out clause until five years unless I say so. I want the acre of land that the house and barn and hen runs and well are on, and he has to pay for the survey of it. That's that, and then I tell a little white lie—big one, as a matter of fact. I tell him another guy stopped me on the street when I left the hotel and he's coming over tomorrow, but I don't say who. You know, if it's one thing those fellows hate, it is to be done out of a deal by one of their own.

Old Jacob—no, that's not his name; I just call all the old Mennonites that—Old Jacob and his sons clump out and I see them standing around their truck and then they come in and yep. Right there and then, he says okay, mister, I buy farm.

You know what? I should have asked for $20,000. Or $25,000. I'da got it.

No matter. I got a deal for the time and that $10,000 and another $3,000 of my own put me in business and I bought another place, and later I sold the acre with the house for $2,500 to one of his sons. I never looked back. I didn't make a killing out of that land, but that's the best deal . . . I mean the one I got the biggest kick out of. Those Mennonite boys maybe didn't go into the service, but I made them pay for it. What I made them pay for was a couple of pennies out of every pound of pork they sold during the war, every pound they probably sold on the black market when there was rationing. That made me feel good.

As I said, that wasn't such a big killing. I made better, lots better, during the crazy times later on, but what the hell, I guess that was the high point of my coming back into Civvie Street. You betcha. Bet your boots on that one.

"ONE OLD TRACTOR, DAMNED TIRED"

I wanted to farm. I honest to God did and I gave it my best shot, but everything was against me because when I got back to the home town, every man, woman, and cow thought I was still the kid I was when I joined up in '42.

You learn a lot over there, in the Army. You know, every kid of seventeen, every man jack of them, should be taken into the Army for two years. What they'd learn there would make this a better country, and there's not much you can find in that statement to say I'm wrong.

Anyway, everyone thought Jack Dickens, that's me, was a wild-eyed cayuse, but they saw me buckle down and the DVA helped me. I must have really given them a good line because they signed me up for the Veterans' Land business and I got the $6,000 credit and I was able to get half a section and a shack of a house and a barn that had a tipping-over look. I guess the whole countryside sat back to watch Jack Dickens make a mess of things. Well, I went belly up, but I didn't make a mess of things. I just couldn't beat the odds. They saw how I worked. Without a word of a lie I must have worked sixteen hours a day and I didn't have no wife to handle part of the load.

Give you an example. I'd grown up on Dad's farm, so I thought a farm had to have a few cows. But I found that was a lot of bunk. There's enough to do without some dumb cows. Cows gotta be milked. So after the second year I sold the cows, the big herd of four of them, and that relieved me of the milking and the bother and, well, I just hate cows to this day and I don't drink milk except in my tea because that's how much I hate cows. I'll say this, the cow is the dumbest goddamned creature God put on the face of the earth. There's only one thing a cow thinks about. Herself. When she's gonna be fed. Just like a woman.

Now about women. Glad you didn't ask. I was twenty-three and folks wondered if I'd sowed all my wild oats, which I guess I had, but I had no mind to go jack-rabbitting around the countryside. Sure there was girls, but so was there guys, driving their old man's shiny cars, taking them to dances or a show and dinner or maybe just taking them down lovers' lane for a goddamn screw, but what did I have? Four horses that I'd rescued from the glue factory when I took over that goddamned Thompson half-section with its Russian thistle and half of it coulee land and a crop of rocks. I didn't have any fancy duds. That hundred they give you for clothing when you get out, it didn't go for Sunday-go-to-meeting duds. I paid that to a lawyer to see that the place was fair and clear to buy.

I showed some of those jackasses, some of those smart-ass Mormons around there, because they laughed at me, right there in the beer parlor, where they shouldn't a been, seeing as how their religion says no beer, but I showed 'em because with four horses and some bust-up machinery I got off a crop in '46. Just enough to pay the bank on my loan and the Veterans' Land people and buy duds and grub and what you'd call the necessities of life.

Then that fall I was the laughingstock because I went to an auction and some widow was clearing out and I bought a mess of junk sitting in one corner of the yard that might have been a tractor. I'd gone over there the day before with my neighbor, so I knew there was nothing good I could afford. But I saw this tractor in the corner of the yard by some trees and I asked the auctioneer's helper to put it on his sheet because it wasn't on there. Mind you, before I done that I'd put quite a bit of time looking around that old tractor and I could see it wasn't as bad as it looked—but it was goddamned old, let me tell you, but she had something about her I liked. Something just told me. The auctioneer's kid asked me what make and year it was, because he couldn't be bothered going over to look at it, and I said I didn't know, just put down one old tractor, damned tired.

On the way home I told my neighbor I was going to buy that tractor and he said he'd seen me looking at it and he wondered why it hadn't been cut up for junk when they was going around to farms during the war getting metal for the war. He figured they figured it had not been worth even scrap.

Next day the tractor, she is on the bottom of the machinery list, and when it comes up everybody looks blank because they don't know what it is. See, they'd looked at everything else but not that. She was just junk to them. When the bid came up the auctioneer said twenty-five dollars and nobody spoke and he dropped her to ten and when nobody spoke he backtracked again and said five and I put up my hand and everybody laughed and that's the way I got her.

After the show—'cause everybody was laughing about me after that, this dumb kid Dickens buying a dollar's worth of junk for five—I went to see the widow because I figured her old man might have been the first owner. Those old guys had a way of keeping stuff like that around. You know, their first tractor. First combine. You've seen it.

"Sure," she says. "You bought that?" She says, "Why, that's Dad's first tractor, the Rumley. He used to call it Ellie. From Model-L, because that's what it sold as. I think he got it in '25 or '26, like just after our second boy was born. The first one born in Lethbridge. I had the first two right here in the house."

She was ready to go on and on telling me the story of her life, but

I asked her how long her husband had used it and she said, oh, she figured up until ten years ago, and I knew I was right. That tractor still had some spark. And then she said something that made my heart just go whoosh, upward. She said she still had the old manual for that Rumley, and next day when I drove over with my tools and things I thought I'd need, she had found it. First thing, I hitched up two of her horses that hadn't gone yet and I towed that thing into the center of the yard and I went to work.

You know, there wasn't much wrong with it. You can't reckon good as new, but in two days I had her apart, cleaned, oiled, fitted, tightened, and another five hours on the rust and I had her looking good. The old lady said to take anything I wanted out of the workshop and I put on some blue paint with white trim and by God, I had me a tractor. She had a good thump to her exhaust when she blew and those old big wide steel wheels, they just kept her steady and even, and I got her home in about eight hours—and by God I didn't take her down any side roads where the going was easy. I took her right down the side of the highway and through town and then I stopped at the hotel for a couple of beer, just so everybody could see what I had done.

People in that part of the country don't come up to you and say what a good job you've done, or that field of barley you've got across from the school looks like the best in the county. No, they're not like that. A lot of them farmers are pretty straitlaced, but afterward I noticed when I went to town those farmers I'd only said hello to or met at some meeting, they'd come around and pull out a chair and order two beer. Listen. Before I bought that five-dollar tractor and made it work, I was just a kid out of the Army trying to make a go of it on a piece of land nobody wanted in those days. They'd jump at that land now, but not then.

They'd talk about the crops or the weather and then bring the talk around to that tractor and finally they'd have to ask how it worked. They was just dying to know. I'd say something like, "She's small but she's light on fuel and she'll out-pull any ten elephants you'd like to know." Things like that. Kind of rubbing it in, a bit.

Seems like this story is more about a tractor than me, but anyway. I guess it had to happen but the next year—that would be '47—I got hailed out and if that hadn't of happened I'd of been burned out, that being the kind of year it was; and if that hadn't of happened, then the Royal Bank would have jumped in and wiped me out. No, it was '48. Yeah, '47 was a poor year and that's why I was in such bad shape and '48 I was hailed out and that did it. I was finished with farming and it did break my heart, but I didn't have much and no wife to grieve with me, so I just turned the key one morning and walked into the bank in Lethbridge and dropped the house key on the manager's desk. Told him there was a farm he'd just added to his collection and he'd better get somebody out there because those four horses had to be fed and there was some chickens scratching around and if he didn't get somebody out quick those goddamned Mormons would be poking around by sundown and they'd lift everything that wasn't nailed down and pry up that what was nailed down.

The Rumley? I sold it to an implement dealer in Lethbridge who kind of liked its style. I got $200 for it, and whether he liked its style or not, I'll bet he sold it for $400. I just wasn't waiting around to do it myself.

"JUST A FARM BOY AT HEART"

I have nothing to say about my war, other than that I found it horrifying and immensely entertaining and I enjoyed it and wouldn't have missed it for all the world. Enough has been written about that part of it, and most of it by generals and politicians and they seemed to have quite a different viewpoint that I had and have today, so shall we let it pass, please.

No, I won't get into that one. Sure, I've read novels on war, but I doubt if many or any of the writers ever saw a platoon go forward or in with a bunch of your guys trying to stop a tank attack. There is just no way to write about it as it actually happens. Suddenly it is quiet and it is all over and if you are still alive and not wounded, you look at your watch and see that it is thirty-five minutes later and you can't remember a single damn thing that happened and what you did. So enough of that. Everything is made up. I'm convinced of that.

No, I didn't have the slightest idea of what I wanted to do when I came out. I was twenty-five. I had two wounds, one of which I get a pension for, small but still my monthly reminder, and it had no effect on me then or now and, to be quite honest, I had not thought a single thought about what I wanted to do. I just couldn't hang around the house listening to the radio and waiting for the paper boy to bring the *Tribune*. If you went down to the Legion the old guys there kind of made you feel unwelcome, as if you were from another war and only their war, my dad's war, meant anything at all. It was summer, you see, early June, and I felt I wanted to get away from everything, so one day I told the folks I was going to hitchhike around and see a bit of the country, which I should say was not easy in those days unless you wore a uniform and I wasn't about to do that again.

So next morning I filled up my kit bag with a few clothes and stuck out my thumb and the first fellow that stopped was a farmer. Yep, in an old farm truck, and I remember I had to keep moving my butt all the time because there was a spring in the seat that kept trying to go up me, and I'm squirming and he's talking and he'd been in Winnipeg looking for a farmhand. I says it looks like he hasn't had any luck because I'm the only body in the cab and there's nothing but a bunch of boxes and stuff in the back.

Portage La Prairie is about an hour and a half down the road and he spent that time trying to convince me that I should come and work for him all summer. When I said I'd think it over, he spent the next half-hour telling me that I wasn't big enough and strong enough and smart enough to be a farmhand and that he'd have to teach me everything. And he spent the next hour trying to tell me I really wasn't worth any money at all and that's when I stepped into the argument. You know, in that short time everything turned right around. Just like my hand is doing now. I knew right then what I wanted to do. I wanted to be in the outdoors and I wanted to do some hard work, some satisfying work, a lot of honest work again, and I wanted to feel good old sweat just pouring down my back and down my legs and into my boots. And I wanted to talk to real people again and to eat some honest-to-God-and-you-better-believe-it home-cooked food and drink lots of milk and smell things growing and pull up a carrot out of the garden and wash off the good prairie dirt and just eat the damned thing right then, crunch, crunch, crunch. And by God, I wanted to eat about six cobs in a row of Golden Bantam corn slathered with butter. Let's put it this way: I just wanted to get away from the whole business and take a look into my head, as the kids say today, and that's why I lit out from the house for the summer. And the first time I put out my thumb, here comes this Dodge half-ton truck with this farmer in it. I can look back on it and call it fate.

We stopped in Neepawa at the Chinese café and I could see the guy, this Webber, the farmer, was well liked as everybody said hi and so on. It was dinner, right on noon, and I had a meal and if I recall it was forty-five cents, soup, meat, potatoes. You always got rice pudding in those days for dessert and they hadn't got around to charging you six bits extra for coffee. But I can always remember, even now, that in those days they'd bring you your cup with the cream or milk in it and you didn't know whether you were drinking coffee with cream or milk with coffee.

If I was going to enjoy a farm holiday doing a lot of hard work, I wanted to get paid for it—but the darndest thing was, I didn't have the slightest idea of the going rate. I'd have welcomed one of his friends to stop by and say, "Hey, Allan, I hear we're going to have to pay ten dollars a day this year for farmhands." Something like that.

I fished and he kept trying to get me to come out and look the place over, and I could see that he had his eyes on me, a big and strong, husky sort of guy and, as it turned out, being of English parents and Anglican, that was just up his alley. And finally I said, "I'll give you four days free, the rest of the week, and then we'll talk it over and if you don't want me, okay, and if I don't like the place, okay, and that's it." No, I don't know what made me say that. It wasn't from any Canadian Army smarts I picked up in those years. Just something that went zing, zing through my mind. You read, a writer says, somebody's eyes lit up. Well, his did. This was just the kind of deal he wanted. It was what I wanted, too, no strings attached and a few days of working, getting into a kind of work pattern, and learning a bit, maybe only a tiny bit, about farming. Farmwork is what I mean.

It was the prettiest farm about fifteen miles away, and I wondered with all this talk of rationing and shortages and the like where he got the red paint for the barn and the white for the house, and everything was kept neat and trim and a monk from Tibet could have seen this Webber was a good farmer. Wheat, oats, barley, green feed, beef, milk cows, hogs, chickens—what a farm is supposed to be and what it isn't today where there isn't even a chicken on the place and no self-respecting crow would sit on the nearest telephone pole.

I knew I would like it from the moment we drove into the yard, and it was at the end of a long row of elm trees and a high caragana hedge and that sort of set the scene. I met his wife and I'll still say she was sure one fine woman, and the bunkhouse was clean as a pin. It couldn't have been cleaner and, you know, there was a coal-oil lamp for reading and a washstand and a towel and soap and a shelf of books—and I could say something about those books—and even quite a few workclothes, pants, shirts, rainwear, boots, and damned if they didn't fit like a glove, and even a bit of carpet on the floor. I didn't tell Old Webber this, but I could have said, you must have known I was coming home. That's it right there. It felt like home.

That Sunday I went to church with them and we had a big dinner and my muscles were still aching more than fiercely and I knew the old bugger had been working the ass off me. I was doing things around that place I knew just weren't done all the time. He had one patch on which he grew rocks, about six, eight acres, and he put me on that for a day, and if you want to break a man's spirit put him picking rocks, and these were daddy-size and mummy-size rocks. No kid stuff. Oh well. I did carpentry and haying, fixed fences, weeded her big garden, and I wasn't putting everything I had into it for him—I guess I was doing it for myself. And I felt good at night and slept like I had never slept before, until six A.M., that is, and ate those wonderful, wonderful, just wonderful meals. She wasn't trying to impress anyone, which was what I liked. She just laid out wonderful meals for her husband and their son and two daughters and me, all those five days I was there and I could just feel that contentment growing in me.

On Sunday night I'm reading a book in the bunkhouse and there's a knock and it has to be old Webber and he comes in and sits in a chair and grunts and takes out his pipe. Funny thing about that pipe. He smoked it a lot but he didn't use tobacco. Nothing. He just smoked it empty. I never forgot that. Maybe guys like us who smoke like chimneys should try that.

He says, "Ronnie, the missus and me have talked it over and she thinks it might be handy to have you around."

Not do you want a job, will you stay, we like you, you're a good worker, Grant and the girls like you, the cows like you, the chickens do, too. No, just that using his wife's name he was saying he wanted me to stay. A lot of people are like that and they aren't fooling a soul. It didn't make me mad or vex me. I kind of had a quiet chuckle. I knew I damned well wanted to spend the summer there with this family, but I wasn't going to work for six bits and a smile at the end of each day, no matter how pretty the daughters were. I just took the bull by the horns, thinking most of the guys overseas aren't back yet and won't be for a few weeks, a couple, three months, and I said, "Mr. Webber, six bucks a day, board and room and Sundays off and I get the use of the truck and your gas on Sunday. Otherwise I'll be off tomorrow to visit my sister in Calgary. She's your bet now."

I thought that was putting it on a business basis, man-to-man, and remember I had had absolutely no experience in job or wage bargaining because I never heard of anyone in the service who could bargain or demand.

He stood up and said, "Fair," and shook my hand. "You're worth four dollars now but in a month, when the real work starts, you'll be worth six, so I'll finance your apprenticeship until then," and I added that I wouldn't be using the truck every Sunday, although I guess I had some old-fashioned country-style courting in mind when I put that into this contract and the Sundays I wasn't away I went to church in my best Sunday-go-to-meeting duds with them, and somehow that pleased them mightily.

Happiest summer I ever spent. Absolutely no doubt about it. The best. I worked myself into wonderful shape and cleared up my mind throwing out great bucketsful of that service junk I'd piled up in five years. I made good money and ate wonderful food and got my courting done right on the farm, and when I could I read those books in the bunkhouse and that gave me the idea: I'd go back to Winnipeg and to the University of Manitoba. Those books were university books—history, literature, economics, poetry. They opened doors I didn't know were there. Who would have thought one of our family would go to college? Those things did not happen. I guess I was the first, as long back as I know of anyway.

As I said, a wonderful summer and I was pretty much part of the family and when the end of September rolled around I had my pay, my six bucks a day, which I hadn't spent a nickel of because I had a chunk of my Army discharge pay. And the day I left, when Webber took me into Neepawa and drew out my pay, I didn't count the roll he handed me, but on the bus I did and it was all in tens. That was like him. A twenty-dollar bill to an old-fashioned farmer like that . . . You know, to the son of the son of the son of the soil, I guess a twenty-dollar bill must have seemed sinful. But there was one twenty in it with a note attached to it and it said, "Good work, good luck and come back." I knew what the come-back part meant. I had a hunch from the beginning that he wanted me to get serious about his eldest daughter, just the right kind of girl for a farm wife although she did become a nurse. But in my first year of university I met another girl.

Now, I did write to them but I never went back and I sometimes kick myself for this, but past regrets don't make rays of sunshine in a man's heart. Yeah, I would have liked to have gone back the next year, but their son had come back from the Army that winter and . . . well, let's put it this way. It is a farm tradition that the eldest son inherits the farm or takes it over when the old folks are too worn to carry on; and if I had gone back next summer, or hell, even visited them or something, I have a strong feeling I might have ended up marrying the daughter. Then there would have been the son, myself, and the younger son, the kid of the family, plus the two daughters, and I didn't think all that would work too well. It was only a section and a half, and not big enough. So, well, what I'm trying to say in my fiddle-foot way is that it was best the way it did work out.

I finished university, got my degree, and set out into the world with about ten thousand other veterans like myself and I think we all did well. I still see their names and pictures cropping up in the paper, in politics, in business, and despite the weird mass we were the first autumn at the Broadway Campus in Winnipeg, I think we all did pretty well. No regrets. Life is too short. I still remember that summer, and while I was city-born and bred and lived in it continuously since the war, I like to think I'm just a farm boy at heart.

6 THE SHEEPSKIN PARADE

6 THE SHEEPSKIN PARADE

On registration day in September 1945 they hit the counters like wolves descending upon the unsuspecting fold. Across the nation the administrators and clerks of Canada's colleges and universities reeled back in shock. They thought they were prepared for the enrollment of veterans, but nobody had told them it would be like this.

Classrooms, corridors, and campuses were never the same again.

At the University of Manitoba I recall there were six or seven of us to every Bunsen burner in the chemistry lab, and every one of us bitching, asking why we had to take all this useless stuff when we were going to be writers and lawyers and school teachers.

Please believe it: it was tough sledding, competing with bright young minds fresh out of high school, whereas many a vet's brain had rusted considerably during the five years he had been out in the world.

There was not much playing around. Hard work was the order of the day. They scrimped and they saved; they got summer jobs so they could have a few extra bucks to make the next year possible. Then, at the end, they got the prized key to the future: the sheepskin . . . the diploma.

"THE CANADA YOU SEE TODAY"

I can't say I succeeded beyond my wildest dreams, but I'd never be where I am today if it weren't for my country. That marvelous opportunity it gave me. Sounds corny? Well, let it be.

I've had my success and my failures over the years, but when I came back, Canada gave me the chance to go to university and that's something that I could never have done. No, no, never. University before the war was something so unattainable for the vast majority of Canadians that it never even entered their minds.

A father would never say, "I want my son to go to university and become a lawyer." He would say, "I wonder if I can convince the foreman to take him on in the roundhouse and apprentice as a mechanic." Oh yes, despite all the things others may say, that was the long and the short of it. Just get a job where you could rise up—slowly, mind you—in pay and be like your father, have a wife, a house, and bring up some kids the right way.

My country provided this son of a roundhouse mechanic with a chance. They gave me a chance in the Air Force to fly bombers and I didn't let them down. They gave me a chance in peacetime to go to university and I didn't let them down.

In the service I was fighting for my country. We all were. We all did one hell of a job. You know that. In peacetime I was fighting for myself, and the wife I would have and the children I would sire.

You know what? Through those years before I graduated from Law, if I ever flagged, if I ever thought, "Is all this crap worth it? Why do I do it?" I would think of one thing. When there was a rush job, meaning overtime, my dad would phone home and say he would be four, six hours late and mother would pack up a cold supper for him and I'd take it down to the CN yards. I'd go in and there were those big steam locomotives, huge, wonderful things, and the noise, the god-awful noise, and the hammering and steel pounding on steel and shrieks of machinery, and there would be my dad, amid all this, surrounded by all this hell. Eight hours a day, and he welcomed, he prayed, for overtime. Why? Plain as the nose on your face. Four hours of overtime, six, would mean a few extra dollars on his paycheck. That's how things were. He prayed for overtime, working in a madhouse like that, so there would be five bucks more in his pocket.

When I was going at it hard, saying these professors are stupid, hopeless, and the law is an ass, I'd think of Dad.

I worked hard. It was all work and no play for most of us. At times I cursed the government because the sixty dollars a month we got allowed you to exist, to carry you on, to pay the bills—but only. It was the carrot at the end of the stick. One more month and you'll get another sixty dollars and that will see you through another month. Keep trying, fellow, keep trying. You'll get there. You're halfway through. Not far to go.

I bless the Canadian government for doing this. It turned out in the DVA program the finest doctors, engineers, lawyers, accountants, teachers, architects. Look around you. The Canada you see today is the Canada those veterans built when they came out. There is no doubt in my mind.

"IT WAS WORK, WORK, WORK"

It was a damn shame, really. Higher education, the university, was there for the asking but just not enough of them could look far enough ahead and see the benefits.

I can think of one, a fellow from Sudbury, and he enrolled with me at the University of Toronto. He was a navigator in the Air Force and we met in the line-up to enroll for studies. We hit it off and in the first month two others joined us, so we were like a little club of four. We'd eat lunch together and have a couple of beers after classes. Harold and Frank and Randy—all three of them had been officers like I had been and all three dropped out after the first year.

We were in Arts, but Randy had high aims of being a lawyer. He would have been a good one. I didn't know what I wanted to be. I guess the idea of going to university appealed to me very much. I suppose I thought it would set me apart from the rest of the Armstrong clan. Teaching, perhaps, but when I look back it was not such a lucrative profession as it is now.

The government paid our tuition and gave us sixty dollars a month during the school year, but you had to keep up your grades, too. It was pinch-penny all the way. You couldn't live on the sixty dollars, not with about forty dollars going for a room in a boardinghouse and two meals. That left twenty dollars for everything, including streetcar, snacks, supplies, clothes, shaving stuff, and there was no provision in the budget for anything of a social nature.

There was also the workload. The math, for one thing. I don't think any of us had seen a table of logarithms for five, ten years, and there were papers piled on papers, and even in first year they had this inhumane system where forty percent of your final mark was from term papers, so they had to be done. Today I understand there is a very widespread system of ghosts in the colleges whereby a person can buy an essay already done, or written to order. Not then. Besides, none of us could afford them, even if.

The dominant thing, I think, was the light at the end of the tunnel. None of us could see it. We knew that if we graduated, there might be no jobs. Remember, the university had a big enrollment even before we came out of the services and made life miserable for the administration. These students, all younger and just as eager and still living at home if they lived in Toronto, we knew these kids would graduate one, two years ahead of us. When they had picked over the jobs, would there be anything decent for the rest of us? That was the problem.

So Frank dropped out at Christmas. He had a girl and they wanted to get married. These chaps who dropped out were the ones who wanted to get going, get moving, not necessarily get married, but they saw the good years ahead passing by and they were still in school. They wanted to make money, get a car, be able to take a girl down to Fort Erie or just take out a girl, anywhere. Of course they couldn't. They were chained to their education, and it was a heavy and short chain.

The day the semester ended, the four of us with probably two bucks to spare went out and got a buzz on. We were trying to persuade Frank not to quit and when it all ended, he had almost convinced Randy and me that it was not worth it. In the end, Harold didn't show up for classes in the new year so I guess Frank's arguments had convinced him. Two down and two to go.

I took the bus down to Guelph for Christmas and got a week in at the Biltmore hat factory where I'd worked for three months after discharge, and it gave me another taste of working and what a lousy prospect my life would be if I just stayed there. Fortunately, I had a mother who was a Scots Presbyterian and you know how strong they were on education. She convinced me to stay. I think the thought of it being free reinforced her arguments. That, and having an Armstrong with a college degree. Hah!

Randy and I slugged it through the rest of the year. The gruesome twosome, as we called ourselves, and our social life was nil and there were no Saturday or Sunday jobs to be had. A blessing, maybe, because it was work, work, work and all these high school subjects they threw at us. Just as an aside, not one subject I belabored for in those four long years has been of the slightest use to me. I suppose I can conduct a more intelligent conversation at a company dinner or a cocktail party, but not one helped me in business.

But, if you could write "Graduated, Arts, University of Toronto, 1949" on a résumé, then that was half the battle. Too much emphasis on a degree, then and now. I'm not sure the universities today even are in the business of teaching. Wouldn't you say they are in the business of providing tenure and jobs for their highly bloated faculty staffs?

Anyway, enough. Randy told me even before the first year finals that he was going back to Sudbury. He had tried higher education and found it wanting. He thought he was still a good enough hockey player to play for the Sudbury Wolves. The Wolves, wasn't that the name? If he could make the team he could get a good job in the smelter and he'd be set for life.

I was beginning to get up some enthusiasm for university then, through no fault of the faculty. With double or triple the previous classes, a student was pretty well on his own. The professors you rarely saw and the assistant professors did little more than direct traffic in those huge classes and hand out assignments. I doubt if they actually marked the papers. I think they looked at the first page of the paper and if it was neat they gave it a B. Untidy, a C. If it was in a girlish hand, a C plus.

No, Randy had had it, and I couldn't give him all the arguments and advice and encouragement he needed, because he had a good brain, but it was, oh, the drudgery of it all and the old buildings and the senseless formality of it all. Education then, you know, really was in the dark ages. The only change, the Parker pen had replaced the quill pen.

So he left the next fall I noticed a great many others had left. Off to get a good job, I mean. A good job meant good pay. Nothing more. It was a shame. Almost a tragedy. That Class of '49 was the brightest of all, ready to build Canada, which it did, but so many of the brightest were missing. I guess you could say the government's intentions were of the best, yes, but the post-war economics of it had stacked the deck against them.

"THE FRILLS WERE CUT OUT"

The University of Saskatchewan was jammed. I've heard every Canadian university was, but U. of S. was something to see. Apparently the student population had more than doubled. The vets, naturally. The DVA made it so easy. I was told almost fifty percent of people in the armed forces had a high school diploma. Now, that surprised me because I know that in the Army the troops I worked with as an educational officer, I know that far, far less than that had their matriculation. I suppose the Air Force and the Navy boosted the percentage much higher.

The setup was that if you were able to handle it, the administration ran courses so you could take your four years to a BA in just over two years. It was sweatshop all the way, long hours, classes, courses during the five month spring/summer break, but you could do it if you had the resolve. I did it. I think about sixty percent of those who started out on that path graduated in two years. The frills were cut out, you see.

This was probably the first major step forward in the Canadian higher educational system in decades, eliminating the frills, the courses you did not need, the frilly-frollery of it all. You were in university to work and that was putting it mildly. But being the academic system, as soon as the crunch was over, they started to put the frilly-frollery back in, and now it is three times worse than it ever was.

You lived in a boardinghouse, or two or three of you shared an apartment. In our case, my wife and I and two other couples shared a big house we rented, and we were lucky to get that. It was work, work, work, and more work and a few beers and a few laughs on Saturday night and that was about it.

I mean, the veterans we knew did not participate in campus life. All they knew about campus life was what they read in *The Sheaf,* which was the campus newspaper. That life was a world away. It was work, get that degree, beat the others out for the vice-principalships, and pray.

You might call it rewarding. You couldn't call it fun by any stretch of the imagination. A lot of the vets were under marital tension. Their marriages were too new, too shaky. The instructors were not of the best, and I can vouch for that. The best probably were in the agricultural faculty.

But we kept going, and my wife and I shared our little triumphs and she did research for us. The other two chaps in the house were also teachers going for the degree. She typed all our essays on a typewriter the three families had rented. Each wife on succeeding Saturday nights cooked a huge dinner for the six of us and that was something, the competition among the women to come up with a feast. On the fourth Saturday of each month we'd all go out for dinner to Saskatoon's one good Chinese restaurant and absolutely eat our fill. For, say, twelve dollars. Fifteen dishes, I believe.

No babies were allowed. If one of the girls had become pregnant that would have been a problem. So, strict birth control. Fifteen hours of hard work before bed time, that was our birth control, I think. Hah!

We made it. We all graduated. We all got jobs. The system needed young male teachers and we all became teachers. We saw each other at the Easter conventions, but that was about it. We had been like a SWAT team, if you'll pardon me being outrageous. We had formed together with our wives for one target: to get ourselves through that degree course in two years. That was our objective. And it was done. So when it was done we disbanded. That was all. Thanks Jim, thanks Rodney, so long Marilyn, so long Helen, it's been good to know you all and good luck.

"GIVING CREDIT WHERE IT IS DUE"

I was like nine out of ten; we came back and eventually found the job we stuck with for the rest of our lives. I suppose you've heard it all before and it can be pretty dull. I'm different, though.

I had Grade Five. I was born on a farm near Rossburn and the Donalds were in that part of the country early and we had small farms. They wouldn't be a patch on the farms today, but remember this was the Depression I am talking about. I was yanked out of school when I was in Grade Six. There were no truant officers in those days. Not in the small farm districts. Couldn't afford them. It was dog eat dog then. It was Depression time, about 1933. I worked around the farm and for neighbors, things like that, and in '40 I joined the Army. I suppose if I had had a high school certificate I could have joined the Air Force, but most farm boys just seemed to head for the Army. I suppose it was because of the outdoor life we had. The Army seemed to be the natural thing. Besides, my father had been in a Scottish regiment in the last war. I think he would have thought of the Air Force as being sissy and the Navy as being unnatural.

In '40 I joined the Army and in '45 I got out. Back from Europe. In the last two years I'd seen more of life and death and general hell than anybody. That was a year in Italy and the rest in northwest Europe. I was glad to get out and it didn't take me long to realize that a Grade Five education wasn't going to get me anywhere, and by anywhere I didn't mean going back to the farm. My brother ran it now and I seemed to be closed out.

In the Army you learn how to fire a Bren and run a carrier and do emergency first aid and forage for food and things, and you learn them well, but the only time you're going to fire a rifle in civilian life is when you're out deer hunting. In short, I had very little education and no skills at all, and here I was out on the street against an awful lot of fellows who had Grade Ten or Eleven and had done some reading and knew what they wanted to do.

That was when I ran into the lady I'm going to tell you about. She, well, you've never heard of her. Her name was Beatrice Brigden. I remember her, she was good-looking and had a good strong jaw that meant business, but she was very kind. All I know is what she told me about herself. I'd say that she would have been called a strong women's liberator today. She was then. She had been a teacher and had gone to college. At the time I'd say she might have been forty-five. Probably a spinster. She seemed that way.

All in all, this is how it happened. I was living in a rooming house and had no job. Remember, there were a lot of guys coming back and getting fifteen dollars a week and happy to have them. Thirty, that would be a good wage. I wasn't even getting the fifteen-dollar type of jobs offered. Humping coal for a fuel company, twelve bucks. That was the kind. I'm feeling blue this night and an Air Force guy in the next room named Ted Bailey tells me I should go down and see the Unemployment Insurance Commission. Be sure and ask for a lady called Brigden. Say you've got to see her.

I go down there next day and sure enough, she is there and her job is to help servicemen like me. Those that don't have much education and have never worked at a steady job and were in the service for four or five years and now we're out on Civvie Street and we don't know what's going on.

I'd been there before, but her little green office was different. It was kind of warm. There were two or three nice little pictures on the wall and she had a vase of flowers on her desk. You remember little things like that. It seemed so ungovernment. Made you feel at home.

We talked that morning and she made me feel special. She talked about education and what I read. I hadn't done any reading since I was a kid. She talked about projecting your personality and putting a bright face to the world and being positive. She was way ahead of Norman Vincent Peale, let me tell you that. Everything she said made sense. In a nutshell what she was saying was she could get me a job, but it wasn't the job I should stay with and I should go to night school and upgrade. Get the high school diploma. It wasn't too late. She said lots of servicemen were doing it and she didn't say, dummy, get smart. Nothing like that. This is forty years past, but I can still see her. She should have married. Somebody would have got a wonderful wife. So there it was. Would I? I said yes and she clapped her hands and said "Good man!" She had a strong voice. I think she would have been a good public speaker. She could tell you things simply, but they were important things.

What happened was this. Right then and there she phoned. In five minutes she had got me a job working mornings as a warehouseman at Marshall Wells. Eight to noon, four hours and at sixty cents an hour, which was good. That made it just about fifteen dollars a week and although it was heavy work, all the big country orders going out, it was only half-day. That woman worked wonders. Just like that. A job. A clean one, too. No more coaldust. No more broken back.

Next thing, she phoned and got me on at a special school, the afternoons. The government paid for that and paid me a little maintenance. It was about twenty dollars a month and that was just fine. With that and my sixty dollars at the hardware, making eighty dollars, and my room and board only forty dollars, I was all set to go.

So I went from one to five at the special school which was filled up with veterans. This was the winter by now and nothing doing much and studying nights I did Grades Six to Eleven in five months and passed. No, that's not a record. I don't think so. They just piled the stuff on you and if you didn't handle it they slackened off. As long as you could keep up, they poured it on. I'd study four hours a night but it was fun. I think that's what maturity does for you. My job at Marshall Wells was brainless; a robot could do it. Load, shove, and unload. Work at the school was hard work, but it was fun and I enjoyed studying. Anyway, six or seven months later, about June end I wrote my Grade Eleven finals and passed.

It wasn't like regular school, naturally. They skipped a lot of subjects, things that they think kids need but that men already know. Commonsense subjects, usually, and in Grade Ten and Eleven they just taught you things they knew were important. I can't think of the school. It was a business school, oh yes. They were getting good money from the government, I'm sure of that. Very sure. But they had good teachers and they used to say it was a pleasure working with us. Not like a bunch of kids. We were desperate to learn. There may have been some dummies in the classes, but they didn't show up too badly. We just pitched in and worked like blazes, like the very dickens. When we got past a course and did well, I remember the bunch of us would trot down to a beer parlor and celebrate. No school kids had ever done that before. No sir. No. That was a new one on the teachers.

In August I got my marks back from the government and I'd passed. A great big B. I think that's the way they graded. I'd been keeping in touch with Miss Brigden, you know, and that day I phoned her and she was happy as I was and I invited her out, but she said no, she'd invite me out. Here I was, one of the dozens she must have counseled, and she was inviting me out. I remember, it was a Saturday and we went to a little restaurant on Portage Avenue. She could have been my mother and here we were on a date and when we finished this little lunch, chatting away like old friends, she said she'd have my teacup read. The old woman had a big wart on her cheek. Funny, but I remember that. She said this was a happy day for me. She could tell by my face. She said I would be doing things to do with rivers and lakes and I said I didn't intend to become a *coureur de bois,* but that went over her head. She was Russian or something. So that was a happy day with Miss Brigden.

The tea lady was right. I worked another year, half a day at Marshall Wells and six hours driving cab for Moore's, and piled up some money and then I went to university. It was easy the first two years because I read all the books ahead of time and that let me go on driving cab, and then into the guts of university engineering course. I graduated in '51.

I did a lot of work the first ten or so years on bridges and dams and construction. So, in a way, the Russian tea lady's prediction came true. She was just guessing, of course.

But this is about Miss Brigden. I'd sent her a Christmas card for a while, but other things got in the way. I never heard of her again. I suppose she's dead now. She was a wonderful woman. A keen insight into people. She turned my life into the right channel. I'm sure she helped a lot of others. I know of at least three, guys like me who would have wound up as foremen doing nothing work.

I believe in giving credit where it is due. That's why I'm telling this story. Miss Brigden.

"IT IS NOT WHAT YOU KNOW"

If you want, I can take you in twenty minutes to the damndest, the very damndest thing that happened to me or anybody on this coast during the war and that was the top thing, the very top thing in my military career.

You see, those eggheads in Ottawa thought the whole Japanese Navy was going to come steaming up through English Bay and take Vancouver, and boom, there would go the war. This was in '38 or so, when everybody was doing their heavy thinking about Hitler and his gang, but out here a lot of people thought about the Japs.

So they put up field guns and anti-aircraft guns, searchlight batteries, and, well, you know how it would have been. If the Japs had shown up saying, oh, we don't want the Pacific, we want the rockbound coast of North America, those little guns would have opened up and the Japs would have just swung their guns around and boom, boom, and our shore batteries would have been blown sky-high. Lucky they didn't show up. We managed to goof up enough anyway.

I was a gunner at the Point Grey Battery this day, September 13, 1942, and it was a Sunday and this fish packer comes around Point Atkinson and keeps going. They were supposed to slow down, be identified, but it kept going. A dumb skipper, I guess, and drunk at the wheel. Our battery got the word to throw an N-E, non-explosive shell, across its bow. It would splash and he'd get the message to stop. It was kind of practice for us. Well, we, the boys of the 15th Vancouver Coastal Brigade, we fired the warning shot and it splashed, bounced, skipped, and I'll be god-damned if it didn't plow into a freighter on the other side. It went through the freighter, a 9,000-tonner, and came out the other side. You know where? Yep, below the waterline. She was on trials that day and the captain gets a report she's sinking and he manages to beach her by Lions Gate Bridge.

Everybody in Vancouver was asking, what the hell is a deep-sea freighter doing beached over there? We couldn't say. Nobody could. Wartime secrecy, eh? The Japs might find out our gunners could sink even our own ships in our own harbor. Well, soon they got her patched up and towed to drydock and later, she was called the *Fort Rae*, she went off to meet the German subs, I guess. I don't know what happened after that.

Oh, sure, an investigation. Very hush-hush. We were absolved. All they told us to do was keep our traps shut, but everybody in town knew. The day after, I suppose. The boys would wind up in the Marble Arch or the Ivanhoe and tell the story from table to table, drinking beer all the way.

Then I got transferred to the Navy. Pull. My old man pulled strings. Nothing to it. I spent months in Newfie doing nothing, building model ships and selling them. Using Navy supplies, glue, wood, tin, the stuff they made the toothbrushes from. I'd melt it down. Months and months of doing nothing, just sitting and wishing it would all end.

I got out with the rest, and none of us had any ideas of what hard work was. I got home here and they gave me thirty days' discharge leave with pay, so after a week I got bored and my old man said, how about working for me? I said sure, and I started out as vice-president in charge of digging a hole. Me and another two guys and they were foreign, grunting away at each other in some language, but they could work. By eleven o'clock I thought I was dying and by five that night I knew I was dead. I was stumbling around breathing, but I was quite dead. When I got home I fell down on the kitchen floor and my old man handed me a beer and he said, "I hope you've learned your lesson. Working with Bohunks at the end of a shovel, that's not the style in this family." He said something like that.

That sure cured me, by God, and I thought it over and talked it over with the C.A. who did the company's books and I started in with them, not as a student. The old man wasn't putting up with that sort of nonsense. I worked with them a year, figured it was a lost year, and went to U.B.C., Commerce, and got my degree.

University was no big deal. I tell kids now, if you've got the common sense to survive this long in the nuclear age and aren't on drugs, go to university, run through it, learn all you can, but for Christ sakes, avoid taking as many classes as you can. Stick in the library reading the reference books, the books recommended for the course, and join the student newspaper, get on the debating club, try your hand at acting with the theater group. Make contacts, contacts, and make more contacts—that's what is going to help you when you get out. Everybody you've met at university will be climbing the ladder with you, and you'll be helping each other. It is not what you know, by God! It is who you know, and how well you know them. So get to know them well, and don't be a goddamned snob. If a guy's name ends with "chuk," he's going to be a Pole, and if a fellow's last name is Mah, he's going to be Chinese, and get to know everybody.

That's what I did, and it worked, and that's the way it happens, and I've made a good life for myself and my family in this town. But you have got to know people!

"THE COMPETITION WAS ROUGH"

I don't think it hit me until I was walking down Yonge Street toward Front Street that day, and there must have been a trainload of returning troops just in because there were a lot of soldiers and airmen and sailors walking up to me and I was ready to take salutes and suddenly I realized I was back in civilian clothes and nobody would be saluting.

It wasn't that, of course. I really did hate all that saluting and I knew they hated it, too, the utter nonsense of it all, but it hit me wham! I thought, God, I'm not a squadron leader anymore. I'm not a man with a great deal of responsibility for my planes and crews anymore. I'm not a guy who can welcome a famous air vice marshal to our mess and introduce him around to my officers and hope they don't drink too much and, by the way, hope our famous visitor didn't drink too much either. Four days ago I was an officer in the Air Force and now I'm walking down the main street of my old home town and I'm a nobody. I looked like every other twenty-four-year-old guy on the street. The fact is, I *was* like every other twenty-four-year-old guy on the street.

Let's face it. It was the moment of truth. It was quite a shock. DFC and bar, that didn't mean anything. The gongery came almost automatically with the rank.

I remember, there was a cafeteria on the corner there and I bought a *Star* at the newsstand and went into it and bought a coffee and sat down and what I was thinking was, what in hell am I going to do now? What in hell am I going to do now?

I looked around me and everybody at lunch seemed to be shoving down liver and onions or fish and chips or beef stew, and I remember thinking, what the hell, is that the only meat they've got and why should the services get all the good meat? Yes, it was stupid, I know, but I remember thinking, the services get all the good food and we get the rest and I had to laugh. I was thinking like a civilian and not any civilian, oh no, because I was a civilian without a job.

The service, thank God, had taught me to think in a straight line, shoving all the rest to the side, and I wrote down my qualifications, which weren't much. I could fly about nine different kind of aircraft. That was just great. I had a little card in my wallet that said I no longer was a squadron leader in the Royal Canadian Air Force. I had a high school diploma and one year of university and one year in a chartered accounting firm and one year in a stock broker's office clipping the tape, and all that hardly qualified me for a giant step into the ranks of business.

Outside those doors on Yonge Street I knew there was a hell of a lot different world, and Toronto, than when I'd enlisted. I thought, I might know quite a bit about them out there, but do they know about me? That was the $64,000 question, which hadn't even been invented then.

Did they know that I was not the same person in '45 as I was when I signed the paper in '41? The answer is, of course I wasn't. There was no comparison and that applied to every man and woman who served in the forces, and I don't care if they saw all the horrors of war or if they were just an Army cook in some training camp in Saskatchewan.

We were different people. In fact, we were a whole new class that had suddenly sprung to life in '45 and we'd be a pretty tough row to hoe for the government and the civilian population if they didn't realize this.

So, there I was this nice day sitting with my coffee and no matter how many straight lines I drew in my mind, they all came together to the one fact that I was a guy who had been a somebody and now I was a nobody and if I started thinking I was a nobody like all the other nobodies out there, then I was in trouble.

Funny how things come back to you and if there are little things that affect one's whole life it was when the luncheon business had cleared out of the cafeteria and two girls came in and took a table near mine. They were busily pushing plates and cutlery off to one side and talking, and if there are two very pretty girls sitting not five feet from you, I think you are going to listen. Do some watching too, eh? Sly man watching. Just like sly girl watching. They were talking about university. U. of T. I even recognized one or two of the lecturers, assistant profs they were talking about. I guess I thought, hah, draft dodgers to the end, eh?

It was not what they said. I can't remember that. But it was the way they said it. Laughing, happy, as though college was a wonderful romp, but not in the hay. This was '45, remember. Girls didn't do those things then. But all the fun and the gaiety and the little excitements I'd remembered in the first and only year I'd taken at Toronto came back, and the foolishness of being a freshie and the common room and the horsing around and the discovery that while the subjects were much the same as in high school, there was a high seriousness, too, about university. I mean, as it came back to me, I remembered I had sort of pledged myself to making myself a better person and also, if you want to stretch a point, pledged myself to making Canada a better place by making myself a more worthwhile citizen of Canada.

Does that sound crazy? It probably wasn't my full thought then, sitting listening to those girls having a snack before they caught a train home for a weekend, but that was close to it.

When I got up I smiled at them and they smiled back. Oh yes, they had been as conscious of me as I had been of them and I said, "Thanks, you've helped me a great deal," and I walked out. I believe I probably left behind me two very puzzled girls. You know, perhaps eighteen. Then, we'd have called them two lovely bits of grub. Just an expression I picked up. I think we all used it. I should have said, "Thank you, you two love-ly bits of grub, you've sure helped me." Then I would have stunned them. But I didn't. Nice boys like me didn't say those things then. Ever.

That did it, though. Everything came together. All problems solved. I'd go back to university. I took that old clanging Yonge streetcar up, then walked over to the U. of T. and poked around until I found the registrar's office, and when I walked in the door into the office they knew what I was there for. Very efficient. They'd been practising on other war heroes like me. I suppose the cranky and who-cares attitude came later, but here was a brand-new war hero to shape, mold, push, and pull into a career. Honest to God, I think the two women who looked after me thought they were doing this. Very friendly. Old maids, of course. Somebody my age, I might have asked for a date.

It seems it took only half an hour. I had one year and they dug out my record and with my accounting year they suggested I take Commerce and I had that in mind anyway. It probably wasn't the faculty I should have chosen. I think Law would have been better but remember, that was forty years ago. A long time. I was thinking I'd probably make a little more than a lawyer when I graduated, not thinking of the long term and never dreaming of the fantastic amounts some of my legal-eagle friends pull in for one case. More than I make in a year, and then they throw it away on MURBs and other dumb financial deals and lose it all. What the hell.

End of this chapter. I went through Toronto as a quite undistinguished student, but I did have a lot of fun, and when I graduated I was hired on at $180 a month by a prestigious Toronto accounting house, which gave me a salary of just over $2,000 a year, and I was twenty-seven, hop-ing to get married, hoping for a lot of things, and let me tell you, the tough slugging began the day I sat at my first real desk in a real office in the real world. The competition was rough and fierce.

But like all the rest of us, I survived quite nicely, thank you, through fair weather and foul. And now that I'm in the position I am, I think it was that bunch of us, the thousands who came out and went to univer-sity or college, who had a very positive and major hand in shaping the Canada we now know.

"I REMEMBER THE GIRLS"

In September I'm home with the folks again and lying around and my uncle and his wife from Brantford had run down for Sunday dinner and we got talking on the porch. Uncle Ted was a lawyer, did a lot of government work. He said what was I going to do and I told him I didn't know, and I didn't. That was when he said I should go to university and I didn't know anything about the benefits, but he did as it was part of his government work, and by the time dinner was finished and the whole family got into the discussion, it was decided I was going to the University of Western Ontario. That's in London and not too far from the town I lived in. We lived in Guelph. There I was, spooning up my dessert and my father and uncle and my mother and aunt had decided I was going to get a degree and then become a lawyer and go into practice and get into politics and in a few years' time I'd be the premier of Alberta and if things worked out, maybe prime minister of the whole country.

I didn't really have much to say about it. Inside me I didn't really object. As my uncle said, get everything you can. The government and the people of Canada owe it to you and it's yours. You can see how well he would get along with those politicians he worked with. You know, a politician. Reach out and grab.

I always had a hankering to be a newspaperman. Even from a small kid. I guess it was those stories by Gordon Sinclair in the Toronto *Star Weekly*, running all over the world with his pen and notebook and camera doing exciting things. But I was twenty-two now and I knew all that was pretty much baloney but what the hell, I guess my thinking was that the government did owe me something. As I remember thinking, I had skated easily through high school and why not university, too? It was the same stuff. It turned out to be just an extension of high school.

Ah, the girls. Time to get to the girls at Western. I enrolled, naturally, and that was no trouble as the administration wanted vets. They'd been starved for students during the war and now here was a huge lump of them and their tuition was guaranteed by the government because it was the taxpayer who was handing out the money for us. It was a perfect deal for them, but thinking back today I can see that the university just was not prepared for the numbers. The sheer numbers. Enrollment, I suppose, doubled and the vets were the reason. Shortages everywhere. Jammed classes. Looking back I can see that the instructors, they left a lot to be desired. I doubt if they would qualify today. No, they wouldn't.

Definitely unsure of themselves, especially when they were in front of a bunch of vets and many as old or older than they were. We were not high school grads; we were tough times and tough war grads. Oh yes, these instructors definitely did not shape up too well and besides, the old question came up: what were these young and mainly husky and healthy fellows doing standing up there spouting off from their notes? Why hadn't they been in the Air Force, the Navy, or even the lowly Army? I think that was another reason why a lot of us had so much contempt for them, and I guess they knew it.

The girls! Damn it all, you keep coming back to them and there's my wife taking it all in. Never mind, Betty, this was long ago. We had come out of a male-oriented society, four years of it. The girls we knew were limited. There were the dances, like the Salvation Army and service clubs and other groups had dances and social evenings where town girls went. I think the girls were screened. No bad girls, but what the hell was a bad girl then? Mothers sure protected their daughters in those days. Wowee! Did they ever!

There were the girls in the service, but when you were in training you had nothing to do with them. They did the office work, drove officers around, worked in the paymaster's office, and did the mail and laundry and work like that. I've often thought, life in the Army for a woman was not the most glamorous of careers and those awful uniforms didn't do much to show off a good figure, but they tried. I don't believe for a minute that they were officers' property, like the word got around. I think they were like us, restricted and even more so, shy, too busy, not enough money and probably damned sick and tired of the whole lousy business of being a soldier.

What I am trying to say is that when I went to Western I was still pretty green as far as women, well, girls were concerned. There was virtually no contact with women overseas. It was celibacy pretty near all the way. Remember, we were in Italy and always in areas which had been knocked around a lot and even if they had spoken English, the class of woman you'd meet certainly didn't measure up in many ways to Canadian standards.

So the first month or so at Western was a shock. There were girls everywhere. Short ones, tall ones, and some a little bit plump. They made their faces up differently then, so they looked natural and pretty. You never saw any of the apparitions you see around today, and Betty, that includes our own daughter. The girls then were young and fresh and clean and they were everywhere in their soft woolen sweaters and pleated skirts and . . . well, you tried to sit beside one of them in class and they were next to you in the cafeteria in the line-up or across the table from you in the library. That autumn you sat on the lawn and talked in a free period and there they were in little groups or with other young people chatting and laughing. The point was this, though. The people, the boys were all their own age. Probably from around London, their school chums, the lads they'd grown up with, played with in the same sandbox. Hay rides in the autumn. Skating on the ponds and rinks. Wienie roasts. Summers at the beach. You get it. Old pals, lads and lassies, although I'll bet there wasn't a lover's duo among the lot. They didn't do such, as Kipling wrote, in those far-off days. It was all nice. But there was no place for us old vets of twenty-two. We were four years and a stinking war down the road.

I know what you're going to say. We could have dated girls who were in their senior year. Don't kid yourself, buddy. You know that better than I do, don't you? Those senior students were just waiting for the day they graduated so they could get married to the fellows they'd dated all through university. They could hear wedding chimes in their dreams. That was the way it was in those days. They sure looked nice from a distance, though.

I found my own girl, right there in London, and she wasn't a girl from Western. She was a girl from home, Guelph, and she's sitting right across the room from you drinking coffee and her name is Betty. Stand up, my love, and take a bow. We met in January of '46, just on the street and we'd been in high school together and it was just coincidence. I was getting off the bus on a Sunday night after seeing my folks, and she was waiting for her bus to go out. Betty was going on a week's holiday from the hospital where she was a nurse. I got her phone number and about ten days later I phoned and we had our first date. A year later we got married and I was on easy street, hey, Betty, right? Going to school, taking the government's money and Betty a nurse bringing home money to our little apartment, and we always seemed to have enough money for a couple of cases of beer and two or three or four couples in on a Saturday night. Those were the days, my friend.

But when you asked me about a post-war anecdote, experience, the girls of that autumn came to mind. At the university. Something about them, and I think it was this. They symbolized our youth, and even though I was only twenty-two, I had lost my youth in that stinking shitty war. Excuse me, Betty. But that's it. They were, well, hell, you know what I mean. I'll put it this way. You got a good feeling looking at them. You kind of felt the world still was all right.

"HE WANTED TO BUILD BRIDGES"

The guy, his name was Wright and one day, maybe it was in
January, I see him trudging down Yonge Street and it's one of those days
where it will freeze the balls off a brass monkey, and you can see a half-
block away the guy is freezing to death and all he's wearing is a light
raincoat.

It's Wright, sure as shooting, and when I get up to him I stop because
I hadn't seen him since we left Holland. In fact, I didn't even know
he was from Toronto. Our outfit, a general hospital unit, got guys from
all over Canada, you know, and we were so busy you only got to know
a few guys in your outfit, the guys in the same tent, you know. This
Wright was a guy who was just around, doing odd jobs, driving trucks,
carrying pails. There are guys you spot even when you're in basic training and Wright would be tagged as one of them by the dumbest farm
boy, and here he was, standing in front of me, right there on Yonge Street.

Oh, he remembers me and I pull him into a store front and it's the
usual, you know: when did you get back? whatcha doing? the like. And
he just says he's doing okay and he keeps shifting this pile of books from
arm to arm, and so I ask him what are the books for?

He says he's going to university and he's slugging his way toward an
engineering degree. I thought that was funny. I'd of thought the way
I'd known him he wouldn't have had Grade Six because that outfit wasn't
noted for guys who were going to become winners of the Nobel Prize
or things like that. We were kind of the Sad Sacks of the Army. Do
this. Do that. Yes sir. And then we'd do it wrong.

I say, "What you doing in your issue raincoat when it's ten below out?"
I mean, that wind is whistling up off the lake and it is one cold day.
He says it's all he's got and I ask, "Where's the greatcoat?" They gave
us that when we got out, so where is it?

He says he pawned it for five bucks and I thought, oh-oh, here is a
Sad Sack. Pawning your greatcoat and a Toronto winter is coming on.
There is this Victoria Hotel across the street and I say, "Come over,
I'll buy you a beer or three." He keeps saying, "I got to go, I got to
go," and I practically have to drag him over, and it's warm in there and
when his goddamned teeth stop chattering he tells me what is with him
and it don't sound too good.

He got home and when he gets to Union Station there's no wife to
meet him and she's living with her mother, so he gets a streetcar up
to St. Clair and transfers, and when he gets there the house is still there

and so is her mother, but there's no wife. The mother takes him in and says he's too late, the bitch has taken off to Vancouver with some other guy she's been screwing around with for a long time and when she gets the word that he's getting home to Toronto that's it. No note. No nothing. He doesn't seem too upset about it. Says he should have known, and that could mean anything. He's telling me about it as though he's talking about somebody else. I get the feeling he just doesn't care.

Anyway, he's going to university. It appears he'd done two years of it before he joined up. Toward engineering, being an engineer. Why he was shoved into our Sad Sack bunch I don't know. But he's having trouble now because he's only getting about sixty dollars a month from the government to go to university and it ain't enough. I'll tell you why.

When he gets out he has the money we all get. He goes to the university to sign up and they've got a kind of desk set up there for students to sign up for summer work. So he signs up on some survey crew for the Ontario government, up around James Bay or Sudbury or some goddamned place like that, and you know what this Wright does? He takes his money with him, his getting-out dough, and he works all summer, say at maybe six bucks a day, and when he goes to the camp boss to get his money, the getting-out money, the guy says what money? Old as the hills. Wright has no receipt. Nobody seen him give the superintendent the money to keep for safety. No evidence. So all he's got when he goes to the government office in Toronto to pick up his summer work pay is that, and not the three hundred or more he got from the getting-out. That's Wright. Toronto has a hundred banks, even just downtown, and he was too dumb to put it in a bank. And he wants to be an engineer. He wouldn't build any bridge I wanted built, I told him.

Anyway, not to make too much of it, we're talking and I'm buying the beer and he's starting to get friendly. We sit for about six or seven beers and then he says he's got to go home and eat and study and then he says, you know, hey, come on over to my place and I'll show you them pictures I took when we were over there. All the guys. Holland. That sort of thing. I say okay, and away we go. It's not far. One of those lousy hotels east of Yonge. You know. I've seen dozens. Little lobby. Dark, and a few old men sitting around wondering if they should go up to their little room and splurge on a whole can of sardines and a piece of bread and tea with the rest of the can of peaches, or should they just have the sardines and tea. That's the way a lot of those old guys lived. Our pioneers. I hate to think how the old widows lived.

We go up to his room. The room is small. Bathroom down the hall.

I didn't have to go there, thank God. I'd gone at the hotel. There is books everywhere and a desk he'd made out of something and a single bed and more books and a little hotplate and some dishes and a pot and pan and the like, and that's Wright's digs.

I don't even know why I'm talking about him; maybe I should be talking about me. But I'm remembering I saw him do something terribly brave once in Holland near the end there, so maybe he needs a fair shake. But here he is in this little snake of a pit, but he seems happier. Maybe it was because he felt safe from the outside world, and he had all these books and a study light, a lamp that sure as hell didn't go with the room, and his few clothes were hung up against the wall and his shaving stuff by the little sink in the corner, and this was his home.

Oh, we talked for an hour, talking over the pictures, and he had quite a pile of them and the old times came back and he sure as hell didn't think we were a bunch of Sad Sacks, our outfit. He was more than proud to be in it.

So, these pictures keep coming and coming and I'm starting to feel good about what I'd done, too. We're like a couple of old World War One veterans cackling over these pictures. Remember this guy? Remember this joker? Lot of remembering that night.

So, I'm thinking of eating by this time and my stomach's grumbling and I suggest he makes a sandwich and he says, well, humming and haw-ing, you see, it's the twenty-seventh of the month, you know, this sort of thing, and it turns out he's out of grub. Not even sardines and bread like those old geezers downstairs. It turns out he gets sixty dollars a month from the government and his rent for this dump is thirty, *thirty*—half his salary—and here he's got two or three days to go before he gets his check for risking his ass in France, Belgium, and Holland.

I ask him where's the money he made on the forestry survey. Then it comes out. He mentions something, he mutters that's where it went. To his little girl. Shit, all the time I'd known him I didn't know there was any kid. Well, turns out there was. Living with his mother in Kingston. So there's another story. When he comes back he finds his wife had effed off with some galoot and packed the kid off to Kingston on the bus. Eight years old. He took out his wallet, not to show me he was strapped, but to show me pictures of the kid, cute kid, a real little blondie. He'd sent his mother three hundred of his money from the bush job and that was to look after the kid. Okay, and what had he left, and he said a hundred and fifty, that was going fast and here he was, stony broke and that was the way the guy was. He wasn't bawling or sniffling about it. No tears, not showing, and no tears in his voice. Know what I mean? It was just that this was the way it happens. He does four or five years taking shit from all directions and he comes home and this is what he gets, and Jesus, I'm telling you, he sure loved that little girl. You could have knocked me over with a feather.

I hadn't one single thing to say. Here was me sitting pretty with all the money I'd made working as a clerk at Woodbine all summer and doing a bit on the side, this and that, some legal and some not so legal, me, planning to go to Florida for two months, not a worry in the world, and there is Wright, sitting on that bed with that wallet in his hand, open, and not a solitary dollar bill in it. I did some fast thinking and I did what I should, but in a different way. I invited him out for dinner but he said no, he had to study. Study? Think about it. His gut is growling and he has to study and here I am offering him a steak and mushrooms and apple pie à la mode. But no, he's got to get at those books. How to build a bloody bridge. A highway. A dam. My God.

So I leave and I have that steak myself in the Royal York, where they still don't do steaks worth a damn, and I'm thinking, and next morning I'm thinking of Wright in his raincoat because it's a stinking day again, cold, and next week I'm off to Miami and the girls, a few hops over to Havana and those girls there. So I go to the bank and I take out ten twenty-dollar bills and I buy a stack of envelopes and I address each one to Robert Wright, Room 11, the hotel which isn't there now because there's a skyscraper there now, and I put a twenty into each one, and I think, who can I trust? I couldn't think of many people I could trust because I couldn't think of many who trusted me, and then I thought of a little Jew named Benny. Now, Benny ran a little place on Yonge, and he sold everything, over the counter, under the counter, out of his back room, or he would give you an address somewhere in Cabbagetown if you wanted and you could pick up the parcel there. Know what I mean? Little Benny sold everything and I'd known him before I got called up and I knew he was as honest as the day is long. I mean real honest. Besides, I was going to do a few kind things for him when I went to Florida. Not dishonest, mind you. Just half-dishonest.

So I went over to see him and I told him I wanted one of these envelopes delivered personally to this Robert Wright every two weeks. Personally. Like, understand, Benny? I didn't trust that hotel clerk. Not as far as I could throw the King Eddie Hotel. He said, sure, sure, I gotcha, and he was thinking, too, I'll bet, of this Florida deal and so he'd send a letter over every two weeks with one of his guys. That was two times twenty, and that would get Canada's next greatest engineer through the winter and then some, because and I hoped he would have the sense to buy a decent overcoat and some King Oscar sardines and not the shit in recycled oil he was probably eating. Done!

I come back in March with a lot of great new ideas in my head I'd picked up from the boys at Hialeah and places like that, and I go and see Benny and he's glad because the Florida business worked out fine for him and maybe we could do the same thing but bigger next year, eh?

I said, "Benny, what about the envelopes?" He kind of sighs and reaches under the counter and pulls out his black change box and he takes them out and says there's nine. I say how come? What happens is, the first envelope one of his boys delivers right on the button and two weeks later Wright isn't there and the room clerk says he isn't gonna be there forever, you know, and that's it. I mean, that is it. My engineer friend has vanished. No forwarding address. Just packed his duds and his books and his photographs and was gone. That's it, buddy.

No, I never heard of him again. Somewhere, if he's alive, on this continent there is a Robert Wright who was in a field hospital unit with me and who was going to build dams and bridges—except I don't think he's an engineer because I phoned the office at the university. No Wright, Robert. He'd checked out of his engineering school, too.

There are about ten things you can think of what he might have done. I know he loved his kid and I knew he wanted to build bridges and dams, but I guess I had him figured different. I gave him his chance. As long as I was doing good, he was going to do good from his unknown Santa Claus. If I ever meet him on the street I'll know him and I'll say, "Hey, Wright, what did you do, rob a bank, and they put you away for ten years?" No, he wouldn't do that. He'd have some answer for me I wouldn't understand.

"MY RETURN TO CIVVIE STREET"

I graduated from high school in '39. I was from a little quiet village called Tavistock, and if my father had owned the farm we had I would have stayed there, but as he only rented it, I knew there was no future for me—or for him, for that matter. That's when I went to Toronto and I worked in the warehouse for Simpson's, which was considered quite a prestigious firm in those days although I'm sure they paid no higher than Eaton's or any other company for a kid of eighteen to

push and shove and heave furniture and crates onto trucks. The pay was
fourteen dollars a week, which was quite good. Things were just so much
different, and besides, the Depression had bred into us that we were lucky
to have a job. Any kind of job. Any kind. Yes, fourteen bucks. I considered I was doing quite well. Another thing, there was the Protestant
work ethic bred into me and also the philosophy that every laborer is
worthy of his hire and pushing crates around a stockroom floor was not
elevating work. Hence, not worth much in wages.

In '41 I joined the Air Force and in July of '45 I came home from
England on the *Aquitania* with about eight thousand other guys, and during
my thirty-day discharge leave I went back to the farm. My father had
decided to buy it, so he was worse off than before. To put it bluntly,
he didn't encourage me to be a farmer.

I went up to the CNE to get my discharge and the last person to see
you after you signed out and got your money was the padre, but you could
skip him if you wanted, but I said, what the heck, what the hell, I mean,
and I saw him and a more bored man I've never seen—I guess he hadn't
many customers in those days. It ended up with me talking to him for
more than an hour. His name was Finley, Finlay, Finnie, something like
that. You'd call him a nice old gentleman.

This old Finley, he talked a lot about life and what lay beyond in Civvie Street and I thought, what the hell does a preacher know about life
anywhere but in the manse and in his church, and I was sure he hadn't
learned much about anything as a chaplain. But he was a nice guy.

I hightailed it up to Church Street and to my old boardinghouse and
Mrs. Cafferty was still running it. Disorganized as ever. I could tell that
as soon as I went into the vestibule. Still the smell of boiling cabbage.
She remembered me. There she came, waddling out of her two small
rooms at the end of the hall, fat as ever, sloppy as ever, but a big smile
on her kisser. She said, "Oh, you're back, you're back. Oh, how I've
prayed for you boys to come back, to come back, and I guess you want
your old room again, your old room again?" That's the way she talked.
The way she talked. Get what I mean? The board and room was thirty-
five bucks a month and that was quite a bit higher than in '39, but by
this time I knew everything was higher, so I didn't mind.

Toronto hadn't changed. It hasn't changed, even today. Take away
the Jamaicans, the Greeks, the Italians, the East Indians, the Toronto
Sun, the subway, that good old spirit the Leafs had, and the fact there
are several hundred restaurants trying to outdo each other in being up-
to-the-minute or, if not that, trying for Old World charm, and add the

fact that ninety percent of the people are much ruder, and no, Toronto hasn't changed from what it was in those days.

One of the things, and I guess the only thing that meant anything, was what the chaplain had told me. He said about ten minutes before our talk ended that I should consider university, and told me the govern-ment would sponsor me. Pay my tuition and so much a month, a month for every month I had in service. Now this was the first I had heard of it. I don't suppose it was a close and dark secret, but when we were waiting in England and taking those lectures and also a few on the ship, I cannot recall anything about that aspect of our coming back. Most of the stuff, as I recall, was about coming back to find a different Canada, and for those who had wives, they would find that they were changed. I suppose that because I didn't have a wife I let the whole business fly over my head.

My next step was to go back to good old Simpson's. They had to take you back, you know. Your old job was secured for you. By law. However, there was nothing in there that you had to be paid what you were worth, and so I found that they'd be glad to take me back. Of course, Sergeant Balfour, welcome home. Glad you've decided to join the happy Simp-son's family again. Had a good war? Good. Found a place to stay? Good. Your pay will be seventeen dollars a week. I thought, not so good. If Mrs. Cafferty could bounce my board and room with cabbage three times a week from twenty-six up to thirty-five, then the high-and-mighty Simp-son's could do better than three lousy bucks a week. The chap in per-sonnel didn't turn nasty when I pointed this out, but he did ask me to sign a form saying I had turned down my old job shoving crates and pianos around the warehouse floor, so to speak. Some fun, eh? A nice way of getting them off the hook, and how was I to know that the form wouldn't wind up in Ottawa against my record? Oh, of course not. Not then. But I guarantee it probably would today. Why not? Today they know everything about you and me but the diameter of our belly buttons, and sometimes I think they know even that, having it as proof that we were all born of women. No, I just walked out.

In fact, I just walked out and down to the University of Toronto where I met some of the nicest people I'd met since coming back to Canada and it was they, not me, actually, that decided that because of my or-dinance work, my supervisory capacity on the squadron, I would make a good engineer. And they went further, or at least once counselor did. He had a list of job openings for summer work, and even though it was the end of July I could still get in six weeks' work and next day, giving my regrets to Mrs. Cafferty and her cabbage pot, I was on my way to a provincial survey job north of Sudbury where they were laying out farming townships in the granite and muskeg and the pay was six-fifty a day and board and room. That was a heap of a sight better than Simpson's seventeen a week, minus Mrs. Cafferty's eight dollars or so for bed and grub. I spent six wonderful weeks up there laying the future for young and eager homesteaders to go broke in one year, and as surveying is part of engineering, I felt I was adding to my list of credits. I was, too. I learned a lot. A lot of short cuts.

University was good. I'd say it was the most pleasurable time of my whole life. The academic atmosphere was congenial and I made a lot of friends. I found the work easy. I just had that kind of mind, an aptitude, if you will. I found it no different from high school in the amount of application I was required to do. In fact, by fourth year and having had three long summers working on engineering projects for the Ontario government, I often doubted whether the lecturers and professors were really qualified to handle some of the subjects. And I'm as sure of this today as I was then, and it is this: with the proper laying-out of the studies and the courses and the method of teaching, the engineering degree could be earned in one year less. But naturally that is heresy, isn't it? Of course it is. Think of the number of professors and lecturers and support staff that would have to be let go. My, my.

One month after I graduated I was in charge of a survey party in the North Bay area and two months later I traveled to Winnipeg to get married to the girl I had gone with for the last two years at university.

I stayed with the government for two years, gaining experience. It was all bush life or camp life or in isolated places, and we loved it. But then it was time for a family so I resigned and went with a development firm, heading up their engineering department at twice the salary I got from the province.

Well, that's about it. My return to Civvie Street, as you put it.

"I DID NOT FIT IN AT McGILL"

Looking back, I would have to look at those first few years after the war in the perspective of those days, the Canada that we came back to, the city, and in my case it was Montreal, the Montreal of the English, the Anglo, and the university, McGill.

Montreal was a cosmopolitan city in those days and it still is, of course.

The business and industry was dominated by the Anglos, the old Scottish families, but the heartbeat, if I may call it that, was French. The Anglo-Saxon was in the minority, but not at McGill, which was—to put it bluntly—a very non-French university. By the very nature of its isolation from the community, it wielded much more power in Canada—but not in Quebec—than I think it deserved. Looking back on it all, I do not really believe that McGill University was a good university, except in a few faculties. I suppose Medicine would be one of them.

It was a foregone conclusion that I would go to McGill. No, it was not a family tradition. But when the Department of Veterans' Affairs offered a university education to each and every one, then it was McGill I had to go to.

Even though I was a captain and had done quite well, thank you, in the rigid caste system of the Army, I found I did not fit in at McGill. An Army friend and I found a nice and clean and warm walk-up apartment there. Watching our money, we could handle it nicely. He was taking Commerce and I was taking Arts and there was no sense of competition or arguing over fine points. I suppose if I had lived in Westmount in a grand home or taken a garret room on Pine Street or the Crescent, which was the rage then, I would have been accepted. I had a flair for writing but the *McGill Daily* was controlled by a clique. So was the debating society and they thought they were the best in the land, but they never seemed to reach the finals of the McGowan Cup. The political clubs were also closed-door affairs and I was interested in a possible career in politics.

Even the girls seemed off-limits. I'd never had a sense of failure with women before but I did at McGill. They all seemed so young anyway, but they were because I was twenty-three and so many of them were entering McGill from finishing schools and high school. I don't think I knew more than three or four students, women, who had been in the services. A pity, really. If even ten percent of those 45,000 women who served in the forces had gone to and finished university, the battle for women's rights might have started much, much earlier. A thing like acceptance of rights for woman has to be in the public eye for a long time before it becomes accepted, and some tough ladies who had been sergeants in the CWACs might have spurred the thing along. No matter. I'd just have liked to see it come earlier.

What I'm saying is that I did not have a happy time at McGill. I didn't expect it to be like the Hollywood movies, the life-is-one-big-party thing, but I didn't expect it to be so dull and staid. As a result I just buckled

down to the books. Let's face it. The young and handsome captain of
infantry was a grind. And I made good marks; some were exceptional.
I remember one young professor, perhaps thirty-five, young to attain such
exalted rank. One had to wonder if his grandfather was rich and had
made an endowment. He called me to his office to discuss a term paper,
one of those silly twenty-five-hundred-word things they were always calling
for, and after much chit-chat and blue pipe smoke he asked, "Jamieson,
did you really write this?"

This was in third year and four years before it would have called for
a sock in the jaw or a cutting remark, but I was so dumbfounded I just
sat there. I did think, this twerp, this academic draft dodger, but I just
nodded and smiled. Just like the Army. Always looking ahead. Don't
get excited. Take an insult. This man may someday help you.

Much more pipe smoke. A swivel of his chair toward the window. Then
back and he said, "Jamieson, yes, yes, you have a definite flair for writing.
History. Very definitely," and I was dismissed. I had been anointed. The
road was open. Victory was mine. Except it was from some young jerk
whose non-academic reading probably consisted of reading "Maggie and
Jiggs" and "Blondie" in the Montreal *Gazette* over his breakfast cereal.

That's just one example of the frustration I felt. I felt I didn't belong.
I even felt I wasn't wanted. Probably it was me and probably the very
high grades I got was my way of showing them. I certainly did show them
but the unfortunate part was, only myself and the faceless markers who
did the essays and the tests knew. So, not quite realizing the future value
of a piece of paper, perhaps ten inches by seven—an Arts degree from
McGill—I quit at the end of third year. It was not a prolonged decision,
not much walking down the midnight streets pondering my fate. No,
it was happpenstance. Through a conversation at a dinner party my sister
had invited me to, I met a man who was an officer on the *Nascopie*,
the Hudson's Bay supply ship, and I casually mentioned that was a voyage
I would like to take. He said something like, "Phone me sometime."
You know how those conversations end. Well, in March I did and I was
invited down to their office and when I walked out of there that afternoon I was a deckhand, one of the lowly, and I would be spending three
or four months in the Arctic. I finished the tail end of the year, wrote
the exams, achieved another round of applause from the unseen and
unknown markers, and that was it. I never went back to university.

I haven't, in retrospect, done anything with my life. I have traveled
the world as a bosun or, if possible, a third or second mate. Freighters.
Always freighters. Preferably passenger freighters. I seemed to function

better on those. I have been around the world several times and in every city there has not been a stamp shop I have not explored. I have done some writing under several pen names—with some success, I might add. The mysterious Upper Amazon. Fierce tribes unknown to man. That sort of business. I have never worked hard for a living and I have never had to. Rewards seemed to come easy to me, although most jobs and careers I have had, most men would scorn. At least most men who are graduates of McGill.

No, I have never married. I have taken my loves as I found them, as the song goes. When autumn comes I shall sit down and think it over, whether I shall make a great career of my life or do something stupid like becoming a senior citizen.

"NO FINER PLACE THAN CANADA"

I was a flight lieutenant by the time the war ended, although I had gone overseas with the Pats. Today if anybody asks me what I did in the war—and I don't think the question has been asked in twenty years—I always say I wore the Red Patch. I'm not sure anyone but those who were there would appreciate that. But if they were young they might think, what a foolish thing to do, sign up with the Army when war broke out, but that's what we did. I had a good job by '39 standards and I guess you would say it was an act of patriotism. I wasn't a hobo and I didn't go from house to house in the winter asking if I could shovel walks or chop firewood for two bits.

My career in the RCAF after I transferred was rather rapid and it could only go upward. I had this knack for accountancy which showed up in the tests I took for the Air Force and it certainly was enough to push me up. I had had seven years in the Bank of Montreal at two Saskatchewan towns and the main branch in Regina. I would say promotion, progress, was almost nonexistent. Somebody had to die. Banking in those days was very, very primitive compared to today.

To make it short, the fact that I had seven years of banking and my high ratings on the tests and the fact that the Air Force must have been desperately short of paymasters, well, caused . . . not caused, but that was the boost I needed. I was yanked from the ranks about three weeks after my transfer and presto, I am a junior officer, a paymaster.

If you remember '46, the great rush of veterans home was over, and as an adviser, which was part of my post-war duties, I had to advise men leaving for Canada that if they had had jobs they were entitled by federal law to get them back; but it didn't work out that way. Thousands of returning veterans found this out to their bitter dismay. A veteran, say in the Army, who has risen to a captaincy, at twenty-six is not the immature kid of twenty which he was when he enlisted many years ago. He is a man. A mature man. A man who has led hundreds of other men into battle, even at times knowing he is sentencing some of his men to death. It is very difficult to give such a man his old job back as stockroom helper at eight dollars a week.

So there you have my position in a nutshell. I had about six years of administrative experience. True, I could not operate a branch bank, but then again, I probably had by that time much more experience in making decisions, big and small, and often the small ones are the hardest, and standing by them, or if events proved different, then revising them or throwing them in the wastepaper basket, and then putting forward new decisions. The Air Force was much the same as a corporation, and a squadron would be the same as a large branch office.

You must remember that in '46 Regina was a small town. Perhaps wearing my flight lieutenant's uniform to my interview at the main branch was a mistake, because nothing went right. I presented a résumé, something that just was not done. It is now, everywhere, even for a menial job, but not then. No, not at all. It was impressive, but I remember the regional manager tossing it back to me, saying that Air Force accomplishments and duties did not apply to banking. Words to that effect, and then he picked up a very slim file, mine, of seven years before the war, and he said I could go back to my old job, at eighteen dollars a week, and if I proved satisfactory, then advancement would come in due course.

I will tell you this. There was no more debilitating experience for a young and serious and ambitious man, which I was, than to work for a bank, any bank, during the Depression and here, the war over, a new day dawning for Canada and its youth, I was hearing those same old expressions. The same Victorian bullshit, if you'll excuse me.

I didn't accept, naturally. I might say that from that day I never did business with the Bank of Montreal again. Call it spite if you will. Yes, it was. And when I took over one firm I changed over, from BM to the Royal. There was a raised eyebrow here and there, but I was in a position where I didn't have to give explanations.

I walked out of that office and I asked a friend of my father if there was a good university I could attend, and he asked me why not go up to Saskatoon. They have a good university there, he said. I said I wanted a good-good university, so when I was asked where I had graduated, I could write down or say, McGill, Queen's, Toronto. It was snob stuff, but I knew that even then. The officers in the squadron who were graduates of Queen's or McGill were considered above the salt and those who went to Saskatchewan were considered far below it. I guess you might say everyone considered the Western universities as little more than agricultural colleges with an Arts and Science faculty attached.

Mr. Johnson instantly knew what I was up to, and he said, "McGill, Queen's. You'll meet sons of Canada's oldest and richest families at McGill. At Queen's you'll have the finest professors." That decided me. McGill.

I sailed through, of course. And I did meet the sons, and the daughters, of some of Canada's oldest and richest families. Four years of college added up to a delightful experience, one I will never forget, and I can say this: I am eternally grateful to the Department of Veterans' Affairs, the pet project of wily old crazy Mackenzie King and the hundreds of nameless men and women who devised it, smoothed out its wrinkles and made it work, and I can say, without fear of a lightning bolt, making it the most worthy piece of work by any government to come out of the Second World War. A great contribution, and one that is not appreciated.

In my letter to you I said I was a very satisfied man. I meant a satisfied war veteran. I wish to define that term, "war veteran." At no time was my life in danger. I was, no more and no less, a paper-pusher and a minor decision-maker. The men I admire are those who flew into danger, men in the trenches, so to speak, and sailors in battle, but we all had our job to do.

I had a good war. It was a wonderful experience. I went to a good university and I benefited from my four years there. I have been successful in business; I have a lovely wife, a daughter who is a doctor and has given me two grandchildren whom we adore and spoil. All in all, I do not believe there is a finer place in the world to live in than Canada, despite its present-day faults. You will cross oceans and climb mountains and you will not find a better land.

7   PLAYING IT
    AS IT LAYS

7 PLAYING IT
AS IT LAYS

People returning from war cannot be categorized.

Sure, there were misfits and mavericks, but most were ready to get on with life—the one they had broken off, or the one they had not started.

Some went back to the mines; others to their fishing boats. Some left the family farm to a younger brother or married sister and struck out on a new course. Some saw a need and filled it—trucking and hauling, repairing and reselling old cars, opening a mom-and-pop restaurant—some headed back to jobs in factories and offices. Some traveled across the country, meeting people, doing odd jobs, making up their minds where they wanted to live and what they wanted to do. Some ended old relationships; others cemented them. Some fitted into peacetime life smoothly, quickly; others bounced around and hit a few bumps and ruts before finding the right groove.

All had to solve personal problems as well as find the answer to that important question of where to go from here. In those post-war years they used their wits, their brain, and their brawn, their imagination, and, true, their good old Canadian know-how, to take hold of their lives, even though they had their private devils to combat, or make peace with.

No one is unchanged by war.

"DOING IS HAVING CHICKENS"

I'm sure our officers were tougher on us than the male officers were to the men. They apparently thought they had to be, and I don't know why. There were a few that made life hell for us. But I loved the Navy, and I loved being a WREN, but I had to be very careful not to end up on Defaulter's Parade and I managed. When I came out of the service in June of '45 I think it was this chip on my shoulder about officers. You know, authority. The way one group of people could have total control of so many and they were just going by the book, and that book had been written by men. I know this, too.

Authority: that's what I'm talking about. When I got discharged at Vancouver I didn't want anybody telling me what to do. I wanted to live my own life. My life was my life and I wouldn't work again for an insurance company like I had. Slaving away. Forms, forms, typing, typing. It is no life for anyone.

I'd go around telling everybody this, and my aunt was a wonderful old gal and independent as anything and she told me one day, she said, "Raise chickens. Eggs. When the hens get old, sell them. People need eggs and they like chicken." She had two acres at Metchosin, which was sort of out in the wilds, outside Victoria, and she said I could have it. She'd sell it to me. She'd take $250 for it and it did have a little house. Living room, bedroom, a kitchen, and a biffy in the bush. It had some sheds like chicken houses and my aunt had furniture and tables and chairs and stuff in her woodshed and a lot of tools my uncle had had. Nails and boards and a lot of things I didn't know about and that's how I started. My, how I started.

You don't start a chicken farm on the puny few dollars I had. It was less than $500, but it was enough to get me going. I was in my aunt's old pants and shoes and shirt through that summer, hammering away and sawing and cutting and fitting. At night I'd be in the house hammering away at the books and pamphlets. You could get pamphlets from the government on everything, but not any about a single woman of twenty-two starting a chicken farm on two acres of bush. I'd burn the midnight oil, and thank God I had electricity. At least there was some measure of civilization. I even got that book *The Egg and I* by that Seattle woman Betty MacDonald, but it was useless, naturally. I couldn't find much evidence that she was actually a chicken farmer. She just wrote that book for laughs. Oh, I laughed at it, but it didn't help me.

There was an old man who lived down the road, Gavin Douglas. A treasure. He had been a carpenter and he did keep chickens, and every day he used to stop by after picking up his mail and he'd give me a hand. He told me a lot and I really appreciated it, but telling isn't doing and telling is like being in a classroom. Doing is having chickens. Mr. Douglas used to shake his head and ask, "Lassie, d'ye ken what yurrr doin'?" I'd say, "Frankly, Mr. Douglas, I haven't a clue." We'd laugh and I'd make him some tea and then he'd go off down the road and I'd be back at it.

In October I quit for the winter and took a job as a waitress in Victoria and I worked hard, pedaling away on my bike before dawn that winter to open up at 6:30 in the morning, and it would be almost dark before I got home with maybe two dollars in tips and a steak and buns and pie and maybe some potatoes from the kitchen, and that would be my supper and breakfast. My lunch was free, too. I lived pretty cheaply and I saved and so on. If I saw paint for sale I'd buy it. I made curtains. I put down linoleum I bought secondhand. If a house was being torn down I'd get things almost for nothing and most times the foreman would give it away. I had that little house looking awfully good and when I wasn't working I was going around on Sunday, my day off. I'd go visit another chicken farmer and hear how hard it was to make a living selling eggs.

One farmer sold me his equipment. He was tired of civilian life after eight months and he got a chance to go back into the Navy and he jumped at it. I gave him twenty-five dollars down and promised to pay him fifteen dollars a month, and that was about the best deal I could have made. Mr. Douglas had a friend who was a retired electrician and he came over and rewired the house and his pay for working one whole Sunday was apple pie with ice cream and coffee. People helped me that way.

In March I quit the job but I had lined up every steady customer as an egg customer. I had it all worked out: every Tuesday and every Friday I'd bring my eggs into town and deliver them and pick up the empty cartons and I'd be rolling in greenbacks. I'd buy a car. A good coat. I'd hire a man to help me. Oh, it was great to be independent!

Then came the day when I was ready. I had all my figures drawn up. I even had pictures taken of the house and the shed and the equipment and I showed everything. Be prepared. This is what the government pamphlets had told me to do. How many eggs I could get from the 500 Plymouth Rocks I had ordered. The cost of feed. Electricity. The price I'd sell the eggs for. How many customers I had lined up. My bankbook, which had about $300 in it. The pledge written by my aunt that she'd loan me back the $250 I had paid for the two acres. Everything was there in my little looseleaf folder. How much I expected to make a month. My living expenses. All in neat rows.

Then I went to the bank. The manager—and may the name Stovell live in infamy—he thought I was something out of a cartoon. He didn't even want to hear me when I said I needed $2,500. He looked at the pictures. This creature Stovell didn't even want to look at my figures, and when I pushed them at him he just glanced at them and set them aside. He said I should have a man running the place and I said I was hiring Tor Haasbeek, who lived in Sooke and was recommended by my aunt who knew the family well. That bastard just smiled.

You know, from the minute I walked in his door, that Stovell had decided he was not going to lend a woman one bloody cent. I still get mad when I think of him. Still boiling mad. He told me, "A woman's place is in the home." What home? I was in my home. I'd bought it with my discharge pay and I'd worked like a dog and I wanted that farm. No way, José. Sorry. Next customer.

That was the Bank of Montreal. Same song and dance at the Commerce. The Bank of Toronto. The Dominion, and finally the Nova Scotia. That was it. Too bad we didn't have the Bank of British Columbia then—it would have been another bank manager to spit on a woman. That finished me with banks.

I did get my chickens. I did get my truck. I worked like a galley slave and when I couldn't pay Tor he worked weekends free, just being the good guy he was. I did have my egg routes Tuesday and Friday and I kept my head above water and I worked like a slave. That went on for two years and then one day one of my customers from the restaurant, an accountant—well, I was dropping off this load of my famous brown eggs and he asked, "Lucy, how is it going?" and I said fine, just fine, and he said, "No, Lucy, I mean are you making any money?" That sort of stopped me. I said I didn't know. He asked where the farm was and I told him, and he said he'd be out Saturday afternoon. He and his wife came and he spent two hours going over everything with me and he said, finally, "Lucy, I figure that spread over a sixteen-hour day you are making maybe twenty cents an hour, and that's for seven days a week."

I think that's when I started to cry.

It was hopeless and I knew it and I did the hardest thing I had to do. I went into Victoria on Tuesday as usual and after I'd done my deliveries I stopped at a real estate company on Government Street and I told them to sell it. A salesman came out next day and if I'd had more courage than I have, I'd have told him to go away. But I was tired. I was worn out. I had problems. He asked me what I wanted for it and I didn't know. I said the first thing that came into my head. I told him I wanted $3,000 and I wanted it in cash. All of it. In twenty-dollar bills. No other way. A big tall stack of twenty-dollar bills.

I signed the contract and he stuck up the sign and the first buyer bought it. Just like that! No quibbling. No bargaining. I got my three thousand and I got it in twenty-dollar bills, you're darned right I did. Of course, twenty-dollar bills, even three thousand worth, do not make such a tall stack. Call it a little stack. I felt sick. Really.

That didn't finish me with banks, though. I put $2,500 in the Bank of Montreal and then I went back two days later and drew out all but a dollar. I did the same with the Commerce and then the Dominion and the Toronto and the Bank of Nova Scotia over the next two weeks and that left just the Royal and that's where I put the $2,950 or so, because that's the only bank that hadn't turned me down. I hadn't got to it, is why. I was just tired of being turned down. So I left five banks with bank accounts of one dollar each and as far as I give a hoot, the money is still there. What's forty years' interest on a buck? No, I guess they've cleaned me out. Some new law they passed, just for Lucy Bawden.

That's all. My fight with reality. Civilization.

"I DIDN'T MIND"

There is nothing to put in your book about me because there is nothing about me. I joined up in Winnipeg when I was twenty-one, September, 1939, just another of about ten thousand fools, even standing in line for two days to get into McGregor Barracks to sign up.

I was with the Pats, a good outfit, but they sure took a lot of wounds. It seems we were all over hell's half-acre and every step of it I carried a mortar and I carried the shells and I set her up and ranged her in and fired when I was told to drop one down the barrel, and I did that month after month and then they sent me home.

Then I was about twenty-six and no job, no education, and there were no jobs in '45 for wrecks like me, so I hung around Main Street for a few weeks until my money ran out. An employment office sign said they were looking for hardrock miners, and I went in and said I was one, and the next thing I knew I was up at the old San Antonio mine. Underground. I did that for seven years and spent my wages in the hotel.

Always. Fifty bucks at the store on my credit sheet to draw on, tobacco and snoose for underground, and the rest on booze.

Then I went to Sherrit Gordon. Then Lynn Lake. All big mines. All underground. I tried Sudbury because the pay was high, but I quit because I could see I was going to die there. Smoke, fumes, dust. You never saw the like of it.

[He began to sing a ditty about "Oh, Sudbury was a killer mine . . ."]

I've mined all my life. I've hurt down below by rock blasting. Seen a man die four feet from me, a chunk of twisted drill in one side of his head and out the other.

I never worked in nothing but mines. Finally workman's comp gave me a pension because of my lungs. The dust. Silicosis. Killed a lot of men but it didn't kill this one. I didn't save no money during my work-ing time, but now I got the WCB thing and the old age and supplements and I'm doing fine. I pay $450 a month up at the house and that's not bad, not considering what some fellows pay for not much better. I go to the Legion 'bout three times a week, have two beers, play couple games of crib, and come home and Mrs. Thacker gives me a long look. Thinks I'm a dirty old man. She's the matron, day matron. I look back at her and sometimes I stick my tongue out at her. She's a good scout and if it weren't for her the house would be a sorry place. She manages to keep a bunch of cackling and mumbling old men kind of happy. She'll get most of the little bit of money I've got saved up when I croak.

I never minded the war, except for the tiredness of it all. Like the monotony. Over one hill, this is in Italy, and there's another in front of you. Me, with the mortar, I used to call myself mule. Once I signed "mule" when I drew my pay and the paymaster, Christ, he was mad. I bet he's a big-shot banker now.

I didn't mind the war. I didn't mind the mines. I don't mind living in the house. Guess you might say I don't mind a goddamned thing. Never have. I won't mind when I die. I hope nobody else minds, too. I ain't worth minding about.

"A RAW DEAL"

You know, that was a long time ago and things have sure chang-ed a lot. I mean, I don't want to talk about being an Indian but a lot of guys like me, we all got a raw deal. You understand? I come back and because there is a lot of guys away in the war I think I can get some work but everybody says no, there is not work. They say things like, times are tough. Things are slow. I need somebody with some experience in this job shoveling out the livery stable. You know, I think I can laugh now about that one. Shoveling shit and I don't have the experience. That's what I been taking in the face all my life and I've still got my Army battle-dress tunic on and there's two confirmed hooks on it and those red wound stripes. No wonder they called them gashes. That's all they meant. Nothing.

Farming didn't work because the two guys and me who wanted to farm, we didn't have no land to farm. They'd hire Doukhobors from Blaine Lake to work for them before they'd hire Indians who could learn to farm this way. We wanted to work but there was no work and, you know, all the time there was this Veterans' Land Act thing, which meant I could have got me and my family a farm, but nobody told me about that. No sir. Nobody thought of even telling me.

You try and get a job and they say, no, chief, but there's gonna be for sure a good rat season this spring and the Jew will give you good prices, so when you're buying you come to my store. I'll give you a bargain. I wanted to learn the storekeeping business and he thought I'd start a store on the reserve and the people wouldn't go into the fort to his god-damned shitty little store and buy things from him. Oh, it was awful, you know.

It was then I decided, no more being an Indian for me. I didn't have an Indian name. Donald is not an Indian name. It's a Scotch name. I'd show them, and this was coming up to the time after Imperial had made that big hole at Leduc and there was drilling everywhere up around Edmonton. I went there and got a job driving truck and nobody asked me to put on a war bonnet and dance around whooping like an Indian and by God, I found out something then. With Imperial you did your work and you worked hard and even for guys working around the rigs and on supply it was good to know a company cared for you. It was pride. They said this is the best company in Canada and we all should be proud of it, and I liked that. I made good pay. There was nothing of this get-ting paid Friday night and showing up on the job next Wednesday. Not for me. I liked that company and they kept their equipment in top shape, so you always were working and anybody says anything wrong, you know, about Imperial Oil, I'll punch them.

I went all over the country for them and when I told the boss I'd like to buy my own tanker and work for them he checked and said okay, fine, we'll do that. I didn't though, because my wife was French, Quebec, and she said her family wouldn't . . . well, she had some song and dance about not doing it, so I didn't. Okay, the truth is, she'd talked it over with them and they wouldn't lend me the down payment. An Indian. That didn't bother me. Not by that time. I just said, well, you know, maybe I wouldn't lend money to me if I knew I was an Injun. Hah hah! A joke.

I worked for Imperial Oil of Canada for quite a while and then I did go on my own and I did good. You get to know people and they know you keep your truck in good shape and if they want you for a tough job at three in the morning you'll be ready to roll, and I guess, well, I'm not sure this is what you want to know but . . . well, it was a long time ago. The truth is, and I'll tell you, it was such a long time ago I've sort of forgotten to remember what it was like being an Indian. Bits and pieces. You know. Pieces and bits. But I do remember, it was tough to be an Indian then and maybe it was because we all acted like Indians.

"SON, DON'T BE A JEW"

I remember my rabbi. When I met him on the street he asked me what I was going to do and I said I didn't know, but I guess I'd have to get a job.

He was a bit of a joker and in those days rabbis didn't joke much. The guys who supported the synagogues didn't make their money joking around, but he got away with it and he asked me if I had much money and sure, I said, I've got more money than most, although I didn't tell him about the Italian stuff I'd stolen.

What was that old geezer's name? Can't think these days. Anyway, we're standing out in the wind and all the crap and corruption of North Winnipeg is blowing south toward the Union Station and he said, come with me, or follow me, and we went into a little café and we talked and he asked me about the war. What it was like? Was I serious about a girl? What did I want to do? He said, by Jesus, I remember his words, he put his hand on my arm and he whispered, that old stained beard just a-waggling away, he said, "Don't do anything Jewish. Don't look like a Jew. Don't act like a Jew. Don't marry one of your kind. Son, don't be a Jew. You're thinking I'm a little lost in the head, but I'll tell you this. You'll do a lot of things, and you'll make a lot of money, but you can make a lot of money not being one of us. But if you're still a Jew you'll have to deal with them, the Gentiles, and I'll tell you this, it isn't going to be much fun."

So, Mr. Rabbi, if you're listening, I took the easy way. I went away from Winnipeg and I went to Tucson and then to Phoenix and they were growing fast and then I went to Miami and I went into business. I made a lot of money and a lot more and I still have most of it and because I don't have that name anymore and I don't act like so many of them and I'm smart, then people say to themselves, he kind of looks like a Jew in a kind of a way and he asks like a Jew in a sort of way but he isn't a Jew but he seems smart like a Jew. Because he's a Gentile maybe he's probably as smart as a Jew. Let's go over to his office and talk business with him and they do and I say, "It's a good thing you came to me and not one of those other fellows," and they know what I mean, and they say, "You're right, and we've got some business we'd like you to do for us and you'll be dealing with those people but we chose you because we think you can deal with those kinds of people."

I shake their hands and I say, let's meet Friday morning at ten and we'll get down to brass tacks, and then I sit down at my desk again and I say, "Thank you, Mr. Rabbi, you were the smartest man I ever met."

WHAT THE WARDEN SAID

One day in about November of 1942 our names were called out and we were marched to the office and the warden said, "Men, I'm going to give you a Christmas present. You're free of here if you join the Army."

I had five years to go on my time, so I jumped at it and two of the other fellows did, too, and when the other two said no, they'd be damned if they would, the warden told the guards, "Thirty days," and those two got thirty days in the hole.

That was in the Stony Mountain Penitentiary and I'd been given eight years. That was for a string of robberies I'd pulled off, from Winnipeg right across to Saskatoon. No, not money. Those small-town drugstore guys took their money home with them. You'd have to hold them up in the street if you wanted to get their money. It was drugs everybody was after. It wasn't too well known then, but drugs were the big thing. You could sell them easily. A lot of people were on drugs. Morphine, codeine. No, nothing big, but it was a big business. I'd hit maybe twenty stores and they wanted me to plead guilty to about thirty more and so I did, even though I hadn't. They said they'd whip me into Saskatoon court late in the afternoon and the newspaper wouldn't be there and I'd just plead to the whole list and they'd tipped off the judge. He may have been tipped off but he didn't approve, so—oh hell, that was a long, long time ago.

Getting back to Stony Mountain. They got about a dozen guys to say they'd sign up and they took us by truck to Winnipeg. We signed, they gave us uniforms and then put us in the digger at Fort Osborne Barracks until after Christmas. We were in isolation—no pack drill, no nothing. Then they took us to the freight yards by the Salter Street Bridge and we got into a prison train, about five cars, and were whipped off to Halifax and onto a ship. About a hundred of us. We weren't bad guys. Oh, yes, B and E, forgery, safe jobs, auto theft. Nothing serious.

Look, if you want to check this out, go ahead, but you'll find it a rough go. This thing was very secret.

When we got to England we were turned loose at Aldershot and took our training and by that time the Army just considered us as soldiers. Nobody knew. Just the officers, the sergeants, the corporals, and about ninety percent of the 12,000 guys who were there.

I went through Italy driving transport. We used to say they wouldn't trust us with guns and I came back with the rest and naturally I got my discharge, honorable, I might say. So I'm not back on the street a week before a buddy and I tap the safe at the old Royal Alex. We don't get much but we do get caught.

Out come the old records and while my record isn't bad, that eight-year jolt looked like a mountain to the judge and I get two years less a day in Headingley. I do about fourteen months and they turn me out and I head for the States. I walk across the border south of Deloraine and keep hiding by day and walking by night, eating from the grub I've got, and after three days I figure I've walked about ninety miles and I walk in at night into this town because I need American money. Somebody's going to ask what I'm using Canadian money for, and they've got a lot of amateur sheriffs down there. I hit a clothing store and get about four hundred dollars and a pair of pants, a sports jacket, shirts, and wire a car. I get about a hundred miles down the road before I drop off the car in this town and catch a bus to California.

I had some close shaves there until I got I.D. and worked in a plane factory, and that's about it. I stayed for thirty-eight years and became an American because I bought a dead guy's I.D.—a bum—off a morgue attendant in L.A. Then I was legitimate and I've been ever since, and when I came to Canada I was me, not the me I used to be.

I live here now, for good, with my wife. Everything is fine.

"CRIME DOESN'T PAY"

I'd say there wasn't much I couldn't do when I got out in June of '45. I wangled every course I could which I figured would help me when the whole bunch of us got back into that rat race of making a living and not having any Army giving you your duds, your grub, transportation, and a rifle to shoot people with.

Every time they wanted to bump me to corporal I'd fight it by doing something stupid, dumb kind of, because if I got a pair of hooks, then I couldn't take any courses. Corporals in the Army were for drill, instruction, and hut duty. Strictly nothing. I wanted courses and by God I got them.

Other guys could tramp all over England, but I was taking courses in advanced mechanics. I took a cook course. A dispatch rider course. Wireless. Weapons. Baker. Everything. Everything that didn't have to do with shooting a rifle. I saw most of England in three years of those fool courses but I knew, sure as hell, one was going to pay off. The best course I took though was stealing. You know, swipe something and sell it to some Limey in the can of a pub. Boots. Butter. Knives. Socks. Shirts. Tea. They'd buy anything, even stuff they didn't need or even want. The whole country was nuts that way. So I'm taking these courses and I'm stealing everything that isn't nailed down, sure as hell, and I've got a great life. The biggest thing, sure as hell, was smokes. Canadian, American, Algerian, any kind. They were the biggest and the next, as sure as hell, was booze. Wow! The money a guy could make on rotgut. Hook up with a couple of guys who worked in a kitchen in camp and rig up a still and you sure as hell were in business. Big money, smokes, booze, butter, boots. They were the best.

Some stuff we just swiped. A lot of other stuff we stole. You know, B and E. Break and enter. A guy would go to the Glass House for that kind of thing. But I never got caught and we lived like kings. Every time you changed camps, like on a new course, the guys in the know, they'd spot you as one of them. Like almost as if they could smell you. Never failed. You were in the club, so to speak, in just a couple of days.

Now, sure as hell, the war ends and I've got the points and heading for home on the *Elizabeth,* about twenty-five thousand of us, Canadians and Yanks, and everybody is talking Japan, Japan, Japan, but I'm thinking money, money, and more money. I'm gonna be a thief. I am going to make a great big pile this high of nice Canadian money.

I get my discharge at Fort Osborne. That's Winnipeg. I move into the Mall Hotel using all this money I've got, the money from jolly old England, the stuff I've been sending back to my mother like watches, rings, bracelets, jewels, stuff I'd bought with money I made swiping and selling. I'd sold it in Winnipeg. They rooked me but good, but I still had enough.

My first job. There's a big drugstore on Ellice and I knew on the weekend the druggist hid a pile, a lot, in a certain place. I knew because I sure as hell had delivered on a bike for him before I joined up and I knew the old bugger sure wasn't going to change his ways. He'd been hiding that money in a hollowed-out big ledger for forty years. So it is Sunday night and I bust in. Easy as hell. Just twist, crank, a shove and you're in. So here I'm crawling around on the floor below the window level this night and I haul out the ledger, she's under a shelf, and I'm sitting there counting it. Just like a kid. Nobody can see me. I'm below the window and it is dark and there's just my flashlight. Nobody can see.

I'm up to counting about eight hundred and still going when all of a sudden, crash, bang, pow, yelling, and there's about four big guys stomping around with big flashlights and they've got me cold. Before I know it, I'm in handcuffs and the lights go on and you're right, Winnipeg's finest. Four six-foot-three Scotsmen. They grew policemen big those days.

I'm thrown into the paddy wagon and the guy guarding me won't tell me what happened. Guess he didn't know himself. But when we get down to Rupert Street and I go before the sergeant I ask him: How come? Nobody could see me. Not a solitary soul.

He smiles that cop's smile and he says didn't I know there was a firehall across the street? Sure, I says. I used to live in that neighborhood. Didn't I know firehalls had hose towers? Sure. Didn't I know they used those towers to haul up their hoses after a fire and drain them, dry them? Sure. Didn't I know there was a fire just an hour before in some house in the neighborhood? I was beginning to get it. He's grinning now. Didn't I know a fireman goes up there to shift the hoses around and such things? Yeah, I knew by this time. I said, yeah, and he looked down and saw my flashlight moving around inside the drugstore. You got it, laddy, he grins.

How do you like that? A perfect deal and a thousand-to-one chance of getting caught and I get caught, just probably because some dumb kid is playing with matches and sets the goddamned woodshed on fire.

I pleaded guilty, naturally. I pleaded guilty next day, matter of fact. I got four years. Stony Mountain, where the bread is hard and stale, as the song goes. Four years. First offense. Today you can chew a guy up with a chainsaw and get only two years.

When I got out I was finished in that town, and I hadn't even started. I came to the coast, thought of a life of crime, but gave it up. Went to work in a mill on the Fraser. Married a Quebec girl. A French Canadian from the village there. Had two kids and built a house and I got my own eighteen-footer and a cottage in the Caribou and I retire in two years. Nobody ever found out. I certainly wasn't telling anybody. Crime doesn't pay. Only if you're in the Army and everybody's crooked.

THE JEEP CAPER

I think you always remember the troop ship you came home on. I was on the *Queen Elizabeth* and she was the world's biggest ship and there was 15,000 on her when we steamed into New York, and there were trains waiting to take the Canadians up to Buffalo and into Toronto where you got onto different trains to go home.

I'd got chummy with an American sergeant named DeWent Carruthers, a Southerner with quite a drawl. Yes, that was sure some drawl. He said it absolutely floored the English girls and I can believe it.

You know, two guys take a shine to each other and in four days, from day one until we reached New York, you're talking and an awful lot comes out and he had this plan and he wanted me to go in with him. He'd thought it out and it was this. If you took a jeep and you changed the reduction and put about five hundred pounds of sand in the back seat and you could weight down the front end, you'd have a tractor. The thing is, of course, that the U.S. had not been making many tractors during the war, but they had been making a lot of jeeps in Detroit, and his brother was an executive for Willys who made the jeeps. See what I'm talking about. His brother had smuggled his plans to Carruthers in the pages of magazines he'd sent him in Europe, past the censor, I guess, or any other prying eyes.

Between the end of the war and the first of December when we'd sailed for New York, old Carruthers had been testing this thing with English farmers. He'd get a jeep out of the car pool and meet with a farmer and they'd slap on this hitch that Carruthers had made in the Army work shops and the farmer would put a plow to it and away they'd go.

Now, they couldn't change the gear ration but even without that, but with the five hundred pounds of sand, the jeep became a good tractor.

And if you can pull a small plow, you can pull a seeder and cultivator and wagon and anything you care to name. So he'd sold a few jeeps to farmers. Sure, just yarded them out of the motor pool and sold them and if the farmer got caught, that was his problem.

He wanted a partner in Canada, and it looked like I was it. Being with the Kent Regiment from Chatham, I was right in the heart of damn good farming country and I was also pretty close to the border. Carruthers would steal the jeeps and get them across the border. Oh sure, his brother had that all worked out and I was going to have them modified and painted and I was to make the assemblies, the hitches, and that was easy. My cousin was a blacksmith. All the jeeps were going to be sold in Ontario because it was too dangerous to work out of Detroit with stolen jeeps—especially brand-new jeeps that had never gone to the Army.

I'll make it short. I did my end of the job. I had my cousin design the hitch and we tried it on a war-surplus jeep and fussed and fooled and got it to work, and believe me, it worked fine. Then Carruthers wrote about the first shipment of jeeps I was to get. By this time I had used up the $1,100 I had and $3,000 I had borrowed from ten farmers who had signed up for jeeps. So I get that letter from Carruthers and he says he's sorry, he can't deliver the jeeps. Not even one. He's in jail for eighteen months. He got caught stealing that first jeep out of the compound in Detroit where they were stored.

Well, I'll tell you, I thought if step one of a twenty-five-step operation fouls up, then everything fouls up and the big foul-up, of course, is that I was in the hole for $3,000 to a bunch of fellows around Chatham and that was it. I went to work. I worked first in a filling station as a mechanic and then I opened one for Imperial two years later and then I got a bit more confidence and I went into the bulk gas, diesel, and oil business in Hamilton. Over the years I managed to pay off those farmers. About five years later and I was clear of them, and I've done well. Just straight and solid old Sam.

But you know something? I've always wondered. That rig with the hitch when you got the jeep balanced right, that really worked. Carruthers, the son of a gun, had a damned good idea. What I could never figure out was this. Why didn't some big outfit take that idea and sell jeeps as light farm tractors? They'd have made a mint of money. When I got the kinks worked out, I was really sold on that deal. Oh, the way Carruthers had it worked out, it was crooked—but done right, maybe I could have made a million.

"MY KICK AT THE MOON"

You see, it was sort of like this. You went in and you had no training and you did your service and there is not much trade in carrying a rifle or lugging a mortar over some of those Italian hills or loading up a carrier with ammo or shells or rations, and that is about all a foot soldier did if he didn't have a halfway decent education, and I didn't have one.

There wasn't much chance for a farm kid from Saskatchewan. When I joined the South Saskatchewans we didn't have machinery on the farm place. It was still horses and I sure knew about horses, but I didn't know about carburetors and gaskets and fuel lines and gears and things like that. So I would have been hell on wheels if there still was cavalry in the Canadian Army, but there wasn't so there I was, a private going in and a private going out and four years and nothing to show for it, and so when I got out I just sort of was losticated.

Nobody wanted to help a kid of twenty-two and there was the old man, maybe fifty, and that is kind of old on a one-man dirt farm. My mother, she sure was no help. The farm was run down and the equipment was run down and the stock was poor stuff and I guess I could say that generally things was kind of messed up. I'd say they was the only people in the whole district that was driving a Bennett Buggy, you know, an old car rigged so horses could pull it to town on Saturday night.

Oh yeah, I had no trade in the Army. I took a driver training course in England but, hell, the way things were waiting for something to happen over there, every man and his dog took a driver course. They had all sorts of dumb courses, and I do mean dumb, like a two-week course in gas identification. I think that is what it was called. What it was, was they was making up courses to keep the troops busy. We couldn't do drill every day or practise digging slit trenches. If we had of there wouldn't a been one square yard of England that wasn't tore up. We'd even of had to start on their old churchyards.

Well I spent that winter messing around the place, sort of fixing up all the things the old man had let go for years, like patching and nailing up that old house and fixing the chimney and the steps and putting in new stalls and cleaning up, and I guess you could say I was just generally fussing around.

Oh, I remember, I hitchhiked down to Regina one cold, bloody cold day and went into this Veterans' Affairs outfit there and asked what they could do for me. When they found out I was still the damned farm kid

I'd always been they said it would be best if I went back to the farm.

Mind you, sir, I wasn't bitter. You wouldn't find me hanging around some beer parlor or Legion bitching that I had served my country and been shot at and is this the way this country is going to treat the vets? No, I joined up and I might have got a exemption because the old man needed me to help work that half-section to grow wheat for the war, and so I had no beef. I joined up because I wanted to see the world. I saw the world, what was left of it over there when us guys and the Germans got finished with it. You never saw such a god-awful mess.

Anyway, there was no place to go, so I just kept busy. I made enough hauling hay for farmers and dumb stuff like that. One day I met an old guy in town. He's got a little cabin out on what we used to call the Big Slough, and he's a mean old customer, but for some dumb reason he always took a shine to me and we're standing in the store where I'm buying groceries and chew for my old man and he says, "C'mon over and I'll stake you to a beer." And over we go and into a corner and he says, "Got a proposition for you. Folks can't afford this government crap but they can afford to buy hooch, and look here, I'll make it and you help me and I got my old customers still and you take it around the district and sell it and we'll split. Fifty-fifty of what's left."

Hell, I was young and you could say I was dumb, and the Army teaches you a lot of things you can't use when you're out of that uniform. But this was one business they taught you a lot about and that was how to survive and how to survive the best way you can. So if I was to go bootlegging, well, I had had a bit of that kind of business in the Army because a whole lot of guys did that and I was one of them, so long as you knew the quartermaster and the master cook so as you could get them supplies.

I told him it sounded like a good idea to me and this old Jake Pinder, he says he could make quite a few batches of potato champagne, and that was not French champagne. That was hooch. So that's how it all started, me and Jake hooching. Call it bootlegging.

This was coming onto spring and I and him would get into his old truck and go around and there was lots of farmers and people who had their potato bins going bad, all sprouting and such, and we'd buy what they had and they knew just exactly what we was doing, what with a half-ton piled nearly half high with old spuds. The guy would wink and ask us to come around with a sample later. You know, farm folk ain't as holy as city folks think. There is a lot of drinking going on in those houses and a lot of gallon jugs hidden in the hay.

The upshot she is that Jake makes the hooch and me going to Regina to buy the other stuff that goes with it and he was really mixing up a lot of batches and once he said, "Remember, the only thing you got to do is remember you ain't supposed to get too fond of this stuff. Sell it but don't drink it, 'cause that's ruined many a hoocher and you're a dead giveaway to the cops."

'Course, the cops was wise but if you did it right they never caught you and they never caught us because a lot of our customers started coming to Jake's shack and we never sold to any fellow we didn't know or to anybody we didn't trust. I think there was kind of a bounty on a bootlegger thereabouts. Somebody turns you in and he gets a reward and nobody in the district knows who the squealer is.

Things were getting a little dicey for me. Old Jake didn't care but the Mounties had been onto us for a long time and they'd stop the truck and ask what I was doing with all those spuds and I'd say for the pigs. My old man had a bunch of scrawny pigs, so he couldn't prove much. But he knew. My gosh, the whole district and all knew. So, we was pretty well cleaning everybody out of their spuds and doing more of the straight whiskey business and that was more complicated, and the Mounties even a couple of times had a light plane up, just circling around, just trying to spot something strange. But the snow was gone, so there were no trails, and they didn't find nothing and besides, they had their hands full, too, because there was a lot of theft in and around and if you don't think farm boys can be pretty good thieves, then you got another think coming, mister.

I was getting a little frisky, too. Old Jake and I was splitting as much as thirty bucks a day usually and that was a lot of money for those times, a lot, and I had got one of those buys of a lifetime in an old car. She was a Model-A and it had been owned by an old lady, and it was against the law to sell a car without government okay, but she didn't want this car anymore 'cause she was moving to Saskatoon to her daughter, so I got it for something like two hundred dollars, and it was a good car. So I'm living in town in the hotel now because I'm twenty-three by now and I'm not putting up with the old man's bitching and I'm buying clothes in Regina and looking pretty sharp and feeling frisky and there is a school teacher from North Battleford and I kind of liked her, and Saturday nights we'd drive over to Davidson for the movie show and things like that. Like, I gotta say, it was looking pretty good but I was getting edgy because I figured the Mounties were getting pretty close and one day it would be all over. It might be a fine, but it could be jail and that would pretty well ruin me in the district and ruin me more than good with Hannah.

One night we're coming back from the show and she tells me to stop the car and I do and she tells me she knows what I've been doing and she's known that for quite a spell and if I didn't quit right there and then, well, then she and I could quit there and then because she didn't want no criminal in the family.

When she said "the family" I just about fell off the seat because I liked her a lot and I hoped she liked me, too, but being a young buck with no experience of that sort, I figured I just didn't stand a chance. I figured I was just somebody to go out with. Right then and there, I told her I had saved more than fifteen hundred dollars in those months Jake and I were doing good and I said, besides, I didn't really like the place. Then I said I loved her and I said I'd quit the bootlegging the very next day and I asked her, right there on that gravel road, I said would she marry me and she said that she would, so long as I quit for good and that she didn't like the place too much anyway, that's the first time I kissed. Kind of sloppy as I remember, and we drove on and that's how I got engaged and married.

Well, sir, there's not much more to say. I guess that was my one little kick at the moon.

"CEMENT FROM EAR TO EAR"

When I went into the Navy I was cement from ear to ear. Wall to wall. I knew nothing, nothing. I was smart, all right, and I had my matriculation, but I was still only sixteen and when the war broke out I was working out of Digby. The Bay of Fundy, Nova Scotia. That's in Canada, if you haven't been following Canadian history lately.

Forty-five bucks a month after full training was better than twelve bucks or so a month working on one of those scallop boats. That's all the work there was. The scallop boats, before dawn to dusk, and every day but Sunday. Three bucks a week and scallops three times a day, boiled, fried, stewed. The only reminders I have of Nova Scotia is my hatred of scallops and my love for my old mom.

I got out of the Navy in June of '43. Broke my back in a fall coming into Halifax. The corvette had to swerve hard starboard and it caught me wrong. Six months in hospital and getting better and then I went deep sea. The first ship was fished north of Ireland. Five of the fellows were lost on that one, and the rest of the war was easy, New Jersey to Trinidad and back, and again, a milk run. Good pay.

Oh, yeah, how did I get in the Navy at sixteen. Easy. I was a big kid, six feet, strong as a bull, and I'd been shaving for two years and screwing like mad around the countryside for a year and my mom's neighbor went in with the rank of CPO, which he'd been in the First World War, and he came back one weekend and he told me if I was going to raise hell with the young ladies around Digby I'd best be doing it against a bunch of German submariners. Something like that. You can put your own words to the tune. Nobody asked for identification or anything like that in the early days. You know, if you could see lightning and hear thunder you were in.

I may have been a cement-head when I joined but when I was in the merchant navy, those Americans taught me a fair number of things and I did a lot of dealing in what you would say was smuggled goods. Remember, Jamaica was awash with the strongest rum you've ever died from and we got other things the Americans couldn't get for love nor money. There was even a quartermaster sergeant in the American Army down there who was selling automobile tires. Government stuff. You'd sell them in any tavern along the Jersey waterfront for three times what you paid, but the real money was in rum and the cigarettes we got almost free. That was big money. It was nothing to get two bucks for a pack we'd paid five cents for. Any brand.

They cracked down just as the war in the Atlantic was over, in '45, and I signed off and came home but the town was dead. Digby, well, don't say this, but if the people who are looking for the end of the world can't find it, then I'll write down the directions to Digby. I read not too long ago it calls itself the scallop capital of the world. Now ain't that just something?

In October I went up to see my sister in Halifax, and her husband got me into the refinery over at Dartmouth, and at a party at my sister's house I met a girl from Annapolis Royal, which wasn't far from my home town. Next year I married her and we got a house and we moved in the day after the wedding. I was on a shift change and I didn't have any holidays coming and I'd put down what she calls my ill-gotten smuggling gains on the house and bought it free and clear. So you can see how much I made. About six thousand bucks, and the real estate salesman just about fell over. The first visitor we had was a man from the insurance company because he'd seen the marriage ad in the paper, and I signed up for a bundle. I wasn't exactly a cement-head anymore because the job with Imperial I was training for could be dangerous. Oh, three kids came along and the insurance guy came by every time the birth notice showed up. The guy must have bought the *Chronicle* just for those notices, I guess, and when I got tired of Halifax and Nova Scotia and their dumb ways of doing things, I put in for a transfer, hoping for British Columbia. I got it, because then I had seven or so years' seniority and because most Nova Scotia people are big on family. They stick together. Some counties are half McDonalds or McLeans and such. You know. Like glue.

We sold the house and with the money bought a house in Burnaby, which was coming along then and right across from the refinery. IOCO. The house had five acres of land with it, and I became a British Columbian with a boat I couldn't afford and this patio and fruit trees.

I could have gotten further up the ladder, I suppose, but all that paperwork and if there's a strike, I'd have to be against the guys I've known for years, so I just keep plugging along. When the company comes up with a good plan to quit at sixty years, I'm going to be the first one standing at the door. We'll just take it easy, watch the kids growing up to be rotten teen-agers and take a few trips. Reno, we like to go there. California in the spring when there's no lousy tourists. That's about it. Except for the smuggling part, my wild oats as the wife says, I guess I'm no different from the next guy. Cheer for the B.C. Lions and curse Trudeau.

THE CIGARETTE MAN

My husband was a captain in the intelligence corps, the Canadian Army, and he always had what people would call a sharp eye. His mother told me he was like that as a kid, always trading and buying and selling and making money every which way. Even when he was knee-high to a grasshopper.

After the war ended he was given a job to go around everywhere and talk to the German people. He said there were so many villages where they had never seen any kind of soldier, and by that I mean the war had passed them by. No shelling, I guess, and no looting and what went on.

Anyway, he was chosen because he spoke fluent German. His name was Miller but the German version was Mueller. His father's name. He used to load up a jeep with as many cartons of Canadian cigarettes as he could buy, and apparently you could buy a great deal if you had the money. He said he could take as many as 10,000 cigarettes in flats. You remember, those tin boxes of Players. He and his corporal would load these in the jeep and tour around for days to these villages and towns where there were people to be interviewed. What he was doing, if you knew Charles, was he was exchanging cigarettes for things. By things, I mean jewelry. Jewelry that had been in some of these families, these well-to-do families for two, three hundred years.

He'd buy wonderful things. Not buy, trade—swap, if you like. Absolutely wonderful pieces, rings, pendants, amulets, bracelets, brooches, necklaces, and they would go for a song. A few hundred cigarettes for something quite priceless. Of course, the Germans didn't want to smoke those cigarettes. They wanted them to swap for other things, such as food and eggs and milk and meat, which they couldn't get with their no-good money, but the black market had it. He said some cities and towns were just alive with German black markets, and, I guess, the black marketers would use those same cigarettes to buy, swap, things that they wanted. Probably even more valuable. I know he sold some of his jewelry in London. He said there were many people who had got rich during the war, producing things and so on.

When he returned to Canada, the box he put his jewelry in, he shipped this box to Toronto to a friend. You could see he was taking no chances, and when he got to Halifax he wired me in Winnipeg to take the first train to Toronto and meet him at the King Edward Hotel where he'd be staying. I did that, and it was some ride, I'll tell you that. I couldn't get a berth on such short notice and I didn't sleep a wink and the coach was like a zoo. I still wonder if train travel was like that all through the war. Women and crying kids and soldiers and sailors and airmen and everybody, and the service in the dining car was terrible, but there I was, on my way to Toronto, and I had hardly been out of Winnipeg before, except to Victoria Beach and the agricultural fair, the horse shows in Brandon.

We met and had a good time, and he got discharged there. He'd arranged that, so we lived well and he got the box from his friend and when he dumped it out on the bed, well I'll tell you. I nearly collapsed. I didn't know much about jewelry then, if anything, but I could see this looked like a fortune. The next day he told me to go shopping. Buy a hat, he said. Buy a dress. Be back in two hours. So I did, and when I did he told me he'd had an appraiser from Birks up to the room and oh clever him, he said it was worth a fortune. The Birks man had given him the name of another man, a Jew, and he came up and the Jew didn't know Charles had had the Birks man up and he appraised the pieces, too, and Charles said he tried to do business, the Jew did, but Charles didn't want it that way. He just wanted two appraisals. They were very close.

The next thing was to sell them, and he did, while we still lived in Toronto. In about three months Charles told me, "Kit, we're home-free. We've got enough to last us a long time," and he said he'd look around to see if there was a business deal he liked. Remember, he was only twenty-four and here he was talking about a business deal. Twenty-four was okay to be a captain but rather young to be talking about a business.

That Christmas was wonderful. We flew to Florida and Charles sold a few more of his pieces of jewelry and kept the rest, the ones he knew would grow more and more valuable. They did, they did more than that. We weren't rich but we had more money than anyone we knew.

No, in answer to your question, I've never really thought about that part of it. We were the conquerors, the Germans were the losers. They'd brought it on themselves and look at the worldwide misery they had caused. A few jewels sold here and there for cigarettes was not going to make up for that, especially when they needed those cigarettes to buy things to keep them alive, or even make more money on those flats. It was business. Everybody did it. A lot of fellows were just content to bring back some fine Swiss watches or a Luger pistol. Charles saw his chance and he took it. He always had a sharp eye, as his mother said.

I thought no more about it, and neither did he. He did what anyone could have done. It wasn't illegal. He just didn't have a business licence to do what he did.

Some people will say this, my story, our story, is not part of your story of returning to Canada and making a new life. I'll say it is, and I'll say it again. It certainly was. That box, about this big by so wide, was our post-war future.

"I SHOWED HER MY WOODEN LEG"

It was right there in the fanciest restaurant in Nelson, near Christmas of 1944, and I'm eating with my mother and father and this woman sees my lapel and she comes up and screams something like, "You got out while my sons are still fighting the Germans over there in the mud and snow."

It was the worst moment I ever had in my life.

My mother said my face went white.

I remember right now, I couldn't think for a couple of seconds, and then I jumped up and it was in a crowded restaurant and everybody was watching because she had yelled it, and I yelled at this bitch, "Do you think I enjoy walking around like this?" I pulled up my right pant leg and showed her my wooden leg.

I yelled, "Italy! I hope your sons don't come back with this kind of hero medal."

Her husband had come up to her and he led her away and he gave me a look that showed he was very ashamed of her but he said nothing and the restaurant was quiet. Even though we hadn't finished dinner I told my folks we were leaving and by the time we'd got out of the restaurant the other couple came out. I remember she scurried up the street and her husband came over to me and said something like, he was very sorry but his wife didn't know what the lapel badge meant, that I was a veteran, but if I was in Vancouver for any reason would I drop in and see him if I needed anything. He gave me his card. He was in the electrical construction business and I won't tell you his name because for all I know his wife might be still alive, but he sounded genuinely sorry for what she had done, although looking back it's easy to see her problem. A mother with two sons in the Army and I don't have to tell you what it was like in Holland that winter. I know what it was like the winter before and that's the place they call sunny Italy. There weren't all that many Army vets back yet. They usually patched you up if they could and let you rest up and then they put you back on strength again. But a guy with one leg shot off, and that was me, there was no place in the Army for me.

It turned out there wasn't much place in civilian life for me. I tried to stand the gaff in the mill but the leg wouldn't take it and there was no work on the railroad and that just about did it. I just wasn't built to work in a bank or sell men's clothing or deliver milk for the local dairy. In January I flipped a coin and was it going to be Calgary or Vancouver?

I was glad Vancouver won because I liked the place and, besides, that's where the government's disability board was and I wanted to get this leg business over soon. I wanted a new leg, too, because I didn't think the one I'd got in Malta, in the hospital there, was working too good. The stump above my knee was hurting. Then no one really knew what they could do with prosthetics and believe me, today is a life and a year further ahead than what they could fit you with then. A guy with two hollow legs is still in the running today if he wants to be.

I went to see the officer in charge of my file and we got some forms filled out and you know what? He and I had to figure them out. He was new at the job and I was the first amputation he'd handled and I told him he'd see a lot more of them before it was all over. He was a nice guy, a civil servant who had been shifted over to Veterans' Affairs, and he asked me out to lunch. He told me I was the first real live veteran he'd processed at that stage of the processing and he wanted to know a lot of things.

I asked him a lot of advice and he told me that there was "veterans' preference," which I didn't know about. Vets got first shot at jobs and amputees like me got first, first shot provided they could stand up to the work. Excuse that awful pun. He gave me a lot of help.

He'd trained for the ministry in the Baptist faith but hadn't taken a parsonage as he didn't think he was qualified to tell his flock how to save their souls, but he was going to be doing a lot of telling this kind of thing to servicemen from now on. That's why he wanted to know how I felt about civilian life. About civilians. How was I treated? Was I bitter? I told him I wasn't bitter. Maybe it was more contempt than bitterness. They're two different things. He wanted to know about the men my age who didn't join up or got exemptions, deferments, and I was able to tell him that women and kids and older men couldn't win the war effort in Canada alone. They needed big, strong, experienced guys for the woods and the iron mines and designers of armaments and administrators and school teachers and bank managers and grocery store owners. You just could not stop the world turning at home because we were at war.

He asked about those who got exemptions for college. I told him that the officers we'd got in Italy, the ones you know who had taken a ninety-day course after getting out of university, well, they were a mighty feeble lot. Too bad, I said. They were always walking out on an open space, a fire field, thinking they were safe. The Germans were 500 yards away, dug into a farmhouse like ourselves. They didn't know that at 500 yards a good man with a good rifle could pick him off like a hawk hitting a slow-flying duck. Oh well.

This fellow, Mr. Raleigh, he asked me about the job situation and I said it looked that with my leg I'd just have to get out limping and dig around because the papers didn't seem to have many ads that fitted me and the war was coming to an end soon. There would be competition. Naturally I told him about the woman who had practically attacked me in the restaurant, and just as an afterthought I took her husband's card from my wallet and said that he had offered me a job, or more correctly, he said if there was anything he could do I was to look him up.

He looked at it and smiled and we made an appointment for next week.

Well, next morning when I came back from breakfast the clerk handed me a message. I thought, oh-oh, trouble back home. No, it was a name and a phone number and "Please call," and it was the name of the man who'd given me his card. How the hell did he know where I was staying? Hell, he didn't even know my name. But it was the same name.

I phoned and he was very friendly and asked me to visit him at the company office, and this was a big outfit. They were electrical contractors and most of their business was war effort. I should have known. Mr. Raleigh of the disability board was a good friend of his and he'd phoned him at home that night and gave him a run-down on me. We talked for a while and he wanted to know about war, battle, shellshock, which we called combat fatigue, and then he offered me a job. It was a good job. An inspector in the plant and I would serve an apprenticeship of four months in which I would be paid sixty-five cents an hour, which came out to $131 a month, and that was good. A one-legger, remember. Then if I worked out, I would become an inspector and that was on salary and my pay would be $162 a month, and in those days you couldn't beat that.

I reported for work the next day. I moved out of the Invermay because the guy I was replacing put me onto his landlord and I got a suite, kitchen, bathroom, bedroom, and little living room, for thirty-five dollars a month. That was furnished. I was in clover.

The workers on the assembly line making the parts I was inspecting were all women. Women, girls, old, young, ugly, beauties, and nary more than a dozen men to be seen. The first one I dated was the one I married. Our first date was a bicycle ride around Stanley Park and dinner at Scott's Café on Granville and then I took her back by bus to her room in Dunbar where she had a basement suite with a friend. After we had coffee and cookies I told myself on the bus going home that she was the girl I was going to marry. And we did. No ifs, ands, or buts about it. Our second date I told her I was an amputee and she said it didn't matter. Why should it? I remember her asking that.

The rest was smooth sailing. You see, I was beyond the extension time you could use your credits for university but Mr. Raleigh, my friend again, he got around that and I went to U.B.C. We lived in a trailer at Fort Camp the first two years. Home-brew heaven on Saturday nights, that's what we called it. I graduated and caught on with a mining firm and that just about takes up the five or six years of my post-war life.

We never had any problems. Life was good. All's well that ends well, I guess.

"DON'T ROB YOURSELF"

Before the war an uncle of mine had been in the mink-farming business at Barrie, north of Toronto, and I had worked summers with him, so I knew a fair amount about the business. He'd made good money and that was when times were really tough but women, if they wanted mink coats and stoles, they got them. I heard there was a mink farm for sale and my uncle told me to stay away from it. No, this genius, me, I went ahead and used up my credits and the money I had saved and after I had been in business for a few months I did some asking around. Sure enough, the bottom had dropped out of the fur business and all my work was for nothing and, besides, I had had bad losses.

Do you know mink? They are the craziest creatures on God's green earth. I went out one morning and found every one of every litter dead. Killed. Slashed and ripped and some partly eaten. The fur was weeks from becoming mature, so I was left with nothing. What had happened was there had been one dilly of a thunderstorm the night before and the mothers had panicked or whatever mink do and they had killed their litters. That was just fine. Just great. It had never happened when I worked for my uncle. It had to wait until I came along. The business was mink and the land and pens were worth nothing. Just three acres of scrub and gravel and old sheds. I didn't bother selling it. I just walked away.

I'm just telling you this because it set the pattern. First, getting into the war was a mistake. Second, flunking pilot training. Third, the great mink disaster.

My family were solid in the United Church and had the connections I needed, so with a loan from my father I studied for the ministry. It wasn't as complicated as today. You just had to have a high school diploma and be able to lift the family Bible off the stand in the living room and talk in holy terms. Know how to christen a kid, conduct a funeral, visit the sick and the poor and the old and the infirm, and be able to rearrange and rewrite the sermons your predecessor had left in the manse and be able to say on-your-mark-one-two-three-and-go at the Sunday School picnic every June. A thunderous voice when you were preaching about the devil didn't hurt. In my congregations it woke people up.

I completed the necessary classes, the course, the terms, and was ready to apply for a pastoral charge when lo and behold, I got malaria. They said I'd gotten it in England, as they knew of nobody who had got it in Canada for many years. That somehow qualified as an overseas disability and they sent me to the old Colonel Flanigan Estate near Toronto, which was being used still by the RCAF as a rehabilitation and treatment center, except there was nobody on staff who knew how to treat malaria. Finally after three months of just walking around the grounds I signed myself out and to this day I don't think I had malaria. I don't know what I had.

At United Church headquarters they were a little leery of me. Who wouldn't be? Anybody who could catch malaria in England must be something else again. But they said they'd do what they could, but this was January and nothing was open by way of a church. I said I'd take anything. They gave me my anything in Saskatchewan. I will not mention the name of this town, village, or whatever it was, or still is, because nice and kindly people may still live there—but when the train stopped I looked out the window and let me tell you, if that was civilization, then they could give it back to the redskins.

I asked the conductor what the next big place was and he said Regina. Now, in '47 Regina was no screaming hell but at least it did have streetlights and a library and a couple of cozy beer parlors fronting the railway yards, the freight yards, and you could get into an intelligent conversation with the farmers who used to come into town for business and were staying overnight. Some of them were the most lively and intelligent men I'd met in a long time. Guys dressed like absolute hoboes but you found out that they could buy and sell a lot of the businessmen in the town. Farming was money in those days. One of them was a fellow who had been a squadron leader, so he wasn't old—my age plus five or so—and he had taken over the family farm south of Regina. He asked me the second time I met him if I wanted to spend the weekend at his place and I said, why not? That weekend lasted for three months, well into spring seeding, and I had a wonderful time. Puttering around, cutting wood, doing the chores, odd jobs, eating good food with his family and his parents, making myself useful, and not being a nuisance.

By the way, I never did square myself with the United Church. I was just a guy who had signed up for a year at this no-name village. A railroad ticket and money for meals, and, boom, I had vanished in the wilds of Saskatchewan.

Then it was time to move on from the Robertsons and I went to Saskatoon. I really liked that city. Along the slow old Saskatchewan River, you know. Friendly people. I washed dishes there in a restaurant, got my meals free, slept in the place, so I was the night watchman and that summer I saved quite a bit of money.

I went to Edmonton that fall and on a crazy hunch I answered an ad for a clerk's job in Weber Brothers Agencies, a real estate outfit. I got in pretty solid because I was fast and accurate and they thought I was honest. You see, what I was doing was drifting West. Instead of putting down my hooks and standing steady I was just moving around, picking up jobs that added to my store of information—although believe me, I didn't know I was doing this. Most of it after Edmonton had to do with real estate, which *can* be as honest or as crooked as you want to make it. I've seen some very rough and cruel deals in my time. For a lot of guys, the customer is just somebody to be taken.

One night, and it was Christmas Day, I phoned my mother. Don't get me wrong; I wrote her, too. But I was feeling sorry for myself, nobody I wanted to visit with or drink with, and I phoned my old mom in her little apartment in Toronto and she's alone for Christmas, too, and we did a little weeping and wailing and then and there I told her I'd come home. That's what I did. I went back to T-O, as we called it. I had been thinking of going to Vancouver and the coast but instead, there I was a few days later sitting in the parlor car of the CPR watching the telephone poles going the other way.

I slept on my mother's couch for two weeks while she stuffed me with every kind of food they had and then I was sitting in a coffee shop on Yonge Street one afternoon. Dead as a doornail and the owner, a guy named Al, came along. We got talking and he asked if I wanted to buy the place. Everything for one thousand bucks. I knew nothing about running a shop, but my mother did—she'd run one at Fort Erie—and on an impulse I said yes. The thousand took everything and the rent was cheap because it was a month-to-month thing. Somebody wanted to tear down the block and build a skyscraper. That's why it went so cheap. Al was a gambler and he wanted the money that day, right then, and he'd be off to the ponies in Florida. I got my mother on the phone and she came down and Al locked the door and Mom went over everything. Poking here. Trying that. Talking to herself. She was only fifty-one or fifty-two at the time, still raring to go. She told me to give Al a check and I did and she wrote out a sale document and Al got the guy next door to witness it and that was it. I never did find out how many millions Al had made on the bangtails. He was a gambler. They always bet one race too many.

We hung a sign on the door, "Closed," and worked fourteen hours a day for a whole week, painting, scrubbing, making out new menus, polishing, and all the while Mom is teaching me how to take orders, handle cash, talk to customers, suggest extra things the Bay Street noon-hour crowd might like. Forget the morning rush. Just shove it at them.

And we closed at four P.M. She said there was no use staying open after the afternoon break. She's in the kitchen cooking away, scraping away, goin' like a blue streak, and we hire a girl to help out and we do fine. Lots of time off. Six A.M. to five P.M., when we go home. Only an eleven-hour day. You don't hear me complaining, because that coffee shop is making money.

Then in '52 the lease is sold out from under us and we've got a month to clear out and, well, we had a good run at it.

Well, that's about the first six years of my life. Pretty spotty, eh?

If you know what you're doing you can make very good money in the restaurant trade and I've been in it, in one way or another, ever since. I love it. I can walk back into the kitchen and get my chef to make me the finest item on the menu and you know what? I pay for it! I mean, I pay for it out of my own pocket! That's my system. Once you start robbing your own till, even for meals for yourself and you own the place, then you are making your first mistake. I started out not making that mistake and that's why I'm successful today. Know where I learned that? Remember I said my mom was teaching me how to run the first shop. That was her number one rule: Don't rob yourself.

NO MEDALS FOR SORTING MAIL

I guess I'm not much different from a lot of the fellows, look-ing back on it. You don't have much of a war when you join up in '39 and the only job you had before joining up was working in the harvest fields in Saskatchewan two summers at two bucks a day and delivering mail and Christmas parcels two years.

So they send me to Petawawa, which is a big army camp near Ottawa, and when I get there I find I've been assigned to the postal corps and I sort letters there for a year and then to England and, you won't believe this, that's where I spend the rest of the war, in the postal corps sorting mail. You don't earn medals for that—but then again, some German isn't cutting you in two with a automatic pistol or something like that.

I got back in '45 and I went to this place behind City Hall, a place called the . . . it had the word "employment" in it and it was where they handed out the jobs. If you threw out the pick-and-shovel jobs and the ones where you needed a lot of experience to do, like plumbing or printing or, say, being a butcher, there wasn't much else. And this is in a town where when I get back and my folks have a party for me, everybody tells me there is this terrific shortage of help and employers will kiss your bare feet if you'll sign on at a good wage.

I said to hell with pick and shovel and I couldn't carve up a steer, so I was walking home and I stopped in at the St. Regis Hotel, and I go in and I see first thing a guy named Teddy Sanderson I'd known in England, and he's sitting there having a beer with some other guys, and so I sit down and he says how's it going? I tell him about the place I'd just been to and he says, hell, join us guys at the post office and he tells me they've got "veterans' preference." A vet gets first crack at jobs and they're looking for posties. I said that's a lot of walking and he says you might get an apartment route, a walk with a lot of apartments on it so there's not much pounding the pavement and dogs and getting your balls frozen, and he said there was other advantages, too. I asked what and he winked. I said, just taking a shot, "You mean knock on an apartment door three times and if the lady inside feels like inviting you in for a cup of tea or something?" He says yes, something like that, and I thought that was pretty good for a young guy like me without a wife or girlfriend in sight, but you know, that never did happen to me and I wonder if it did happen to anyone.

I got a job, of course. Just like that. Snap. No problem. Just sign here, my boy, glad to have you in His Majesty's Mail, and I'm not sure there even was a medical and I figured they thought if you could survive six years in the jolly old Army and not get a scratch you must be intelligent. No, just kidding. The thing is, I had been corporal for the last three years in the postal corps and that did it and, by golly, I got River Heights on a good route with big houses. Fairly big good houses where the husbands had good jobs and I was there, oh, about nine years. Everybody called me "Bunny" as a nickname, and in the summer when people were away I'd check out their houses, try the doors, for burglars, and more than quite a few times I'd find they left doors open. They'd even arrange for me to feed their dog if they were away for a couple of days or something during the week. One man, quite a big shot in some insurance company, we got to be friends when he retired and he was moving to the coast and he offered me his cottage. Five hundred dollars. That was a steal, one hundred dollars down and twenty a month, and that's how I got the cottage. There was always good gifts or money or a bottle at Christmas, too.

Things were so nice I could have used seniority when a downtown office walk was posted, but I didn't, and then about '55 they put me inside and they made me take that. Being the post office the way it was, they probably figured I was too happy where I was. So that good time ended, but inside was easy, but I missed my friends and the chats I had.

So I just settled in for a long wait until I could retire and spent my time thinking and going about fixing up my little veteran's house I got from the government. I added two rooms and put in a basement and now it is a dandy of a house. We spent a lot of time at the cottage and I put in a big garden. We? Oh, we. Yes, I got married in '50. January 26 and we had a four-day honeymoon in Minneapolis. Don't ever call that a honeymoon town. It was colder than it was in Winnipeg and nothing much to do. I was glad to get back.

That's about it. You couldn't call it a career. I did nothing. Didn't make a lot of money. I think my starting pay at the post office was about one hundred and six a month, which was okay and enough. Then again, I took a lot of goof and guff and everything they, post office, could throw at us guys and believe me, in the last ten years, that was a lot. Things in that place really went haywire. You wouldn't believe it. You could call it inhuman treatment, I guess. But I stuck it out and then four years ago when I came up to sixty I said to aitch with all their stupid little mean rules and regulations and how they tried to treat us like slaves and animals and I took retirement. Early. It was the best move I ever did.

About fifteen years ago I took a couple of courses in lapidary and then a course in engraving, bracelets, watches, and stuff. The engraving came from my interest in making jewelry and you'd be surprised how much work I've gotten in the past four years. Fifty here, thirty there, and it comes in steady. I do work for some jewelers and any time I make a piece of jewelry in my workshop I can usually sell it because I'm not trying to be Birks and make 300 percent profit.

Anyway I get the old-age pension next year. I've already applied for it. Six months ahead, you know. And my wife gets it in '87 and we're sitting pretty now, and when that pension money comes in we'll be sitting even prettier. I can't say sitting there in England for four years sorting and handing out V-Mail did much for me. I could have done it on my own, and I can't say being in the Army was anything either. I was just plain bored all the time. Now I'm not. It sure is nice to know like me that at sixty-four life is just going to get better and better.

Epilogue

Forty years have passed, and time, like a silent river, has carried away the Canada we knew then. The war—and Canada's great military achievements, as well as our astonishing industrial contribution to the war effort—changed the nation forever.

The veterans came back intent on improving their lives, not on taking charge of things; but they inevitably moved into significant positions in every segment of our economy and society, and their leadership helped Canada achieve great growth and prosperity, world stature and respect.

The Canada we know today is largely the creation of the veterans of World War Two. Now, their average age is sixty-six, and 1945 and victory seem a long way away. But what of their lives today? I have two letters before me, and the first tells of how one man's struggles to succeed failed despite his every effort, and he writes: "I feel now as I did in 1946, used, discarded and forgotten."

The other veteran writes: "We have had five children and I have had a wonderful life and a lovely wife who has made it all possible. It has been said there's winners and losers in war. In my case I won it all."

I feel after writing this book that the first veteran is one of a tiny minority and that the second speaks for most of us.

But Canada was the real winner, and the vets, with their desire to get ahead and their determination, have earned themselves a place of honor in Canada's hall of heroes. And I salute them.

Printed in Canada